A Guidebook to *Piers Plowman*

A Guidebook to
Piers Plowman

ANNA BALDWIN

First published 2007 by
PALGRAVE MACMILLAN
Houndmills, Basingstoke, Hampshire RG21 6XS and
175 Fifth Avenue, New York, N.Y. 10010
Companies and representatives throughout the world

PALGRAVE MACMILLAN is the global academic imprint of the Palgrave Macmillan division of St. Martin's Press, LLC and of Palgrave Macmillan Ltd. Macmillan® is a registered trademark in the United States, United Kingdom and other countries. Palgrave is a registered trademark in the European Union and other countries.

ISBN-13: 978–0–230–50714–2   hardback
ISBN-10: 0–230–50714–X   hardback
ISBN-13: 978–0–230–50715–9   paperback
ISBN-10: 0–230–50715–8   paperback

This book is printed on paper suitable for recycling and made from fully managed and sustained forest sources.

A catalogue record for this book is available from the British Library.

A catalog record for this book is available from the Library of Congress.

10 9 8 7 6 5 4 3 2 1
16 15 14 13 12 11 10 09 08 07

Printed and bound in China

In memory of Margaret Thomas

1930–2006

As on a walnote wiþoute is a bitter barke
And after þat bitter bark, be þe shelle aweye
Is a kernel of confort kynde to restore (11.258–260)

Contents

List of Text-boxes

List of Illustrations

by Jonathan Brockbank

Acknowledgments

In writing this book I have been given much encouragement by James Simpson, whose *Introduction to the B-text* was the inspiration to this *Guidebook*. I am grateful to Carl Schmidt for permission to use his text, glosses and even his choice of cover-image. I have been given a great deal of positive support by Kate Wallis, Sonya Baker and Brian Morrison at Palgrave Macmillan, and also by Sarah Hutton, Margaret Thomas, and above all my brother Stephen, who discussed ideas with me in detail, and even checked the proofs. My husband Tom has as always supported me throughout the journey.

Introduction

Why read *Piers Plowman*?

To read *Piers Plowman* is to encounter a highly original and perceptive poet, one who was extremely popular in his own time and has
fascinated readers ever since. What is most immediately striking
about the poem is its variety and inclusiveness. There are scenes in
the London markets, in the King's Council, in the households of
lords and beggars, in the church, in the field, on the hills.
Everywhere we see human drama, as men and women struggle to
gain status and wealth or merely their daily bread, oppress others or
try to control oppression, indulge in pleasure or try to love one
another. The poem shows the world as a whole; its shifting cast of
characters is confronted by political, economic, social and religious
forces at once, as we are in real life. This universal confusion is
roughly shaped into a series of dreams, retold by the bewildered narrator, Will, who travels through the world and through his own
mind, reporting the struggles of others while also struggling with
himself. His very name, Will, is ambiguous, suggesting at once an
individual called William and the general human will. This ambiguity makes his personal questions into ones which touch everyone.

The poet's understanding of the complexity of his world is fired
by his passion to make it a better place. It needs laws and law-
enforcers to protect the weak from the strong, but it needs moral
leadership even more, so that all people can turn from what he calls
"unkindness" to love. Who is to provide this moral leadership? The
obvious candidate, the Church, is given an ideal voice in the poem,

1

but it is also constantly castigated for its worldliness and loss of principle. But another candidate for moral leadership steps forward, a ploughman called Peter or 'Piers'. This enigmatic character seems at one time to be a real farm labourer, at another time to be St Peter the chief apostle and first Pope, and at yet another time to be Christ himself. His ambiguity reflects the poet's refusal to give easy answers to the questions the poem raises so honestly, and his capacity to swing from satire into vision.

In describing the experiences of Will and Piers and of the characters they encounter, he consistently offers us the values of truth, of justice, of love, of faith. But he does not fully interpret his own narratives, and he does not explain how Piers reflects God or epitomises human goodness. He seems to expect his readers to work things out for themselves, and to find their own routes through the scenes and characters which confront them at every turn. This Guide will try to help you, the modern reader of the poem, to do this. It will point out some of the signposts embedded in the text, and try to remove some of the barriers (linguistic changes, historical facts, theological assumptions and the like) which might impede your understanding. But essentially it will pass on to you the interpretive pen which the poet gave to all who read *Piers Plowman* for themselves.

The texts and date of the poem

The poem exists in four main versions, known as the Z, A, B, and C texts, though the boundaries between them are fluid. It is generally accepted that a single poet wrote the various versions, but controversy abounds about the order in which he did so. Indeed it seems quite possible that no version is truly "final", but merely represents a stage in a constantly evolving task. Although the different versions cover many of the same episodes, they differ in wording and in length, each having a different number of sections, or *Passus* (meaning "steps"; note that the singular and plural forms of this word are the same). There are two shorter texts: the Z-text with a Prologue and eight Passus, found in one manuscript, and the A-text with a Prologue and twelve Passus, found in 17 manuscripts, most of which are late. These texts are comparatively conservative in their criticism of society, and relatively uncluttered by Latin quotation. Does this make them less mature work, or abridgments made for a less educated audience from an earlier text (see Mann 1994)? There are also two longer texts: the B-text with a Prologue and 20 Passus, found in 16 manuscripts; and the C-text with a Prologue and 22 Passus, found in 18 manuscripts, including some of the earliest. Both are even more outspoken in their criticisms of Church and State, though in different ways, than A or Z. In addition there are seven composite manuscripts, starting with A and completing it with the second half of C. Counting all the versions together (though discounting additional fragmentary versions) we reach a total of 54 medieval manuscripts; among literary texts in Middle English only Chaucer's *Canterbury Tales* can boast more. Although a few are handsome and decorative, and one (Douce 104) is illustrated, the majority are modest and on paper rather than parchment. This and the evidence of wills and signatures suggests they belonged to middle-class rather than aristocratic readers, priests and laity (that is, non-clergy) including some women, throughout England. The poem was influential enough to have fathered a new group of poems such as *Piers Plowman's Crede*, which imitate its methods and sometimes use its characters (see Barr). To read it is to hear the authentic voice of the common man.

Historical references in the three main texts, and possible quotations from them in contemporary literature, can be used to show they were written in the 1370s and 1380s. The A-text mentions the Normandy Campaign of 1359–60 (A 3.176) and the 1362 hurricane (A 3.14), which may suggest that it was finished in the early 1370s during the last years of Edward III's reign, though of course it may have been written after this period. The B-text must have been finished after 1378, because it seems to allude both to Richard II's coronation in 1377 (B Prol. 112) and to the "Great Schism" beginning in 1378, when a second Pope was elected while the first was still in place (B Prol. 108). The C-text seems even later, as it removes the reference to the Normandy Campaign of 1360, replacing it by a passage which appears to criticise the personal rule of the young

Richard II between 1382 and 1386 (C 3.203–209). It also adds an 'autobiographical passage' in C 5 (see p. 105) which suggests a knowledge of the Statute of Labourers of 1388. If these references are valid then the texts *were* probably written in the order A-B-C after all.

The most widely known version of the poem is the B-text and it is on this that this Guide will comment as you read. This text is clearly more complete than either Z or A, and includes some famously vivid and controversial passages which are omitted from C (though other passages in C are equally interesting and disturbing, and I will refer to them when appropriate). The B-text is easy to get hold of in student editions and translations in both England and the USA, where the Norton edition with facing-page translation has just been brought out. My quotations are from Schmidt's parallel text edition of all four texts, which uses a B-text manuscript (Trinity College B 15.17), probably written out by Chaucer's scribe, Adam, and which is as authoritative as we are likely to find. It is also the text of Schmidt's Everyman edition, and the basis of his translation. Langland seems to have actually lost his own holograph of B, and to have used an inferior scribal copy when revising it for C. Thus chaos informs Langland's writing as much as it bedevils his world.

The author

Whereas Chaucer was a public figure, whose life and writings are well documented, we know scarcely anything about the author of *Piers Plowman*, particularly if we look for evidence outside the poem itself. A note in the very early manuscript in Trinity College Dublin claims that he was 'willemus de Langlond', the son of a gentleman called Stacey de Rokayle who had died in Shipton-under-Wychwood (a village in Oxfordshire). It was not always the case that a son took his father's name, and the line 'I have lyued in londe,' quod I, 'my name is Longe Wille' (B 15.152) seems to be a cryptogram of the name by which the poet preferred to be known. Alternatively this could be seen as a nom-de-plume, signifying the "long field" in the human will which Piers must plough. More contemporary evidence is provided by one John But, who made an 18-line addition to an A-text manuscript (Rawlinson, *Poetry*, 137) claiming that the poet, William, had recently died, punished by God because he 'medleþ of makyng' (meddled with poetry; A 12.109), and commending himself to King Richard. In the sixteenth century the antiquarian, John Bale, noted on the Huntingdon manuscript, though also without providing any evidence, that 'Langland' was born in Mortimer Cleobury in Shropshire 'within viii myles of Malbourne Hylles' (presumably the Malvern Hills where the poem begins). As many C-text manuscripts can be traced back to the area around the Malvern Hills it is attractive to imagine that Langland retuned to his childhood home to revise his poem yet again and died in the early 1390s, but this is (as so much of his biography) speculative.

All other evidence about William Langland has to be gathered from the poem itself. Conventionally the author of a dream-poem gave the dreamer his own name and biography in those parts of the poem which are not dreamed, and indeed several C-text manuscripts seem to make this assumption by ending *Explicit liber Wiliemi de Petro Plouȝman* (here ends William's book about Piers Plowman). Many details about Will's life are given in the 'autobiographical passage' when he is supposedly awake (see p. 105), and we can flesh these out with some of the dream testimony, and – with somewhat more reliability – by looking at the topics of concern to him and the level of knowledge with which he discusses them. But you should judge for yourself how much of what follows describes William the poet, and how much the developing and multiple *personae* of his protagonist Will.

It seems then that William / Will presented a tall, uncompromising figure (C 5.24, B 15.5), and that he had a voracious appetite for reading and a passion to teach what he knew or believed. As he gives his dream-age as 45 in B 12.3 (completed after 1378), he could have been born about 1330, probably near the Malvern Hills which appear at waking moments in the poem and from where the dialect of several manuscripts can be traced. He clearly went to school (see C 5.36) and University, for his poem shows distinct signs of an Oxford education (such as his Psychology, see p. 123). He would have taken the 'minor orders' of priesthood to do this and shaved his

head in a "tonsure". From his 'autobiography' in C 5 we learn that
the 'frends' who had supported his education died (C 5.40), possibly
in the Plague of 1348, and he seems to have left Oxford before
taking his degree, for he became neither a theologian nor a lawyer,
though his knowledge of both disciplines was prodigious. Nor did
he become a celibate priest, though he retained his tonsure and clerical garments all his life – that is if C 5.41, 56 really describes
William as well as Will. If so, perhaps this was because his passion
extended to women (B 11.7–33 – but dream testimony again), or
perhaps simply because he could not obtain a parish (without which
one could not be ordained; see C 5.78–79). At any rate he later
married and settled in Cornhill, a cheap area of London, with his
wife and daughter (see B 18.428, C 5.2). He seems to have earned
his living by copying legal documents (see A 8.43–44, B
11.303–306), by performing spiritual services for his neighbours
(see C 5.45–49), and by visiting the London intelligentsia as a witty
satirist (to judge from the dream in B 13), and as an increasingly
famous poet. If his hosts were the important clerics and statesmen of
the later fourteenth century, his knowledge of both Church and
State becomes more comprehensible. As the demand for religious
poetry written in English was increasingly high he could even have
earned money by selling his poetry to the London booksellers. If he
died in the early 1390s (see previous paragraph), he would have been
at least 60, and fitted the contemptuous description of 'himself' in B
20.182–194, when his wife wishes her bald, deaf and gouty husband
were finally stowed in heaven.

The times

The poem was written in the second half of the fourteenth century,
a period of change and turmoil and also a period in which literature
in English came into its own. *Piers Plowman* is unlike most of the
medieval literature read by undergraduates in being partly a chron-
icle of its times, giving its fictional and allegorical characters a real-
life setting with which to engage. Langland would certainly have
been alive in 1348 when the Black Death began to ravage the

country, reducing the population by almost 50 per cent by 1400. The resulting changes in peasant society are reflected in the way in which Piers Plowman (on his first appearance in the poem) sets up his own farm with a reduced labour force. He has to deal with workers who are no longer "feudal serfs", bound to an estate by traditional obligations to work for their lord, but free men who must be persuaded somehow to keep the contracts they themselves negotiated. The old feudal bondage is used throughout the poem both as a positive and as a negative metaphor, as though the author appreciated its value but knew its time was over. However he never goes as far as the peasants who marched on London in the Revolt of 1381 demanding (among other things) that they be freed from bondage immediately, though there is evidence that the rebels used the words of his poem as a code in their letters to one another (see p. 138). A new sense of freedom was also developing in higher places. During the 1370s and 1380s, when much of the poem was written, the King was either very old or very young, for the senile Edward III was succeeded in 1377 by his ten-year-old grandson Richard II. This gave opportunity for power to the nobility both in Parliament and Court, and in the country at large. The struggle of Parliament to control nobles who cared nothing for the law is a feature of the period, and is reflected in the poem in the story of "Lady Meed" and her protégé "Wrong", whose criminal oppression is eventually punished by the officers of the King's Council in Parliament.

Some members of the contemporary Church were also breaking traditional bonds; for example the theologians Richard Fitzralph in the 1350s and John Wycliffe in the 1370s both gave an influential series of public sermons which questioned the Church's right to own so much property and wealth when Jesus himself had been a poor man. *Piers Plowman* includes a famous passage which suggests that the king should purify the Church by confiscating its lands (B 10.316–329); sixteenth-century readers were to see this as prophetic of the Protestant Reformation when Henry VIII did "disendow" the Church in this way. Several characters in the poem attack other examples of the Church's worldliness, such as its methods of raising money and its use of such funds to fight wars. It is by no means the only text to voice such criticisms, but the number and range of its attacks associate it particularly with the writings of Wycliffe, who died in 1384, and his early followers. His later followers anticipated the Reformation in wanting more sweeping reforms, and although some of the views expressed in *Piers Plowman*, particularly by the more unreliable characters, seem to lead in this direction, the poet constantly insists that people cannot be saved or even live well without the sacraments and teachings of the Catholic Church. Indeed the tragic ending of the poem seems the direct result of the divisions in the Church.

These breakdowns in social and religious cohesion are linked, and the poet searches for ways of replacing such divisions by "kyndeness" or charity between individuals. Yet his charity towards the poor and sinful is subversive in an age when hierarchy and order were honoured, for his narratives seem to reverse the importance of peasant and knight, of soldier and enemy, of professor and pilgrim, of cleric and ploughman. The poet's ideas do not undermine either the kingdom or the Church, but they are radical in the way that Jesus' own teaching was radical. Therefore he is not sparing of evidence from the Bible (and from his favourite commentators on it) to support his ideas. Indeed his habit of translating the Latin quotations which so liberally scatter the pages, although used in some devotional writing, may remind us again of Wycliffe, whose followers dared in the 1380s to promote a translation of that most dangerous book, the Bible, so that all should be able to read for themselves the secrets of salvation.

The language and metre of the poem

In the middle of the fourteenth century the demand for poetry written in English began to increase rapidly. One group of poets, who flourished in London and included Chaucer, responded by imitating French and Italian rhymed models. This suited their "East Midlands" dialect, which had a high proportion of French words, and in fact developed into Modern English. But another group of poets revived the native *alliterated long line* (explained below) characteristic of much earlier Old English verse, and exploiting the rich pool of consonants in Middle English words derived from Old English and Old Norse. The "West Midlands" dialect of their poems suggest their authors came from around Worcestershire where Langland is likely to have been brought up, or from further north, on the Cheshire and Lancashire border, the setting of *Gawain and the Green Knight*. Most of the first generation of these poets developed a rather ornate style, often using rhyme as well as alliteration and incorporating a specialist or archaic vocabulary which must have limited their readership. *Gawain* for example uses ten different words for *man*, each beginning with a different letter. Though Langland is a central figure in this group, he seems from the first to have wanted to appeal to a wider audience, particularly as he lived in London. To judge from the large number of manuscripts and their wide distribution around the country, he succeeded. But his western dialect and the need for alliterating syllables means that he uses more words which have not survived into Modern English than Chaucer does, and modern editors retain the letters *yogh* (ȝ – pronounced *gh*) and *thorn* (þ – pronounced *th*) which Chaucer's editors generally replace. In addition, though Langland does not use as many unusual words as other alliterative poets of his generation, he does use some; there are not ten words for *man*, but there are six. Because these features make Langland initially more difficult to understand than Chaucer, I have provided a translation for unfamiliar vocabulary in my quotations.

The metre of the poem is the *alliterative long line*; this is a four-stress line divided in the middle by a *caesura*, but held together by (generally) three alliterated words or *staves* beginning with the same consonant or vowel. The staves usually coincide with the first three stresses of the line in an *aa/ax* pattern (where *a* indicates alliteration, *x* indicates no alliteration, and / indicates the *caesurae*), though there can also be subsidiary alliteration (marked *b*) and rhyme. Langland's version of the long line is unusually informal. He does not use rhyme, he constantly varies the number of unstressed syllables, and he often alliterates on unstressed syllables or unimportant words (an effect known as *modulation*). Langland's reader feels she is hearing natural speech often in everyday words, while a whole world is

brought to life by this most flexible poetry. The plainness and sub-
tlety of Langland's style can be judged by comparing the lines in
which Will first falls asleep:

> I was wery [of]wandred and wente me to reste
> Vnder a brood bank by a bournes syde;
> And as I lay and lenede and loked on þe watres,
> I slombred into a slepyng, it sweyed so murye. (Prol. 7–10)

with the equivalent passage from the late fourteenth-century alliterative poem *The Parliament of the Three Ages* where that dreamer also
falls asleep beside a brook:

> Als I habade one a banke be a bryrnne syde
> There the gryse was grene, growen with floures,
> The primrose, the pervynke, and piliole the riche
> The dewe apon dayses donkede full faire   (*Parliament* 7–10)

habade: abided; *pervynke*: periwinkle; *piliole*: pennyroyal (medicinal mint);
The dewe … faire: the dew on the daisies was beautifully dank

The description in *Parliament* is much more formal: the poet has a
very regular stress on each stave and has resorted to the obscure
words *piliole* and *donkede* and the "fillers" *riche* and *faire* to maintain
this. The effect is of an enamelled casket rather than a real meadow.
Langland's lines are less decorative, using no unusual words, and his
more relaxed alliterative metre conveys the reality of the dreamer's
experience. The four stresses in the third line quoted (*lay*, *lene*de,
*lok*ed, and *wat*ers) are evenly spaced in its fourteen syllables, and the
gentle l sound of the staves is appropriately soothing. But the preceding line quoted has only eleven syllables and its stressed monosyl-
lables are placed next to each other in two pairs (*brood bank*, *bourne*s
*sy*de), which stops the forward movement and so suggests a pause in
Will's wandering. This static effect is reinforced by the *modulation* of
beginning the line with the stressed but not alliterated '*Vn*der'. The
last line quoted has fourteen syllables and two of its four s staves are
separated by as many as four unstressed syllables (*slomb*red into a
*slep*yng). This increases the movement and suggests the rippling
water. Because of this wide variation, all three lines have the natural

rhythms of speech. We will explore some of the dramatic and poetic effects Langland can achieve with this "plain style." Indeed it became the model for all the surviving alliterative poems of the fifteenth century.

The structure and genres of the poem

The poem can be divided into two unequal halves, the first (Prol. 7 in the B-text) is known as the *Visio*, and the second, longer half (B 8–20) is known as the *Vita*. There is some doubt whether it was Langland who gave the names to the various manuscript sub-divisions I shall refer to in this paragraph, but it is convenient to adopt them. The poem is constructed as a series of 'Visions' dreamed by the narrator, Will, linked by generally only the briefest of waking interludes. These Visions are grouped in pairs, as indicated in the Contents (p. vii). In the *Visio* Will has two Visions, but he plays little part in either of them, merely watching events unfold in the countryside and in London. This is the most accessible section and contains some of Langland's liveliest poetry, and is a good place to start your reading. Will becomes the centre of events in the two Visions which make up the first part of the *Vita*. Here he discusses the Christian life with various characters apparently living inside his own head. Some manuscripts call this section *Dowel* because Will is searching for a life that "does well". As this section contains a good deal of didactic, almost hectoring verse it is often omitted by readers, though its experimental nature makes it intriguing. In the next part (sometimes called *Dobet*) Will first has a Vision of Faith, Hope and Charity allegorised in different ways. He then has a Vision of the life and death of Jesus Christ, a moving drama which has become the most famous part of the poem and is not to be missed. In the two final Visions (*Dobest*) Will first watches the life of the early Church and then participates in the struggles of the Church of his own time. This section returns to some of the themes and structures of the opening Prologue but from a darker, even despairing perspective. This unusual structure of a series of dreams allows Langland immense freedom to switch from one kind of narrative or genre to another and so there follows a brief introduction to the major genres used:

Dream-vision

When a Middle English poet wanted to discuss general truths, he often pretended to be describing a dream. This allowed him to use symbolic figures and landscapes in an "allegorical" narrative generally including himself as the Dreamer and protagonist. Under this cover he could explore difficult or even dangerous topics: he could describe his inner life (as in the enduringly popular thirteenth-century *Romance of the Rose*), or comment on the contemporary political situation (as the strange creatures in the Biblical *Book of Revelation* were thought to do) or analyse man's relationship to God (as the anonymous fourteenth-century poem *Pearl* does). Langland wanted to do all these things and more, and as we shall see, seems to know several literary examples. These literary dreams are not very like real dreams. In them we meet not only symbolic landscapes and creatures but also personified characters who deliver long speeches. They can be understood better if we look briefly at medieval dream theory, usually drawn from the Roman author Macrobius, referred to by Langland and paraphrased by Chaucer in the *Parliament of Fowles* and in the *Nun's Priest's Tale*. Chapter 3 of his early-fifth-century *Commentary on Scipio's Dream* divides significant dreams into three kinds:

- the *somnium or* enigmatic dream, which 'conceals with strange shapes and veils with ambiguity the true meaning of the information given'
- the *oraculum*, in which the dreamer is addressed by authority figures who tell him 'what action to take or to avoid'
- *visio* or prophetic vision

Langland uses all three of these types of dream in the series of eight Visions which make up his poem. Passus 6 and 16 include allegorical landscapes characteristic of Macrobius' *somnium*; Passus 1 is only the first of many *oracula* in which imagined authority-figures give moral homilies; and Passus 20 is on one level a *visio* of the end of the world. He also makes use of some of the other characteristic features of English dream-visions. Like the dreamer in *Pearl* he is generally lulled to sleep by natural sounds (a brook in the Prologue, birdsong in Passus 8) in a briefly beguiling landscape. Like "Geoffrey" in Chaucer's *House of Fame* he gives himself the *persona* of a somewhat cantankerous Dreamer, bewildered by all the changes of narrative, and inclined to argue with the authorities he meets. Like other English poets of the time, Langland uses the dream-vision as a flexible and unobtrusive structure on which he can hang his observation not of a fantastic fictional world, but of the world of here and now.

Allegorical journeys

Some of the features of Langland's dream-vision can be related to two originally French forms, the *chanson d'aventure* and the *Pilgrimage Allegory*. Both these forms depend on the idea that man is a sinful wanderer in this world, in need of some emotional and spiritual direction (and we are told in the third line that Will is 'vnholy of werkes'). In *chansons d'aventure* the poet-narrator encounters a guide and experiences an adventure which, in English versions, tended to be edifying rather than romantic. In the Pilgrimage Allegories of Ruteboeuf and Guillaume de Deguileville (1330–60) the poet-dreamer, guided by allegorical characters like Reason and Patience, is confronted by various temptations and Sins on his way to the Holy City. Deguileville's *Pélerinage de l'Ame Humaine* (*Pilgrimage of the Human Soul*) was extremely popular in both England and France and could have inspired Langland to construct his own poem as a series of dream pilgrimages and maybe also inspired the pilgrimage structure of the *Canterbury Tales*. Although by no means the only pilgrimage that takes place in the poem, the Dreamer's journey to find a virtuous life is a narrative thread for the whole poem. As he is called Will, it can be read both as a symbolic autobiography of William Langland, and as the journey of anyone's will.

Political and social commentary (satire, complaint, debate and advice)

The dreams and allegories just described often seem, particularly in the first part of the poem (the *Visio*) a pretext for Langland to criticise his own world by exaggerating its failings in *satire* or voicing the laments of the oppressed in *complaint*. There was already an established tradition of satirical and complaint poetry in Langland's England, some of which (like the satire known as *The Simonie* composed in the 1320s) seems to have echoes in *Piers Plowman*, as will be shown below. Poets were however not the only group to satirise or complain about society. Preachers attacked the sins of all classes of men, using what is sometimes referred to as the *sermon ad status* or *estates satire*; these clearly influenced Chaucer's *General Prologue to the Canterbury Tales*. Chronicles attacked what they saw as degenerate elements in society, and reformists of all kinds attacked the Church. Langland can be distinguished from other writers not in his social concerns or even his examples but in the haunting effect of his verse and the complexity of his analysis and poetic method. It is characteristic of complaint, for example the early-fourteenth-century *Song of the Husbandman* which complains of the burden of taxes, to voice the wrongs of those who cannot speak for themselves. But rarely is the voice as authentic as Langland's, for in spite of his learning he seems to have suffered with the poorest and most ignorant of his fellow subjects.

The First Vision of the poem also includes a good deal of *political advice* which is at first general, but becomes focused with increasing directness on Langland's own King, Richard II. An example of general advice literature is the *Secret of Secrets* falsely attributed to Aristotle, which was translated several times in the fourteenth century and suggested the virtues appropriate to a king, such as justice and prudence. More satirical and politically sensitive were the texts which addressed the King directly, such as John Gower's 1399 addition to his Latin *Vox Clamantis*, which, like Langland in the C-text, castigated Richard II. This First Vision is also the context for several *debates* or *flyghtings* between pairs of allegorical characters. This was a popular form (examples include *The Owl and the Nightingale* and *The Parliament of the Three Ages*) in which the opposing sides generally attack each other's weaknesses rather than listing their own strengths, and their (often unequal) debate is usually ended by an umpire of some kind. However like the debate in the mid-fourteenth-century *Wynnere and Wastoure*, which Langland had almost certainly read, Langland's debates are generally inconclusive, open-ended.

Religious genres (sermon, confessional handbook and Biblical commentary)

Most of the texts available in the fourteenth century were religious, and they cover a large number of traditions and genres. The friars' mission included teaching both at university and in the wider community, and they had had developed a new kind of sermon, characterised by a complex division of material into sections and sub-sections, by frequent references to the Bible, translated where necessary, and by the use of lively anecdotes, allegories and examples. The long discourses in *Piers Plowman* have much in common with this kind of sermon, and Will meets several school or University teachers who debate theological issues like the nature of salvation with their rather obtuse pupil.

The Friars were also prominent among those who produced materials for priests to use in the parish, such as the "Confessors' Handbooks" which analysed the types of sin and the ways in which different classes of society were likely to commit them (Chaucer translated one in his *Parson's Tale*). Langland's detailed analysis of sinfulness in Passus 5 and 14 suggests he was well versed in such *fraternal literature*. But his references to friars are almost always unflattering, sometimes even reminiscent of the attacks made on them by the followers of Wycliffe. Langland's eagerness to quote and translate from the Bible also parallels the efforts of the Wycliffites to give the laity an English translation of the Bible. However Langland's commentaries on his quotations draw on the much older authority of the Church Fathers and their traditional exponents, so that his understanding of the Bible is generally quite orthodox. Unlike the Wycliffites he supports the traditional teaching of the Church though deploring its failure to live up to its ideals.

The presence of so many genres under one roof is disruptive. The whole poem has the accumulative effect of the *Canterbury Tales* where each section is linked to, rather than being a clear development of, the preceding one. And yet certain characters – notably Piers Plowman, Conscience and Patience – do recur, and the poet visits and revisits key ideas and concerns. Above all the figure of Will the Dreamer turns the different Visions into a single experience which enables him and the reader to change and grow. But if the characteristic of a "post-modern" text is its simultaneous use of different narratives and perspectives to conceal rather than reveal the viewpoint of the author, then *Piers Plowman* often feels postmodern. It is the reader who must make sense of the discontinuous sections, and map out Will's development and Piers' significance. And perhaps Langland kept writing and rewriting, never really finishing the poem, because he felt that writing and reading can only be completed by "doing well" in the world.

The purpose and organisation of this Guide

This Guide is designed as a commentary to help you understand as you read. I have contextualised each section within the relevant historical situation and literary sources and analogues, and also indicated where Langland's thinking differs markedly from that of his contemporaries. Most of the time I use available scholarship on the poem, but in some areas, for example on his relation to debt law, or to the writing of St Augustine, the research is new. I also offer my own way of disentangling Langland's creative confusion, showing where he is going and what previous lines of thought he is returning to. But the aim of the Guide is to make it possible for you to solve the enigmas for yourself.

The book is divided into chapters corresponding to the different Passus, grouped in the eight separate Visions. Each chapter will contain the following parts:

- an opening paragraph relating it to the previous Passus and briefly introducing the genres and possible sources for that section

- a boxed plan for the Passus with line numbers
- sections of commentary on the component parts of that Passus
- introductions (for example, Who is Lady Meed?) to the major characters
- informal questions to guide your personal approach to the poem
- a conclusion leading to the next Passus

Historical and other background information is generally confined to text-boxes, which will be referred to by page number when appropriate. Links between the different parts of the poem are made by bracketed references to line numbers. Quotations are from A. V. C. Schmidt's *Piers Plowman: A Parallel Text Edition* (Longmans, 1995a), and translations rely on Schmidt's Everyman edition of *Piers Plowman: the B-text* (3rd edition, London, 1995b) which has the same line numbers as the parallel text edition.

Further reading

On texts and dates of poem, see Benson; Burrow (1982); Hanna (1993, 2000); Justice (1994); Mann (1994); Warner. On readership and works inspired by *Piers Plowman*, see Barr (primary text); Bowers; Kerby-Fulton (2003); Scattergood. On Langland's life, see Bowers (1995); Hanna (1993); Donaldson, Ch. 7. On Langland's language and alliterative style, see Barnie, S. A.; Davlin (1989); Samuels; Schmidt (1987). On Langland's genres, see Adams (1985, on rubrics); Burrow (1993, Appdx A on Deguileville); Cooper (1991); Godden (1990), pp. 12–14; Davidoff, Chs 2, 3; Mann (1973); Middleton (1982a); Shepherd; Trigg (1993: essays by Justice and Finke).

The Prologue

Langland's Prologue is a *tour de force*. It not only demonstrates that he will be looking at all society as it is and as it might be, but also introduces some of the genres he will be using (see the Introduction for definitions). First and foremost it is to be a *dream-vision* (or *allegorical dream*) but this form will include other genres as well. Allegorical dreams can be subdivided according to the kind of dream the author is supposed to be experiencing. In the Prologue it is a *somnium* or symbolic narrative set on an allegorical "stage", here a field between a tower and a deep ditch. This is a backdrop for a passage of *estates satire*, where we meet figures representing different groups in society. Langland's version is organised both by social classes (like Chaucer's *General Prologue*, which may have been influenced by it) and morally, by the kinds of sin typical of those classes. The estates satire culminates in a short *mirror for princes* in which Langland seems to be describing the recently crowned Richard II. Finally there is an *animal fable* (like Chaucer's *Nun's Priest's Tale*) involving a *debate* reminiscent of one actually held in the Parliament of 1376. All these genres recur in the poem. For example, the diagrammatic allegory of the *somnium* set in a field is extended in Passus 6 into a ploughing scene, the moralising estates satire is the basis for Passus 7 when the good estates are pardoned their sins, and the advice offered to the king is put into practice in Passus 4. In Passus 1 Langland introduces us to the another kind of dream, the *oraculum*, in which the personified abstraction Holy Church gives a sermon on Truth and Love. Sermons by such personified characters will be a recurrent feature of the poem and these two qualities will be the centre of much of their discussion. The Prologue and Passus 1 therefore act as a double prologue to the issues and the allegorical method of the poem as a whole.

The following chart shows how the Prologue is organised:

Prologue	
Dream introduction and landscape	1–19
The folk of the field	
Secular (that is, non-clergy) workers and parasites	20–45
Religious workers and parasites	46–99
Religious rulers	100–111
Secular rulers and nobility	112–145
The fable of "Belling the Cat"	146–210
The mixture of classes in London	212–230

Dream introduction and landscape 1–19

Langland's opening lines are not only very beautiful; they are full of clues about himself and his *persona* in the poem: Will the Dreamer. At this stage in the poem Will seems to be both morally and socially lacking:

> In a somer seson, whan softe was þe sonne,
> I shoop me into shroudes as I a sheep were,
> In habite as an heremite vnholy of werkes,
> Wente wide in þis world wondres to here.
> Ac on a May morwenynge on Maluerne Hilles
> Me bifel a ferly, of fairye me þoþte. (1–6)

> I shoop me into shroudes: I dressed myself in wool like sheep;
> Me bifel a ferly: I was visited by a vision

Although Will's dream in this Passus will be chiefly of London, he falls asleep in the hills of Worcestershire, where Langland probably grew up. He dresses himself in the poem as a social parasite – false hermits are scathingly described at 53–57 as 'Grete lobies and longe þat loþe were to swynke' (great tall fellows unwilling to work, 55).

He also seems to have an unhealthy curiosity for 'wondres' and is on the lookout for fairies. But the landscape he finds himself in is not so much like fairyland as a medieval pageant wagon. Plays were staged on a three-level structure with heaven on the upper storey, earth on the cart, and hell beneath the wheels. So Will dreams of two castles (tour / dungeon), one on a hill and one in a ditch, and a field between them:

> I sei3 a tour on a tofte trieliche ymaked
> A deep dale byneþe, a dongeon þerinne ...
> A fair feeld ful of folk fond I þer bitwene (14–17)
>
> trieliche ymaked: excellently made; fond: found

This allegorical setting introduces the moral and social framework for this – and perhaps every – Vision. If we use the analogy of a 'vertical' axis to describe an individual's relation to God, then this three-level backdrop conveys a religious outlook on the world, in which people choose either to go towards God (high) or towards the Devil (low). We can then use a 'horizontal' axis to describe their relation towards each other. The folk in the field live 'as þe world askeþ (asks, 19) and so their social roles extend 'horizontally' across society. But they should also be able to see beyond other people's demands on them, to the demands being made on them by God, or the enticements laid for them by the Devil. It is the mixing of the two axes on which human beings live which makes Langland's estates satire so subtle.

The folk of the field: the two lower estates 20–111

Secular workers and parasites

Medieval social classes or "estates" were traditionally seen as three interdependent groups placed below one another: the nobility or "those who fight", then the clerics or "those who pray", and lastly the peasantry or "those who work". But Langland replaces this social hierarchy by his individual moral hierarchy, so that the most important estate seems not to be the nobility but those who support the others by either work or prayers. Whereas Chaucer began his Prologue with the knight, Langland begins with those who 'putten hem to þe plouȝ' (20), and those who live 'for loue of Oure Lord' (26); these are contrasted with those who 'putten hem to pride' (23, who might well include knights) and those who enjoy a 'likerous liflode' (lecherous life, 30). At the same time we seem also to be offered an economic value-system, for the ploughmen are contrasted not only with the proud but with the wasteful, as they 'wonnen (produce) þat þise wastours wiþ glotonye destruyeþ' (22). This seems more like the antitheses in *Wynnere and Wastoure*, another dream-poem, written about 25 years earlier, and which Langland probably knew. Its author satirised the gluttony of the nobility (Wastour) and the avarice of the farmer (Wynnere), but seemed to suggest that both vices are necessary for society to flourish:

> Whoso wele shal winne, a wastour moste he finde (390)

Langland does not restrict "wasters" to the wealthier classes in this way – indeed as we will see in Passus 6, there are wasters among the ploughmen themselves. And he too seems to allow that wasters must be permitted in society, but with the important proviso that if they are not going to contribute anything on the horizontal social axis, they must contribute on the vertical, moral axis. For example the 'mynstralles' or poetic entertainers are said to be 'synnelees' (33–34), but not if they are liars and vagabonds. Virtuous hermits and anchorites (itinerant and enclosed solitary religious men) are seen winning 'heueneriche blisse' (27–28) for themselves and those they pray for, but mere wasters if they are hypocrites (53–57). 'In Langland's age a significant and valued number of hermits were laymen (that is, not in holy orders) and labourers, and some at least of these were neither holy nor celibate' (E. Jones, 79). What then of the Dreamer himself, who writes verse as a minstrel does, and is dressed as a hermit? Is he so 'vnholy of werkes' (3) on the vertical axis that he must be considered merely a social parasite on the horizontal one? And even if he does improve morally, does that let him off the social obligation to help produce food? This question of whether religious worthiness justifies social dependence preoccupies the whole poem; each of its central characters (Piers, Will, Patience, Hawkyn, Conscience) will at some point turn away from the social good of the provider to the moral good of those who try above all to save their own souls. Which way of life is the more selfish? which is the closest to God? which, in short, "does well"?

Religious workers and parasites 46–99

The section on false pilgrims and hermits (46–57) is the start of Langland's survey of the second layer of society: those who pray, or the clergy. Nowadays English clergymen are almost all "secular", deacons, parish priests and bishops who live in the everyday world. In Langland's Catholic England however there were also great numbers of "religious" clergy, that is to say, monks and friars who were members of religious orders and supposedly lived apart from the world (see Monks and Friars, p. 000). Such men had an even higher moral standard of behaviour to live up to than the secular clergy, who took a vow of chastity but not the vows of poverty and obedience. The pilgrims and hermits whom Langland mentions first are not within a monastic or fraternal (that is, of Friars) community, but are also living "religious" lives in this sense, at least for a while, because they have undertaken a pilgrimage:

> Pilgrymes and palmeres pli3ten hem togidere
> To seken Seint Iame and seintes in Rome; ...
> Heremytes on an heep wiþ hoked staues
> Wenten to Walsyngham – and hire wenches after (46–54).

> Palmers: professional pilgrims; Seint Iame: St James the Great buried in Compostella; an heep: lots; hoked staues: crooks. Wenten ... after: Hermits went to Walsingham with their crooks, followed by their girlfriends

Pilgrimage was a part of the sacrament of penance (see The Sacrament of Penance, p. 89), through which people tried to repair the damage done to their souls on the vertical axis of eternity while they were fulfilling the demands on the horizontal axis of social life. Throughout the poem penance is seen to be crucial for the laity (non-clerics), and Langland here attacks three groups who undermine it. First the hermits and palmers (professional pilgrims who are paid to perform pilgrimages for others) are shown robbing pilgrimage of spiritual value. Shortly afterwards we see friars on their way to hear lords' confessions and allow them easy penances for their sins (64). Then at 68 we meet a pardoner, a minor cleric licensed to "sell" pardons or "indulgences" to raise money for hospitals and other religious foundations. The pardon replaced a pilgrimage, and supposedly absolved the purchaser from a period of suffering in Purgatory – a wonderful way of ascending the vertical axis by money rather than virtue. The satire is scathing in the little vignette where the pardoner rakes in offerings with his rolled-up licence which grants him authority to absolve everyone there of their sins (68–82). Langland clearly does not blame the friars and pardoners alone for this spurious sale of 'heueneriche blisse' (27). The people themselves are at fault (as they are in the similar scene in Chaucer's *Pardoner's Prologue*) for taking this easy option rather than performing penance properly. But they lack leadership because the priests are neglecting their duties, running off to London to be chantry priests singing masses for the dead, or highly paid secretaries and stewards (86, 95–96). Even bishops who are ultimately responsible for the conduct of the priests prefer to 'seruen þe King and his siluer tellen' (92) – Langland may be thinking of bishops like Wiliam of Wykeham, the bishop of Winchester, who had recently been stripped of his enormous wealth as a punishment for his conduct when the King's Chancellor. Consequently the laity, the non-clerical folk in the field, are losing the chance to perform proper penance for their sins. They and their priests need proper leadership.

Religious rulers 100–111

At line 100 Langland turns to this leadership. It was supposedly provided by the cardinals and the Pope who were at the top of the clerical hierarchy and had the ultimate power over the sacrament of penance and the issuing of pardons. This 'power of the keys' to Heaven had been given by Jesus to St Peter who became the first Pope:

Thou art Peter, and upon this rock I will build my Church, and the
gates of Hell shall not prevail against it. And I will give unto thee the
keys of the kingdom of heaven, and whatsoever thou shalt bind on
earth shall be bound in heaven, and whatsoever thou shalt loose on
earth shall be loosed in heaven. (*Matthew* 16:18–19)

This "power of the keys" was delegated by Peter's successors in the
Papacy to the cardinals, bishops and lesser clergy they ordained (see
picture, p. 25). But Langland points out that the 'hinges' of the
doors of heaven, the cardinals (a word derived from the Latin for
hinge), are themselves corrupt, for have not some of them recently
presumed to give 'the power that Peter hadde' to a second Pope
(77–79)?

> Ac of þe Cardinals at court þat kauȝte of þat name
> And power presumed in hem a Pope to make (107–118)
>
> kauȝte of þat name: appropriated the name of 'hinges'

Langland is referring here to the Great Schism which began in 1378
when a faction of cardinals elected Clement VII to be Pope (living in
Avignon) after Urban VI had already been elected in Rome the previous year. This is both a clue to the date of the B-text, and of
Langland's position in the "reformist camp" of contemporary critics
of the Church in England. Like the Master of Balliol College
Oxford, John Wycliffe, he was prepared to speak against the Pope
and the cardinals, but unlike Wycliffe he does not question whether
the passage from St Matthew did actually authorise the Papacy.
Wycliffe's later followers would even claim that any good man could
be priest or even Pope without election by any cardinals (which is
close to the views expressed by the 'Lewed Vicar' of Passus 19, see p.
254). Langland does not go as far as this; having mentioned the
Schism, he refuses to 'impugnen' (criticise, 109) the Papacy any
further and certainly does not imply that the Christian can do
without the Church hierarchy or its authority to pardon sin. He
wants to reform rather than to replace it.

St Peter with key

(after a sculpture, Wentworth, East Anglia, mid 12th century)

Rulers and nobility: the Coronation Scene 112–145

The estates satire has swept from the ploughman to the Pope but has not found good leadership. It is logical then that the Dreamer should now see a vision of secular leadership, and his dream switches without comment from estates satire to something more like a "mirror for princes", that is to say, a poem advising the King how to rule. This is cast as a kind of "Coronation Scene" (112–145) which seems to be modelled on the actual coronation of Richard II on 16 July 1377. Langland also seems to have used the influential study of the *Laws and Customs of England* written by Henry Bracton in the middle of the previous century. This scene will be followed by an animal fable (145–216) relevant to the Good Parliament of the previous year. The whole section appears for the first time in the B-text, suggesting that these had been recent events. However it can also be read more generally as an allegory of the constitutional principles by which the English king reigned.

On the day before his coronation the ten-year-old Richard was led from the Tower of London by his barons and knights to Westminster Abbey through the crowds lining Cheapside. This had been decorated with elaborate constructions, including a turreted tower from which a golden Angel leaned to present a model crown (see Donaldson, 116–17). Langland's King is also escorted by 'Kny3thod' (112) and addressed by an Angel. On the next day, in the Abbey, Richard swore the royal oath to his people, promising he would 'uphold and guard the rightful laws and customs which the community of his realm will have chosen'. It was for allegedly breaking this oath that his great-grandfather, Edward II, had been deposed in 1327, and that he too would be deposed in 1399. The following lines convey the sense of this important oath:

> The Kyng and þe Commune and Kynde Wit þe þridde
> Shopen lawe and leaute – ech lif to knowe his owene. (121–122)

Kynde Wit: leaute: justice/loyalty; Natural Reason; knowe his owene: know what belongs to him.

As in the oath, the king is said to act with the 'commune' – the community of Parliament (the hereditary Lords as well as the elected Commons). He is also advised by 'Kynde Wit', which has already been associated with the clergy in lines 113–116, and here suggests the Natural Law (see, Kynde, Kynde Knowyng and Kynde Wit, p. 000). Natural Law was defined by Bracton as 'that which Nature, that is God himself, taught all living things' (p. 26). Kynde Wit helps the King and the Community to shape 'leaute', which means both justice and loyalty, and is further defined by the

Roman law principle of knowing what is one's own. Thus the king, clergy and commoners unite to provide a just regime under which men keep faith with one another because they know what is legally theirs, and what are the responsibilities of their estate (Baldwin 1981a, pp. 12–15). However, although the lines quoted seem to fit with the English constitutional principles defined by Bracton, they do not insist, as he does, that the king should keep the law himself.

The words of the Goliard (vagabond poet) and Lunatic, who now enter the scene, do however advise the king to obey this law 'so leaute þee louye' (126). Indeed both characters can be seen as *personae* of Langland himself, advising the King as only a mad poet can. The Angel reinforces the point, warning the King of retribution if he fails to be merciful as well as just. The only group who seem ready to release the King from all restraints is the 'commune' who suddenly discover an ability to speak Latin (but do they understand what they are saying?):

> *Precepta regis sunt nobis vincula legis* (145)
>
> The king's orders will have for us the binding force of laws

This tag from Roman law should not apply to English subjects, but it will be the real Richard II's ambition to make the law lie in his personal will, which is why he will lose his crown. As so often, Langland has put his finger on the crucial issue. But writing in about 1378, he seems fairly optimistic. If the king is wise, he will limit himself both on the vertical axis, by the laws of God represented by the Angel and Kynde Wit, and on the horizontal axis, by the laws which the Goliard and Lunatic refer to, the English laws he has inherited and by any future laws he will make *with* his Parliament.

The fable of "Belling the Cat" 146–210

If this Coronation Scene suggested that the king should consider Parliament a partner in making the laws, then the *animal fable* which follows it seems to suggest the opposite. This very fable of the rats who failed to hang a bell on the cat who tyrannised them, had been used in the sermon which opened the "Good Parliament" of May 1376. It urged Parliament to take action against several greedy courtiers who were exploiting the weakness of Edward III. The rats of this remarkable Parliament *did* succeed in belling the cat at least for a time, for they "impeached" (condemned) two of the courtiers for corruption and had the King's extravagant mistress Alice Perrers (said to cost the Treasury over £2,000 a year – an enormous sum at the time) banished from the court. This significant advance in the power of Parliament was however counteracted by the King's eldest surviving son, John of Gaunt, in the following autumn, when the "Bad Parliament" reversed the impeachments and allowed Alice to return. The historical context may be relevant in the following ways (although, like the Coronation Scene, it can also bear a wider interpretation):

- The cat may suggest John of Gaunt, who was protecting not only the Court party but the rights and privileges of the Crown. Alternatively, the cat can be seen as any strong but unjust ruler.
- The 'raton of renoun, moost tenable of tonge' (158) who proposes belling the cat, can be seen as the first Speaker of the Commons, Peter de la Mare, who led the group of Commons and Peers in their attempt to purge the court, and was immediately afterwards imprisoned by Gaunt. Had he succeeded, he would have represented the power of Parliament to curb the king.
- The 'kitoun' (194) can be seen either as the ailing Edward III or the boy king Richard II. Alternatively it can represent any ruler who allows parliament to detract from his power.

Though the Dreamer, Will, at first sides with the rat who proposes controlling the cat, he seems to give more lasting approval to the 'mous þat muche good kouþe, as me þo þouȝte' (182), who points out (in rodent terms) the disadvantages of allowing commoners to control their rulers:

For hadde ye rattes youre wille, ye kouþe noȝt rule yowselue. (201)

couþe: be able to

Was Langland a supporter of John of Gaunt, preferring a corrupt court and even a rapacious royal mistress to a Parliament with too much power? Or was he simply presenting two contrasting views of kingship: first an idealistic Coronation Scene where the 'comune' (community) actually helps the king to shape the law, and then a more cynical demonstration of how helpless that same 'comune' is against royal power. Where do you feel his sympathies lie? It is difficult to assess Langland's political views from the Prologue, but he returns to the question of good government in Passus 4, where royal corruption is epitomised by a character who could have been modelled on Alice Perrers: Lady Meed.

The mixture of classes in London 211–231

The Prologue has introduced a vision of English society in a state which cries out for reform and leadership. The peasants are exploited by the numerous parasites on their labour, the clergy prefer to corrupt rather than to lead their flocks, and the king and his nobles cannot be compelled to keep the laws they make. Yet it is also a vision of the bustle and variety of life as it is actually lived. It ends with a cacophony of voices from London, including some (the mumbling lawyers, the shouting retailers) who will take centre stage in Passus 2–4. But first Langland gives us, in Passus 1, another prologue, one which focuses not on the horizontal axis of men's relations with each other, but on the vertical axis of their relationship with God. He has sketched some of the problematic areas of his society, failures of obedience, justice and loyalty, and the failure of the mechanism for their correction: penance. Reformation of the Church can be supposed to be the key to the reformation of society as a whole. It is therefore appropriate that we now meet that Church in its ideal form.

Further reading

On estates satire, see Mann (1973); Owst. On hermits, see Dias; Jones; Godden (1984). On politics in *Piers Plowman*, see Baldwin (1981a); Bishop; Donaldson. On contemporary political theory and practice, see d'Entrèves; Holmes; Saul.

The First Vision: Passus 1–4

Passus 1

Passus 1 is intimately connected with the Prologue; it can be read both as a commentary on it, and as a second prologue in the *sermon* genre. Though Will has not woken up, he now experiences a different kind of dream, an *oraculum*, in which a female authority-figure speaks to him. Like other authority-figures met in dream-visions, she treats Will quite roughly but offers him reliable advice; she will be succeeded in the poem by many other less reliable authority-figures of both sexes. As well as commenting on the Prologue, she introduces the key ideals of the poem, so much so that some critics see her sermon as 'the poem in miniature'. In particular she explores the meaning of the word "truth", which in Middle English suggested love and faithfulness as well as honesty and justice, so that his section includes some inspired poetry on the love of God. This "treasure of Truth" is contrasted with earthly treasure, whose potential to corrupt will be the subject of the rest of this first Vision. In trying to grasp what she says, Will reveals himself to be lacking in 'kynde knowyng', whose meanings range from "experienced understanding" to "God-given wisdom", and he initiates an endeavour to turn verbal advice into practical goodness characteristic of his whole journey, and in which he will experience truths which he heard first from Holy Church's sermon.

The Passus is in two parts, divided by an introduction to the speaker, Holy Church:

Passus 1	
Commentary on the Prologue:	1–70
Introduction of Holy Church	71–84
Sermon on the Truth that God is love	85–209

Who is Holy Church? 71–84

The Church as an institution is fiercely satirised in the poem, but Lady Holy Church represents the Heavenly Church, the ideal community of the blessed. Allegorisations of the Bible often depicted this as a woman: the great Old Testament love-poem, the *Song of Songs*, was supposed to express Christ's love for his bride, the Church, and the tribulations of faithful Christians on earth were supposedly revealed by the sufferings of the 'Woman clothed with the Sun' in Chapter 12 of the *Book of Revelation* (or the *Apocalypse*). In the many illustrated manuscripts of *Revelation* she stands in opposition to the personification of earthly kingdoms, the Whore of Babylon, who has much in common with the personification of Meed (reward) we will meet in the next Passus. So in giving Will a sermon on the true treasure, she is partly talking about herself in opposition to the false treasure he is about to encounter.

Commentary on the Prologue 1–70

Holy Church's explanation to Will of what he has just seen is not as well organised as we might wish. Langland seems easily distracted from large patterns by immediate concerns, and he often prefers a specific and practical truth to a generalisation. So although Holy Church does comment on the three places Will has just glimpsed, Heaven, Earth and Hell, she spends most time on an apparently new issue: the question of property – what men need, and what they want. This looks forward to the next three Passus, where the way in which people use property determines their position on the two axes of moral and social value. Most people ignore the vertical axis, but have 'worship (honour) in þis world' (8), enjoying the goods of the earth which have actually been given men 'to worshipe [God]' (16). The test Holy Church offers to judge whether men are misusing the 'Þree Þynges' (the essentials of food, drink and clothing) is 'mesure' (moderation). One can judge what is 'mesurable' by how much one needs, and this measure can then become the foundation of social justice, for God

> comaunded of his curteisie in commune þree þynges:
> Are none nedfulle but þo (20–21).
>
> nedfulle: necessary; þo: those

Langland reveals the often radical implications of this traditional principle throughout the poem, most crucially in Passus 7 and Passus 20 where he discusses begging (see p. 110 and p. 261). So far so good, but anxiety about property involves not what one absolutely *needs*, but what one *wants* and can afford to buy. When Will asks Holy Church about money, she refers to Jesus' cryptic words at *Matthew* 22:21 and says he should use Kynde Wit (natural intelligence) and Reason (who understands Divine Law) to interpret them (see Langland's Psychology, p. 123):

> For riȝtfully Reson sholde rule yow alle,
> And Kynde Wit be wardeyn youre welþe to kepe (54–55)
>
> wardeyn: guardian; Kynde Wit: natural intelligence; kepe: protect

Will draws her back to his first vision, and asks her about the 'dongeon in þe dale' (castle in the ditch, 59), which she interprets psychologically as 'castel of care' (61) where Wrong dwells:

> He is lettere of loue and lieþ hem alle:
> That trusten on his tresour bitrayed arn sonnest.' (69–70)
>
> lettere: barrier; lieþ: lies to; bitrayed: are betrayed

It will be no surprise to learn in the next Passus that Meed is the daughter of False (2.25). Holy Church has therefore placed worldly treasure on the vertical axis between False and Truth, and now warns Will to treat it with great circumspection if he wants to avoid the fate of Adam and Eve and Judas (65–70). Will thanks her for her good advice, but receives a scolding in return for not having recognised her. He was brought to her as a baby by godparents who stood as sureties ('borwes') for his obedience:

> Thow brouȝtest me borwes my biddyng to fulfille (77)
>
> borwes: sureties; biddyng: commands

In the hierarchical world of fourteenth-century England her words also imply that she is a feudal lady who expects loyalty and obedience from her 'serf' or bondsman. Her kingdom is God's, not man's, and we have already seen (using the analogy of the vertical and horizontal axes) that men and women can be distinguished according to which kingdom they give their allegiance to.

If Holy Church represents the heavenly kingdom then Will's moral failings can be seen as a kind of breaking of allegiance, and he at once falls on his knees and asks for forgiveness and instruction.

Sermon on 'God is love' 85–209

Holy Church's sermon text 'God is love' is from St John's *First Epistle* Ch. 4, a chapter so important to Langland that it may even be seen as the text for the poem as a whole (see Davlin 1996). Verse 16 claims that 'God is love, and he that dwelleth in love dwelleth in God, and God in him'. Holy Church calls this the unlit mate treasure, and names it as Truth:

> Whan alle tresors arn tried,' quod she, 'treuþe is þe beste.
> I do it on *Deus caritas* to deme þe soþe; (85–86)
>
> *Deus caritas*: God is love

What is Truth?

The affinity between love and truth is less clear to us than it was to Langland's early readers, for truth is a word which has changed its meaning. It derives from the Old English word *treowþ* meaning 'faithkeeping' (still preserved in the phrase 'I plight thee my troth' in the *Prayer Book* marriage service). In Langland's time the most common definition was *fidelity* – to a person or an oath (*MED*, 1, 2); this meaning could include love. As faithfulness began to be applied to principles as well as people, it had come to mean *honesty* and *integrity* as well (*MED*, 3, 4). This meaning came to be associated particularly with keeping the law or the principles behind the law, and so truth also meant *justice* (*MED*, 13). Since a principal attribute of God is his righteousness, truth was coming to be used as a synonym for God or spiritual reality (*MED*, 6: 'every lesyng [lie] is against treuthe, for Crist is verray treuthe'). From this it is but a short step to the modern sense of 'that which accurately and completely represents a state of affairs' (*MED*, 11, 12). The word carries all these meanings at different places in the poem, and sometimes all at once, for when Holy Church says that 'Truþe' is within 'þe tour vp þe toft' (12), she may want Will to think of God's loyalty, justice, honesty and divinity. The word *leaute* also combines loyalty and legality (it derives from *lealte* and *legalitas*) though it does not extend into the Divine as truth does. (For the construction of her sermon, see Sermons and Religious Education, p. 78.)

Holy Church's sermon on 'the 'tresor' of 'Treuthe' (85), mostly used truth to mean justice, and loyalty. In the first part of her sermon (85–138) truth seems to mean the justice and loyalty expected in society. The 'kynges and knyȝtes' that keep Truth (94) show their loyalty for their king primarily by enforcing justice, when they:

> taken transgressores and tyen hem faste
> Til treuþe hadde ytermyned hire trespas to þe ende. (96–97)

transgressores: law-breakers; faste: securely; ytermyned: judged; trespas: crime

Langland's contemporary knights did in fact have a responsibility for apprehending and trying criminals in their capacity of Justices of the Peace.

Holy Church contrasts such examples of loyal 'knights' (the JPs, David's followers, Christ's apostles) with Lucifer and his fellow angels, who 'brak buxomnesse' (broke their obedience, 113) to God in Heaven. The story, derived from *Isaiah* 14:13–14 and dramatized in, for example, *The Fall of Lucifer* from the York Cycle, was that Lucifer and a band of rebel angels tried to overthrow God, and were banished to Hell and transformed into devils. Langland has already described Lucifer as the 'lettere (preventer) of loue' (69) and now dramatically evokes their fall:

> And mo þousandes wiþ hym þan man kouþe nombre
> Lopen out wiþ Lucifer in loþliche forme
> For þei leueden vpon hym þat lyed in þis manere: ...
> [They] fellen out in fendes liknesse [for] nyne dayes togideres,
> Til God of his goodnesse gan stable and stynte
> And garte [to stekie þe heuene], and stonden in quiete. (116–123)

> kouþe nombre: can number; loþliche: loathsome; leueden: believed; stable and stynte: make them stable and stationary; garte [to stekie þe heuene]: stuck Heaven up again

The strong active verbs of this passage not only convey Lucifer and his followers' treason (lepen, leued, lyed – all alliterating with Lucifer) but also God's restoration of stability (sticke, stable, stynte, stonden) which is a materialization of the principle of firm faithfulness.

Perhaps finding this a bit remote, Will requests Holy Church to show him how to recognise truth:

> 'Yet haue I no kynde knowynge,' quod I, 'yet mote ye kenne me bettre' (138)

> kynde knowynge: natural knowledge(?); kenne: teach

This leads into the second part of the sermon (139–208), in which Holy Church works out the moral and religious implications of her text. As explained in Kynde, Kynde Knowynge and Kynde Wit on p. 153, 'kynde knowynge' is a kind of inner wisdom for which Will seems to be searching throughout the poem, using experience rather than books to recognise it in his heart. It becomes increasingly associated with Love; in Passus 18 indeed we will see Jesus himself learn it on the Cross. It is appropriate then that Holy Church should answer Will's question by defining truth as the love of God (143–145), using her text from St John that 'God is love'. She describes the Incarnation of Jesus and his return to Heaven as the journey of love:

> 'For Truþe telleþ þat loue is triacle of heuene:
> May no synne be on hym seene þat þat spice vseþ; ...
> For heuene myȝte nat holden it, so was it heuy of hymselue,
> Til it hadde of þe erþe eten his fille.
> And whan it hadde of þis fold flessh and blood taken,   155
> Was neuere leef vpon lynde lighter þerafter,
> And portatif and persaunt as þe point of a nedle
> That myȝte noon armure it lette ne none heiȝe walles. (I 148–168)
>
> triacle: medicine; heuy of hymselue: heavy in itself; fold: world; leef vpon lynde: linden leaf; portatif and persaunt: bouncy and piercing; lette: stop, resist

Love 'ate' flesh and blood when Jesus was born on earth from the body of the Virgin Mary; this made love both heavier and also even more of an ideal, so that after the Crucifixion Jesus pierced the walls of Death and Hell and was resurrected to life, soon to ascend back to Heaven like a leaf whirled upwards by the wind. The verbs move from the stative (is, be, was) to the dynamic (eten, taken), demonstrating the movement from an abstract ideal (love is the 'triacle' or medicine of heaven) to its incarnation in Jesus. Contrast the verbs and adjectives in this passage with those in the last passage quoted in order to savour the palpable difference there is for Langland between lies and truth, the treason which 'lettes' (obstructs) love and the love which no walls can 'lette'.

Holy Church finishes by teaching how this heavenly love can be experienced by those who love others. She is building on (though not quoting) the rest of her text: 'God is love, and he that dwelleth in love dwelleth in God, and God in him'(*1 John* 4:16) which she interprets much as St Augustine did in his fifth-century treatise *De Trinitate* (*On the Trinity*), a text which Langland uses throughout the poem:

So it is God the Holy Spirit ... who fires man to the love of God and neighbour ... and he himself is love. Man has no capacity to love God except from God. That is why he says a little later, Let us love God because he first loved us (*1 John* 4:19; *De Trinitate* 14:31).

So Holy Church says that the 'kynde knowynge' which Will said he lacked will be given him by God:

> And in þe herte, þere is þe heed and þe heiʒe welle.
> For in kynde knowynge in herte þer [coms]eþ a myghte –
> And þat falleþ to þe Fader þat formed vs alle,
> Loked on vs wiþ loue and leet his sone dye
> Mekely for oure mysdedes, to amenden vs alle. (164–168)
>
> welle: source; might: power; falleþ: belongs to, is the work of

Love links earth with heaven, and the love that wells from the human heart was first sent by God. But we only know this love 'kyndely' when we experience it through charity towards others, for when men have 'ruþe (mercy) on þe pouere' (175) they are imitating the pity of Jesus for his executioners, and disposing God to have pity on them. This social love is a more important meaning of truth than mere being verbally honest ('trewe of youre tonge', 179), or sexually chaste (180), or sexually honest; we are reminded of St Paul's famous words: 'Though I speak with the tongues of men and of angels, and have not charity, I am become as sounding brass, or a tinkling cymbal' (*1 Cor.* 13:1). Holy Church has returned to the point she made at the beginning about the use of property. Honouring the treasure of truth is sterile unless it leads to sharing one's material treasure with the poor:

> '*Date, et dabitur vobis* – for I deele yow alle.
> And þat is þe lok of loue lat leteþ out my grace,
> To conforten þe carefulle acombred wiþ synne.'
> Loue is leche of lif and next Oure Lord selue,
> And also þe graiþe gate þat goþ into heuene. (201–205)
> *Date* ... : give and you shall receive (*Luke* 6:38); leteþ: allows;
>
> carefulle acombred: those full of care and burdened; leche: doctor; graiþe gate: direct way

To unlock God's grace towards one's own sinfulness, to heal one's weakness, to find the path to heaven, it is necessary first to help the poor man oneself. But to deny help to others, to act with unkindness and covetousness, is to follow the False and to choose Meed instead of the Divine treasure and to deny oneself God's pardoning grace. This truth, stated so eloquently by Holy Church, will be demonstrated and relearned by Will throughout his journey; it is in a way the meaning of the poem.

Thus the speech of Holy Church has introduced the central opposition of the Fist Vision between the love which comes from God and the covetousness which comes from the Devil. It is with a dramatic demonstration of the effects of making this choice wrongly that Will begins his journey to 'kynde knowynge' in the next Passus.

Further reading

On JPs, see Harding, pp. 117–18. On the faculty of Reason, see d'Entrèves; Alford (1988b).

On Lucifer, see Russell. On Langland's personifications, see Griffiths.

Passus 2

The next three Passus tell the lively story of Lady Meed, a personification of monetary reward. This kind of allegory is known as *venality satire*, that is to say, satire against the unscrupulous acquisition of money. Contemporary satire of this kind can be seen as a response to an economic change in society – the emergence of a *wage economy* where services and labour were paid for in money, as distinct from a *feudal economy* where they were paid for in land that the peasants were allowed to work (though not to own). As England's feudal economy waned, accelerated by the reduction of the population in the Black Death from 1348, lords were increasingly having to pay their servants in wages rather than land. And the development of a bourgeois middle class also meant that professional men like lawyers, clergymen and administrators expected good wages and (unless restrained by a strong monarchy) were not above taking bribes. Langland is not alone in attacking the profit motive; sermon-writers and satirists alike often targeted the officials of the Church and Common Law courts. But Langland's satire is by no means predictable, and his use of personification allegory characteristic of allegorical dreams (see p. 12) is particularly subtle in the case of Meed herself. On the one hand her femaleness, her readiness to make friends with all comers, suggests the indiscriminate availability of money and its vulnerability to abuse. But as we will see in the next Passus, she has her own victims, and suggests not only the wealth but also power of the great. Her story thus becomes increasingly political until she is unmasked in Passus 4, and it provides a window on late-fourteenth-century misgovernment. Passus 2 is organised as follows:

Passus 2

The attempted marriage of Meed to False

  Meed's introduction by Holy Church and her effect on
    Truth in society   52–75
  The marriage settlement   76–114

The intervention of spiritual and secular authorities to stop the marriage

  Theology claims Meed should be married to Truth   115–143
  False and his followers arrange to accompany Meed to
    London   144–188
  The King intervenes   189–217

Who is Meed?

Meed literally means *reward*, and can be used in a positive as well as a negative sense. The character before us, however, dripping with jewels and surrounded by unsavoury companions, does not seem 'morally ambiguous' as some critics suggest. Bearing in mind how easily Langland moves in and out of allegory, allowing meanings to overlap and even conflict with one another, you may be attracted by all of the following interpretations. The first two are more moral, more on the 'vertical axis' discussed in the last chapter; the second two are more socio-economic, more on the horizontal axis introduced in the chapter on the Prologue:

1. She is simply a personification of reward, and therefore could be given justly, for example by God in heaven as 'amends' for good works or for suffering in this world, or as the king will claim, as reward for faithful service in the kingdom. On the other hand she could be given unjustly, as bribery before a service is performed, or as a reward for a service which does not merit it. If 'Langland consistently uses economic imagery to describe spiritual relations' (Simpson 1987, p. 85) then should the profit motive be condemned or turned to good?

2.   She is a dramatisation of St Paul's teaching that 'the love of money is the root of all evil' (*1 Timothy* 6:10; see Robertson and Huppe, 51ff.). Consequently she is both attractive and dangerous, and should be linked with the Whore of Babylon, seen seated on the seven-headed dragon in the Biblical vision of the end of the world 'arrayed win purple and scarlet and bedecked with gold and precious stones and pearls ... having a gold cup in her hand, filled with the ... filthiness of her fornication' (*Revelation* 14:8, 17:4–5; see picture on p. 43). The dragon was generally thought to represent the Seven Deadly Sins, and these sins are all named as Meed's dowry.

3.   She is a type of all the wealthy nobles who were 'as Kings in the country so that right and law are almost set at nothing' (*Rot. Parl.*, 100b; see Baldwin 1981a, p. 39). The monarchy passed in 1377 from a very old Edward III to a very young Richard II, and without a strong central government powerful local lords were building up their retinues by offering both financial rewards and protection from the law in return for loyalty and services. If Meed is seen as such a noblewoman, her retinue of administrative and judicial figures becomes an allegory of the recent breakdown in justice and public order. Edward III and Richard II responded not by punishing their nobility, but by building up retinues of their own, and Meed's appearance and actions would certainly have recalled Alice Perrers, on whom Edward used to lavish gifts of pearls and money in the 1370s, and who 'would sometimes sit by the judges on the Bench ... or in the Consistory Court, and play with the truth' (Trigg 1998, p. 19). Corruption was becoming virtually institutionalised.

4.   She is a woman, in need of protection, and represents the need that the wealth of the kingdom has for regulation and nurture. She cannot then be blamed for the abuse which others subject her to, or seen simply as a stereotype of the promiscuous female (see Aers 1994; Lees; Burrow 2005).

Are these interpretations compatible with one another? And how does Langland's use of the horizontal axis of social comment (where

The Whore of Babylon

(after the Peterborough Apocalypse, c.13th century)

Meed seems to represent a failure in society) relate to his use of the vertical axis of salvation (where Meed seems to represent some failure in ourselves)?

Church Courts

As well as courts of Common law, England had a system of Church courts. The higher Church courts, or *Consistory courts*, were directly administered by the Bishops and Archbishop, whose appeal court in London was known as the Court of the Arches from its venue in Bow Church (see 2.51). Here the Bishop's Official (legal representative) and Register (clerk) heard privately brought cases involving marriage settlements, divorce, wills etc plus some 'moral' cases. Criminals convicted under Common law who could "prove" (by being able to read a "neck verse") that they were in Holy Orders escaped hanging and were sent to the Consistory courts for imprisonment or release instead. Cases were argued by special advocates ('vokettes') and clergymen ('proctors') trained in both the Roman *Civil law* and the collection of Church ordinances or *Canon law*.

Far more people were brought before the bishop's lower courts, the *Commissary courts* administered by local archdeacons. The most important one was held several days a week in St Paul's cathedral, presided over by the Commissary-general. These courts dealt with "criminal" cases, trying the accusations made against large numbers of parishioners by churchwardens, or by unnamed neighbours, of drunkenness, vagabondage, prostitution, fornication, adultery and so on. They also heard defamation cases, probate cases, and supervised Church property. There were no lawyers to argue cases, but the archdeacons employed *summoners* or *aparitours* to summon the accused to court. The method of trial was "compurgation", where a jury of neighbours swore to your guilt or innocence. This system worked well enough in a village, but in London it was all too easy to arrange for complete strangers to swear to your innocence and trustworthiness, and consequently only a very small proportion of London cases (about 20 per cent of adulterers, and 30 per cent of fornicators) resulted in convictions. As so often, the attempt to cleanse society simply resulted in greater opportunities for immorality.

Bibliography
The Simonie; Wunderli, Chs 1 and 2.

Meed's introduction by Holy Church and her effect on Truth in society 52–75

We are first introduced to Meed by Holy Church, as the figure at the other end of the vertical moral axis from Truth, who has been the subject of Holy Church's sermon. We might have expected Wrong (Satan) to occupy this position, so it is no surprise that Holy Church says she is the daughter of False, whom we were told at 1.63 was the son of Wrong, King of the Castle of Care or Hell. Whereas Truth represented both the faithfulness and justice of God and the

heavenly reward for our obedience to such standards, Meed undermines faithfulness and justice by her promiscuous use of money to
bribe and corrupt. This is epitomised by her opposition to Leaute
(justice and faithfulness) the 'lemman' of Holy Church (21), and by
her marriage to Fals Fikel-tonge, which occupies the rest of the
Passus. Her bridegroom confusingly has virtually the same name as
her father, this allegorical incest reinforcing the point that earthly
reward both attracts falsity and cannot itself be trusted. Both Falses
are said to have a 'fikel tonge' (25, 41), and the marriage is pro-
moted by Favel (flattery), Liar, and Guile; this emphasis on lying
throughout the Passus suggests that Meed is also opposite to Truth
in the sense of verbal veracity. The lavish description of Meed which
follows (8–16) recalls Holy Church's opposite in the *Book of
Revelation*, the Whore of Babylon, yet she clearly attracts Will, who
seems to have forgotten Holy Church's puritan strictures on
'mesurable' clothes (19):

> Hire array me rauysshed, swich richesse sau3 I neuere (17).
>
> I was blown away by her clothes; I had never seen any so rich

Here it seems to be Will, not Meed, who is the first to be 'carried
away' in a Passus full of sexual abductions. Is he wrong to be so
seduced?

Having warned him against Meed's corrupting influence, Holy
Church leaves Will to his own observations (52). It soon becomes
clear that Meed corrupts truth particularly in the sense of justice,
and that this is having a pervasive effect upon society. The apparently disparate group who surround her includes many officers such
as 'sherreues and hire clerkes / Bedelles and baillifs' (59–60) responsible for royal administration and justice. Their presence supports
Interpretation 1 above, for such officers were notoriously open to
bribery, and also Interpretation 3, for as we will see in Passus 4, they
were likely to come under the influence of the powerful local lords
whom Meed resembles in appearance. This interpretation is also
supported by the presence of the 'forgoers and vittailers' (61) who
made compulsory purchases of provisions for the higher nobility
from the common people; their crimes will be detailed in Passus 4.

However in this Passus Langland is more concerned to show how Meed undermines the justice of the Church courts. These had power to judge people's private lives, and so were even more open to being bought off

> Ac Symonie and Cyuylle and sisours of courtes
> Were moost pryue with Mede of any men, me þou3te. (63–64)

> Symonie and Cyuylle: explained below; priyue: intimate.

The system of Church courts is explained in the inset on p. 43, so that I will only deal here with the opportunities for abuse which placed so many of their officials in Meed's retinue. The higher Consistory Courts, such as the 'Court of the 'Arches' (61) in Bow Church in London, dealt with Benefice and marriage disputes where money was always an issue, and 'vokettes' (advocates, 61) and judges settled cases themselves using a version of the Civil (Roman) law. Here were opportunities for Simony (the sale of Church benefits) to work with the Civil law to secure success for the rich and influential suitors. The officials of the lower Commissary Courts (such as the 'sisours and somonours' mentioned, 59) had even more opportunities to extort money from the great numbers of people brought before them on moral and sexual charges. Even if you failed to pay enough to the 'summoner' to take your name off his list, you could bribe the 'sisors' or jury of neighbours to swear to your innocence, particularly in London where scarcely a third of those accused were actually convicted. Though the venality of the Church had been the stuff of satire for generations, it must have seemed to Langland that it had never been more appropriate.

The marriage settlement 76–114

Simony and Civil, being versed in the marriage disputes heard by the higher Consistory Courts, have drawn up a deed of conveyance transferring property from the bride's father (Fals / Satan) to the married couple (Alford 1988, p. 40). On one level this suggests the dangers in mercenary marriages, for Meed is married for 'hire goodes' rather than her 'vertue' (76–77); Langland will expand on this theme in Passus 9. On another level the contract is evidence for the second interpretation of Meed suggested on p. 42, that she shows the love of money to be the root of all evil, for the property in question is the Seven Deadly Sins. Or using the third interpretation of Meed as well, we can see her harming the individual soul (on the vertical axis) and also society (on the horizontal axis). Chaucer's Parson, like many other preachers, attacks the deadly combination of wealth and pride in the retinues of great lords:

> certes pride is greetly notified in holdyinge of greet menyee ... For certes, swiche lordes sellen thanne hir lordshipe to the devel of helle, whanne they sustenen the wikkednesse of hir meynee. (1.435–440; Robinson, p. 241)
>
> menyee: retinue; sustenen: allow and protect

It is interesting to analyse the relationship between wealth, sin and social misbehaviour, and the ironic tone of triumphant success, in the terms of the settlement itself. As Keen has shown, it draws on the tradition of the Devil's Letter 'promising riches on earth during life and punishment in hell after death' (p. 53), and should be contrasted with the other charters of *Piers Plowman* (see for example pp. 215 and 240).

The intervention of spiritual and secular authorities to stop the marriage 115–237

At this point Theology intervenes to assert Meed's moral ambiguity. He insists that she is a 'moillere' (legitimate) the daughter of Amendes and promised in marriage to Truth himself (119–120). This is incompatible with Holy Church's claim that her father is False; the first and second interpretations of Meed are now in collision, and you could look at the implications of privileging one over the other. If we agree with Theology that even God can offer reward, then Meed's marriage to False should be seen as a *disparagement*, the union of a nobly born and legitimate woman to a bastard like False;

such a marriage could be annulled by the Common Law courts (see Ravishment and Disparagement, p. 52). Consequently Theology tells the wedding party to ride to London, presumably to the Court of Common Pleas to see if the Chancellor will allow a match which corrupts his kingdom, or (now using the third interpretation of Meed) would prefer to use her to reward one of his own following. This interference does not worry the wedding party unduly and they make arrangements to travel on the backs of the people one might meet in Common law courts:

> And Fauel fette forþ þanne foles ynowe
> And sette Mede vpon a sherreue sheod al newe,
> And Fals sat on a sisour þat softeli trotted (163–165).
>
> fette: fetched; foles: horses (or fools?); sheod: shod (like a horse); softeli: quietly

This lively allegory is even illustrated in one manuscript (Douce 104; see Pearsall and Scott edition or cover of Norton edition). Focusing on Meed's association with sexual promiscuity (interpretation 2) they enlist some Church Court officials (see p. 52):

> Lat sadle hem wiþ siluer oure synne to suffre –
> As deuoutrye and diuorses and derne vsurie – …
> And cart sadle þe commissarie – oure cart shal he [drawe]
> And fecchen [oure] vitailles at *fornicatores*. (175–181)
> suffre: permit; deuoutrye and diuorses: adultery and divorces; derne: valuable;
>
> cart-sadle: put the cart traces on; vitailles: victuals; at: from; *fornicatores*: those who have sex before marriage

Though divorce (through annulment or the 'discovery' of a previous marriage) was usually treated in the Consistory Court, adultery and fornication were material for the Commissary Courts and *The Simonie* explains even more clearly than Langland how easy it was to protect the sinners by finding '*compurgators*' to swear falsely (presumably that he was *already* married to his new love):

> If a man have a wif, and he ne love hire noht,
> Bringe hire to the constorie ther treuthe sholde be souht,

And bringge tweye false wid him and himself the thridde,
And he shal ben to-parted so faire as he wole bidde
From his wif.
He shal ben holpen wel i-nouh to lede a shrewede lyf. (199–204)

souht: sought; tweye: two; to-parted: separated; bidde: ask; shrewede: wicked

And as is appropriate for Courts that depended on gossip and hearsay to initiate cases, and where about a quarter of the total cases concerned defamation, Liar leads the procession.

The king however sees Meed much more kindly, as a vulnerable heiress in need of his protection from both *ravishment* and *disparagement* (see Ravishment and Disparagement, p. 52), in harmony with the fourth interpretation of Meed on p. 42:

'Now, by Cryst!' quod þe Kyng, 'and I cacche my3te
Fals or Fauel or any of hise feeris,
I wolde be wroken of þo wrecches þat wercheþ so ille,
And doon hem hange by þe hals and alle þat hem maynteneþ.
(193–196)

feeris: companions; wroken: revenged; hals: neck; maynteneþ: support/keep in their retinue

The king was guardian of the heiresses of his tenants-in-chief, and his consent in the marriage of this 'cosyn' (cousin, 133) was necessary in feudal law (and of course a king directly benefited from this opportunity to reward loyalty by promoting a valuable match). All those with rights over an heiress could ask the sheriff to 'arrest and deliver' men who *ravished* or abducted her, but it was generally the king who summoned the culprits to appear before him or the Chancellor in his own Court of Chancery. That is what this king does, summoning the couple to London, though Favel and his entourage manage to melt away on the journey. In the next Passus we will see him accuse Meed of marrying without his leave, and offering her an alternative husband (3.105–110).

How should we read this allegory? If we use the first and fourth interpretation of Meed offered on p. 41–2 we can see the king is in a sense the guardian of the wealth of his kingdom, trying to eliminate or control corruption in the administrative and judicial processes.

But if we use the third interpretation, we must see him more darkly trying to profit by Meed himself, building up his own sphere of influence by offering the marriage of a valuable heiress to one of his own followers in Passus 3. And what of Meed's own wishes in the situation? Walker points out that 'Women allowed themselves to be abducted in order to affirm their own choice of a husband, and force their families to accept the relationship' (p. 237). Should we see her, and wealth itself, as beneficial to society, as morally neutral, or as promoting falsity? And can she provide the remedy if she is the source of the disease?

Further reading

On Meed, see Cooper; Harwood and Overing (essays by Lees and Aers); Trigg (1998); Mitchell, pp. 175–8; Simpson (1987). On her marriage and charter, see Keen, pp. 53–60; Tavormina, pp. 20ff.

Passus 3

Our impression of Meed in this next Passus is hardly that of a victim. She is quite a superstar in London, courted by everyone, and well able to build up a new retinue. It include some new targets of the venality satire of the previous Passus, notably friars and London traders. However when the king attempts to arrange another marriage for her, we at last meet someone who can resist her charm: Conscience. He achieves the overthrow of Lady Meed through a *debate*, though the king is not convinced until he receives proof of her true nature in the next Passus. This debate is wholly within the tradition of alliterative verse, and comparable to *Wynnere and Wastoure*, though more daring in its topical political reference. This is particularly true of the C-text which includes some *advice* offered directly to Richard II. Both texts end with some more general advice couched as *political prophecy* (these generic terms are explained on pp. 12–15).

Meed's progression Passus 3 takes the following form:

Passus 3	
Meed builds up her position in London	
The corruption of the Central law-courts at Westminster	1–34
The corruption of the friars	35–75
The corruption of London Borough Law	76–100
The Debate between Meed and Conscience	
The proposal of Conscience as bridegroom	100–113
Conscience's first indictment of Meed	113–169
Med's attack on Conscience and defence of herself	170–229
Conscience distinguishes two types of Meed	230–283
Conscience prophesies the reign of Reason	284–353

Meed arrives at Westminster and corrupts the central law courts 1–34

When the king has got Meed to Westminster he continues to behave as though she were his ward. The tone is all softness and courtesy, certainly, but he says he will only pardon her attempt to marry without his leave if she will accept his choice of bridegroom. Meed readily agrees – as Mitchell pointed out, it is her way to be complaisant. Nevertheless she begins to build up a retinue among the judges and clerks who frequent Westminster Hall, where three central Common law courts sat (see Secular Law Courts, p. 65). The higher judges and barristers (*sergeants*) regularly received fees and robes from important clients to keep them permanently in their service, and Meed's success with them indicates how partial these central secular law courts were, how inaccessible to the poor. She also brings her "feminine" touch to the Church courts, promoting lecherous clerics and ensuring that 'konnynge clerkes shul clokke bihynde' (limp, 34). Priests who broke their vow of celibacy one way or another were a familiar target of satire (see *The Simonie*, 51–4, for example), and the evidence suggests that the Church courts (see p. 43) scarcely ever convicted or punished them; indeed in the in the later fourteenth century the London Mayor and Aldermen began to prosecute such priests themselves, and imprison them too, in the Tun prison.

Ravishment and Disparagement

Although the Church insisted that both parties give her consent in the marriage ceremony, in practice high-born women had little defence against a marriage arranged for financial reasons by their parents, overlord or guardian. The law against *disparagement* (being married to someone of much inferior status, such as a rich peasant) restricted their choice even more. Both the father and the father's overlord had rights over the marriage of heiresses, and gave them as rewards for faithful service. If a couple eloped the guardian would lose this benefit, and bring a charge of *ravishment*; if the couple were convicted, their marriage could be annulled (if it was not too late) and the 'abductor' fined or imprisoned.

But the occasional heiress, like Lady Meed, did still manage to disparage herself and allow a favoured suitor to 'ravish' her; he would pay a fine to her parents or overlord to avoid imprisonment when it was too late to undo the match. For example, during Edward III's reign one Roger Jolyf was accused of both ravishment and disparagement for having abducted an heiress called Alice in order to marry her to his bastard son John. However the royal judge found that Alice had married John of her own free will, so the marriage was not annulled and Roger did not have to pay damages. And in 1477, after months of suffering, Margery Paston finally married Richard Calle, her father's bailiff. Determination seems to have sometimes succeeded.

Bibliography

Pollock and Maitland, I, pp. 318–29; Walker; Helmholz; Sheehan; Lucas, 100–3.

The corruption of the friars 35–75

Before Meed is shown asking the Mayor for similar mercy in the Borough courts, we see her buying mercy for herself from a friar (see The Sacrament of Penance, p. 89, and Monks and Friars, p. 187). Friars, who lived a religious (that is, monastic) life within the secular community, had been given three privileges directly by the Pope and exercised them against increasing opposition by the bishops and parish clergy. These were the right to preach, to bury the dead around their convents, and to hear confessions, and the charges they made for these services were a major source of their income. Indeed they were notoriously willing to absolve sinners in return for donations to their convent. Compare Langland's lines from 3.40 and 11.74 with *The Simonie*'s complaint that friars will

> preche more for a busshel of whete
> Than for to bringe a soule from helle out of the hete ... (165–166)
> And if the riche man deie that was of eny mihte
> Thanne wolen the freres for the cors fihte. (181–182)

busshel: measure; hete: heat; mihte: might; cors: body; fihte: fight

However, whereas the *Simonie* poet only looks at the complicity of penitent and confessor, Langland has Meed asking for mercy for all her followers in return for her commitment to join their fellowship as a 'sister' and 'Wowes to whiten and wyndowes glaȝen, ...' (whiten walls and glaze windows, 61). The wording reminds us of Jesus' attacks on the Pharisees as "whited sepulchres" (*Matthew* 23:27); such noble donors are indeed morally as well as economically affiliated to their order (see Clark-Maxwell). Langland follows this understated satire with 14 lines (61–75) of explicit attack on such donors; which do you find more effective?

The corruption of London Borough law 76–100

Meed's kindness is shown to have an even more damaging effect in the next section, where she asks the mayors and aldermen to 'siluer to take' (88) from illegal traders who come before the Borough courts (see Secular Law Courts, p. 65). Once again abandoning his allegorical voice, Langland voices the complaint of the poor who must buy 'parcelmele' (piecemeal) rather than the brewers and bakers who should be punished:

> For þise are men on þis molde þat moost harm wercheþ
> To þe povere peple þaat parcelmele buggen ... .
> Thei richen þoruȝ regratrie and rentes hem biggen
> Wiþ þat þe pouere peple sholde putte in hire wombe. (80–85)
>
> molde: world; parcelmele: piecemeal; regratrie: retail; biggen: buy; wombe: stomach

In the C-text Langland expands his attack on the London retail trade and accuses the London mayors of selling freeman status (which gave considerable trading rights) to 'vsurers oþer regraters' (113); he even suggests that a recent serious fire was a punishment for such laxity (C 3.86–114). Why is Langland so passionate here? In what sense are such practices against truth and reason (85, 92)?

The proposal of Conscience as bridegroom 100–113

We now turn to another aspect of Meed's characterisation, her ability to build up a sphere of influence, as the rich and powerful did in Langland's day (see the third interpretation on p. 42). It is significant that the king himself does not bring her before a public court to answer the charge of 'ravishment' but brings her into a 'chambre' (10), where only he and his justices are present; we are later informed (101–103, 114–115) that this is the king's (Privy) Council, recently established as an occasional court, which met in the Star Chamber of the Palace of Westminster (see Secular Law Courts, p. 65). It is there that in the next Passus she directly interferes with a particular case, and so reveals to the king her potential for harm. However, now, in this intimate setting, he falls into her merciful ways and pardons her immediately, as the real king generally did pardon runaway wards (though the 'abductor' would still be liable to damages). He then offers her a marriage of his choosing, to which she readily agrees. So far he is behaving like any feudal king who uses his control over the marriage of his wards to reward his followers and build up their support for him. Assuming that Meed really is his to dispose of, is this not a good use of his royal patronage? Why shouldn't the king's advisors receive a reward for serving in his household, his Chancery or on his Council? Surely they were entitled to be granted wardships and marriages, or payments for mustering troops, or (if they were clerics) lucrative benefices? It would have been difficult to attract anyone to royal service without them; and yet, then as now, such rewards tended to attract the wrong sort of public servant. And how could local officials be expected to administer justice impartially if their superiors seemed to be managing the system for their own benefit? In a period when England was not being fairly administered at any level, it is not surprising that Conscience now launches a lengthy attack on the whole system of using Meed to buy loyalty. Is Langland wholly on his side?

Who is Conscience?

Conscience is an important character in the poem; only he, Will, and Piers recur as recognisable identities throughout its length. He represents the *demotic* habit in one's mind, that is to say, the spokesman of duty. Yet Conscience in *Piers Plowman* is no preacher; indeed, apart from here, he seems generally eager to please and is eventually taken in by a hypocritical friar (see 13.58, 113; 20.242–245; Jenkins). He even seems to acknowledge this own weakness by asking for support from Reason in Passus 4, and from Patience in Passus 13). Medieval teaching on Conscience (*Conscientia*) always acknowledged that it might be mistaken, that for example heretics thought they acted in conscience when they killed Christians. (Langland sees the reverse of this, by condemning Christians equally when they killed heretics). Conscience literally means "private knowledge", and the Greek word for this, *synderesis*, was used by scholastic philosophers, like the thirteenth-century friars Bonaventura or Aquinas, to distinguish the abstract incontrovertible duties (such as the duty to obey God) from practical specific duties which *conscientia* tries to determine and makes us want to obey. Indeed Aquinas specifically linked *synderesis* to Reason (see Langland's Psychology, p. 123). But if Langland's Reason and Patience represent only more general truths, how can Conscience be expected to apply them correctly, or to persuade us to live by them? Is his weakness the cause, rather than the effect, of his courtesy?

Conscience's first indictment of Meed 113–169

Conscience's rejection of the king's proposal could not be more direct:

> Quod Conscience to the king, 'Crist it me forbode!
> Er I wed such a wyf, wo me bitide' (120–121)

Crist me forbode: let Crist forbid me!; wo me bitide: let misfortune happen to me!

When Richard II came to the throne in 1377 he was only ten, but his councillors immediately began to develop a series of unprecedented or downright illegal methods to raise money, including the dispossession of tenants from royal lands, the raising of forced loans, and the imposition of the notorious Poll Taxes of 1377–80, sparking the Peasants' Revolt of 1381. These institutionalised 'customes of couetise' which arose from his 'vnsittynge suffraunce' redoubled when in 1382 Richard dismissed the Parliamentary Council which was supposedly governing the country and took over government himself. Parliament tried to take back power in 1386 but the abuses continued; by then 'Meed' was too firmly ensconced at court and Henry Bolingbroke could only oust her in 1399 by deposing the king. Conscience's warning of the dangers in using Meed to build up a political party were all too prophetic.

Meed's attack on Conscience and defence of herself 170–229

Meed begins her defence against the charge that she destroys kings by boasting of her exploits in the recent French wars, and claiming that kings are in fact supported by the large retinues which we have seen are so damaging to the poor and weak:

'It bicomeþ to a kyng þat kepeþ a reaume
To yeue [men mede] þat mekely hym serueþ – (209–210)

bicomeþ: becomes, suits; mekely: meekly

Her promise to make the king 'biloued and for a man holden' (beloved and thought a real man, 212) points to the historical cause of 'bastard feudalism', as the growth of local retinues is known (see McFarlane, 102–21). As Edward III realised he could no longer expect his feudal tenants-in-chief to provide soldiers in return for their land, he began to offer them financial 'indentures' or contracts to bring a private company of paid men into the army, and it was

these private companies which developed into the peace-time retinues of Richard's reign, with all their associated problems of 'main-
tenance-at-law' (protectionism). If we can take Meed, a woman, to
represent this essentially masculine nexus of power-relations (and
Aers 1994, pp. 64–7 argues that we cannot) then Meed is right to
see herself as the force behind the king's newly "privatised" army,
and so as the upholder of his prestige both at home and abroad. In
this allegory do we sympathise with Meed's *realpolitik*, or do we
begin to question the assumption that a king is entitled to reward his
followers and fight his enemies?

Having defended her own position, Meed castigates Conscience
for opposing the war and encouraging the king to make peace.
However imperfect the faculty of Conscience may be, it is surely
unlikely that Langland wants us to take Meed's side against him.
Indeed as the war dragged on into the 1380s, and England lost
nearly all the gains of 1360, and moreover came under threat of
invasion herself, an increasing number of voices were asking for
peace (see Barnie, J., pp. 133–8). In the C-text, written probably
at around this time, Langland makes his opposition to the war
even more explicit. He removes Meed's references to the painful
but ultimately successful Normandy Campaign of 1359 and the
Treaty of Bretigny of 1360, under which the king renounced his
right to the French crown in return for 3 million gold écus from
the 'poore men' of France (B 3.189–208). Langland replaces it by
a deeply ironic attack by Meed on Conscience's cowardice – or
moral scruple:

> Ac thow thysulue, sothly, ho hit segge durste,
> Hast arwed many hardy man þat hadde wille to fyhte,
> To berne and to bruttene, to bete adoun strenghtes.
> In contrees there the Kyng cam, Consience hym lette
> That he ne felde nat his foes tho fortune hit wolde (C 3.235–239).
>
> sothly: truly; segge: say; arwed: frightened; bruttene: destroy; lette: prevented

The aggressively plosive verbs of line 237 evoke the violence of the
dampnum, or *chevauchée*, the march of devastation which the

English army repeatedly inflicted on the French in the 1370s and 1380s. This scorched-earth policy did not win the English any more territory, and we feel Langland's sympathy to those who suffered it, although they were French (as we did with his earlier reference at B 3.195 to the 'poore men' of France who paid the ransom). It is worth looking back at the debate between them so far to see if we are persuaded that doing the opposite of what Meed advocates would ensure a more united and just kingdom, or if on the other hand we think that Meed is the true defender of England and Conscience is being characteristically unreliable.

Conscience distinguishes two types of Meed 230–283

At the very end of her own defence, Meed had attempted to associate her kind of reward with legitimate wages

> Seruaunt3 for hire seruyce, we seeþ wel þe soþe,
> Taken mede of hir maistres, as þei mowe acorde. (217–218)
>
> soþe: truth; mowe acorde: might agree

Now Conscience ends his speech against her by trying to define where the desire to give or take rewards becomes a force for evil rather than good. His argument is long-winded and confusing, particularly in the B-text, where he distinguishes between two kinds of meed:

- *mesurable meed* (244) or legitimate reward, which God gives to those whom 'truþe helpeþ'. This suggests Theology's identification of Meed in Passus 2 as the daughter of Truth and Amends who is *disparaged* on earth by False's attempt to marry her (Interpretation 1 on p. 41). This legitimate kind of reward is 'mesurable hire' in wage packets, or a 'permutacion' (fair exchange) in the marketplace. In the C-text Langland replaces this plethora of terms by the Latinate coinage *mercede* (true reward) which depends on there being a right relationship or 'relacion rect' between the giver and the receiver.

- *mede mesurelee*, which Lady Meed uses 'to mayntene mysdoers' (246–247).
- In the C-text the word *Meed* is only used to refer to this illicit reward, which arises from a false relationship or 'relacion indirect' between giver and receiver.

Earlier *venality satire* had simply condemned the profit-motive, preferring an idyllic but impossible feudal past where services were exchanged without the need for money. Langland is both more realistic, and in a way more idealistic, for Meed's parentage indicates that God is also involved in the system of giving rewards. And as Simpson shows (1987, p. 95), divine meed tends to be "measureless" (*de congruo*, of grace) rather than earned (*de condigno*); Langland will continue to agonise about the justice of divine reward throughout the poem. However in neither text does Conscience himself seem to recognise Meed's ambiguity, which is presumably why in the C-text he manages to find another word for honest reward – 'mercede'. To him it is not the men of the world who use her rightly or wrongly, but she who corrupts them. His attitude prepares us for her demotion into 'whore' in the next Passus, in a world where whores were more to blame than their customers. But should we accept his viewpoint? After all, can we really do without her in either the earthly or the heavenly worlds?

Conscience prophesies the reign of Reason 284–353

Conscience suddenly changes gear. In a passage much discussed by scholars he foretells a time when Reason and 'David' (presumably Christ, the descendant of David, 288) will rule with a Christian king, and under them 'Shal na moore Mede be maister as she is nouþe' (a master as she is now, 290). Prophecies were fairly common in satirical writing: the writer supposedly protected himself by adopting a fanciful pseudo-religious form, though no-one was fooled and there was even legislation against such writing in the early fifteenth century Robbins, xliv). Langland himself claims at the end of the *Visio* that what he is writing is an uninterpretable dream (7.14, 173 and see Introduction, p. 12 on the genre). He claims that Kynde Wit (see p. 153) has promised that one day England would be transformed into a land where Holy Church's ideals of ideals of love, truth and leaute were living realities:

> And whoso trespasseth ayein truþe, or takeþ ayein his wille
> Leaute shal don him lawe, and no lyf elles ...
> Ac Kynde Love shal come ʒit and Conscience togideres
> And make of lawe a laborer; swich loue shal arise
> And swich pees among þe peple and a parfit truþe (293–301)
>
> offends taketh: steals; Leaute: Justice; no lyf elles: no-one else; Kynde Love: natural
> love; make of lawe: turn law into a labourer

He concludes with a riddle (325–327; its solution may be "love", like that of Patience's riddle in 13.151–156; see p. 172 below and Galloway 1995) to detach the prophecy even further from the here and now. However this future world is not without crime and punishment, but simply a world without Meed, where the right relation between act and penalty will return. The vertical axis of personal salvation will support the horizontal axis of social obligation; justice will replace indiscriminate mercy. Could this happen? Is this vision meant to be *realistic*, a social goal something like the one which John Ball would be said to preach to peasants of the 1381 revolt (see Langland, Wycliffe and the Peasants' Revolt, p. 137). He said it was their duty, telling them to be imitate a good 'husbandman tilling his field' by:

> first killing the great lords of the realm, then slaying the lawyers, justices and jurors, and finally uprooting everyone whom they knew to be harmful to the community in future. So that at last they would obtain peace and security ... (Walsingham, *Historia*, transl. Dobson, p. 375).

Though writing the B-text well before this, does Langland know of their plans and want to insist that it is not by turning ploughshares into swords, but by doing the opposite (305–308, referring to *Isaiah*

22:4) that peace and security would be realised? Or should we see the prophecy as *satiric*, a Utopia where the opposite of all Conscience has condemned will flourish? Or is it *apocalyptic*, a version of the Millennium or thousand years of peace initiated by the Second Coming of Christ, prophesied for the end of the world in *Revelation* 19:11–20:3? There is a problem with all these readings. For how could flawed humanity, who are not 'so trewe' (304) fit into such a millennarian kingdom, a world of strict justice without mercy for their sins? Is not God's gracious gift of heaven to men far closer to a Meed than to a 'mesurable hire'(256)?

The Passus ends with some Latin point-scoring, and without a real resolution to the debate between Meed and Conscience. During it we have seen Meed corrupt many areas of society, but Conscience's unrealistic prophecy seems to suggest that society will never be rid of her. In the next Passus Langland will not only bring matters to a head, but suggest a way in which Meed could be controlled.

Further reading

On Conscience, see Jenkins; Potts; Morgan. On warfare, see Barnie, J; McFarlane; Palmer, I. J. N. On London, see Pearsall (1997); Myers, pp. 118–27, 196–203.

Passus 4

Passus 4 concludes the First Vision by showing the triumph of Reason and Conscience over Lady Meed. After all the talk of law and justice, it is appropriate that she is finally exposed in a law court, one moreover in which the king himself presides with his justices and councillors. This material not only continues the political advice offered in Passus 3, but is itself a model of good government, based on a contemporary procedure: in genre it is therefore a very practical *mirror for princes*. In it Langland can draw together the threads of his *venality satire* of Meed in society, and the *political allegory* which had begun with the Coronation Scene in the Prologue. He can moreover return to the principles of Truth which had been established in Passus 1 by Holy Church, and so brings the First Vision to an optimistic close. By combining satire with allegory Langland particularises the problem while also offering the solution.

The Passus is in four parts:

Passus 4	
Conscience brings Reason to court	1–46
The trial of Wrong	47–109
The (impossible?) reign of Reason	110–148
The downfall of Lady Meed	149–195

Who is Reason? 1–46

The Passus opens with the King trying to arrange a reconciliation between Meed and Conscience, who responds both disobediently and uncompromisingly.

> But Reson rede me þerto, raþer wol I deye. (5)
> rede me: advises me (to be reconciled with Meed)

As Conscience has just described how Reason's reign would be a golden age of justice and truth (3.285ff.), the King asks for him to be fetched. What does Reason mean here? And what is his relation to Conscience?

The extremely authoritative theologian Aquinas taught that Reason was planted by God in a person's soul to raise him or her towards Himself. One way it does this is through *synderesis*, the faculty which understands moral principles, and recognises, for example, that we should obey God, though it is the more practical Conscience which is left to work out how we should do this (see Langland's Psychology, p. 000 and Who is Conscience?, p. 123). But as Reason is being summoned here to a law court we should probably focus on another of his functions: his awareness of the underlying principles of Natural Law, which the civil lawyers placed above human law, rather as we place a code of human rights: 'This participation in the eternal law by rational creatures is called the natural law' (Aquinas, *S. T.* 1a–2ae 91 art. 2, transl. d'Entrèves, 43). This legal and political function can be summed up by the words of thirteenth-century Germanic Emperor Frederick II (a man greatly admired by Richard II):

> Although our imperial majesty is free from all laws, it is nevertheless not altogether above the judgement of Reason, herself the mother of all laws (quoted Baldwin 1981a, p. 10).

However on another level Reason suggests the human ability to reason, and this is not always directed towards justice. Two lawyers, Waryn Wyseman and Witty, try to join the party so as to pick Reason's brains about financial cases they have in the Exchequer and the Chancery (28–29). It is a demonstration that Conscience is the more practical faculty; that it is he who warns Reason against them and their preference for Meed over 'loue and leautee' (36). An association with such qualities, or with characters like Tomme Trewe-tonge (18) can help us to distinguish true Reason from mere cleverness (see Alford 1988b). We also seem to be invited to distinguish the allegory of the journey to Westminster from Meed's ride there in the previous Passus. When he arrives, Reason – as befits someone of his Divine connections – is given the place of honour at court, sitting between the king and his son (42, perhaps referring to Edward III and the Black Prince, as the line also occurs in A; Richard II had no son, but then he had little Reason either).

Secular Law Courts

The non-religious law courts of England can distinguished by the authorities under which they were held. In simplified form, the system was as follows.

The king

The king as the 'fountain of justice' was responsible for upholding the laws and customs enforced through the Common law courts. The law concerning the organisation of property, contracts and other civil (non-criminal) matters were heard in the *Court of Common Pleas* which sat in Westminster Hall. The King's Peace was under the protection of the Common law criminal courts, chief of which was *King's Bench* which also sat in Westminster Hall, while the travelling *Assize* and *Commission* judges brought royal justice into the *County courts* at least twice a year. This left the bulk of the criminal cases to the county Sheriffs and Justices of the Peace, local landowners sitting in the *County* and *Hundred courts*, and their increasing powers gave them increasing opportunities for abuse of the system, which resulted in a notorious loss of respect for the law. The local *juries* ('sisors') were more character-witnesses than independent adjudicators, and they too were very open to influence, even when they were transported to London for the central courts. From the later fourteenth century the king tried to correct these miscarriages of justice by using his Parliament, Council and Chancery as *prerogative courts* to over-ride the Common Law courts in cases where justice had not been obtained in the lower courts (as in Passus 4).

The mayors

London Borough law was ultimately based on international merchant law principles and contained in the Calendar Books and other collections of city ordinances. It was enforced by the Mayor in the Court of Hustings and the Mayor's Court, and by the two Sheriffs in their own court. These all dealt with civil disputes between traders (such as contracts and debts), but the Mayor's Court was also particularly responsible for "criminal" offences of public order, petty theft, and unfair trading practices such as those detailed in Passus 3 and 5. Commonest among these were profiteering through the retail (the 'regratrie' of 3.83) of staple goods like ale, bread and cloth. The Mayor's Court was held in the Guildhall, and the Mayor was generally represented by a professional *recorder*, but like the other courts outside the Common law it used the corruptible system of *compurgation* (here an oath taken by six reputable character-witnesses) and so was vulnerable to the influence of Meed.

The lords of the manors
There was a complex system of local laws and customs which were administered through the *Manor* and *Leet courts* under the jurisdiction of lords acting as landowners (rather than as Justices of the Peace). They heard disputes about land use, services on the manor, minor misdemeanours and the like under the higher authority of the County courts.

Bibliography
Harding; Myers, pp. 118–27; Pollock and Maitland.

The trial of Wrong 47–109

The scene now reverts to the King's Council (called a 'parlement', 47), which had recently started sitting as a court in the Star Chamber, usually under the Chancellor but occasionally under the king himself. The business of this very high court and the Chancellor's other prerogative court, the Court of Chancery, included cases which had suffered 'maintenance' or interference by powerful lords like Sir William Mainell, whose men had in 1355 committed 'diverse felonies, trespasses and other outrages' against the Abbot of Burton-on-Trent. To prevent them being convicted, Sir William threatened the Abbot's men 'that as soon as they commence any suit against him he would burn down the said abbey'. The Abbot asked the king in Council to give a writ commissioning 'to some valiant man to seize the body of the said William, to bring him before you and your Council to answer for the aforesaid felonies' (*Cases before Council*, pp. 41–2). Such cases had to bypass the corrupted processes of Common law; they needed what became known as 'equity' or a 'court of conscience', where 'law and reason' might be obtained (see *Select Cases in Chancery*, pp. 9, 121, 132). Under the weak government of Richard II's reign the problem of maintenance grew and grew, one petition in 1392 complaining that the criminals were 'so great in their county in kinsmen, alliances and friends, that the said supplicant cannot have any right against them by any suit at Common Law' (*Select Cases in Chancery*, p. 48; for these cases see Baldwin 1981a, p. 39; other examples given in Scattergood, pp. 143–59). The court in *Piers Plowman* could also be called a court of Conscience and Reason; indeed in the C-text they are given the appointments of Chancellor and Judge at the end of the Passus (C 4.185–186).

Before this court comes a petitioner, Peace, who must also have been frustrated in his efforts to get redress at Common law. His very name shows this, for crimes committed 'against the King's Peace' are classed as *felonies*, matters for the criminal courts. Peace's oppressor is called Wrong, who has begun his life of crime by acting as a *purveyor* (who requisitioned goods and services for a nobleman or king) and seized Peace's 'gees', 'grys' (pigs), a horse, and wheat, offering either much too little money or merely a 'tally' (a wooden token of debt). This kind of requisitioning had been legal in the early days of the Hundred Years War, but after a Statute passed in 1362 (*36 Edw. III* st.1 c.2) only the king's household was allowed to purvey. The difficulty of prosecuting the king's own servants was however recognised, and victims were invited to present a 'bille' or petition to the Chancellor. Do we get any sense that the king in Passus 4 is embarrassed by this charge?

Wrong also seems to be oppressing Peace on his own account, committing rape, highway robbery, interference in markets, and murder. He and his gang are acting like the armed bands whom the Commons complained of in the Parliament of 1378:

Many evil doers from the counties of Chester and Lancaster ... go
wandering from day to day in order to kill your leigemen and ravish
their daughters ... and lead them away ... Others in other counties of
the kingdom, for confederacies and false alliances ... and make great
and evil extortions against the poor people of the county, and take
their goods and menace their lives, so that they dare not plead against
them. (*Rot. Parl.* III.42b–43a).

The problem continued and got considerably worse during the reign
of Richard II, who was not above using the men of Chester for his
own purposes. It is clear that Peace has suffered oppression and that
the king has so far lacked the political will to end it:

The Kyng knew he seide sooþ, for Conscience hym tolde
That Wrong was a wikked luft and muche sorwe wroȝte. (61–62)

wroȝte: brought about

Having heard the evidence the court proceeds to judgment. We
might expect a more formal trial with a jury, but it was a feature of
cases in Council and Chancery that the court could decide the
verdict upon information and the advice of the judges. But at this
point we are given a demonstration of maintenance in action. The
two lawyers who had already tried to nobble Reason now reappear
and hint to Wrong that his only chance is to use influence of
someone rich and powerful – like Meed:

Thanne wowede Wrong Wisdom ful yerne
To maken his pees wiþ his pens, handy-dandy payed.
Wisdom and Wit þanne wenten togidres,
And token Mede myd hem mercy to wynne. (74–77)

yerne: earnestly; pens: pence; handy-dandy: under the counter: myd: with

At the same time Wrong uses the intimidation tactics which have
helped keep him out of the courts all along:

Pees putte forþ his heed and his panne blody (78)

putte forþ: stuck out; panne: crown of head

Langland was not exaggerating when he depicted this shameless attempt to corrupt and intimidate even this highest of courts. In 1389 the Earl of Devonshire, who wanted to protect his murderous retainer Yeo, called the local Justice Esturmy 'false traitor', and said 'he knew all the roads by which he must come and go' and would punish him for proceeding against Yeo. Esturmy petitioned in Council and the Earl was summoned to appear before it with his retainer to answer the charge that he had 'harboured' Yeo, and had threatened the justice. The Earl admitted the crime and was condemned to be imprisoned, but at once

> all the foresaid Lords, spiritual as well as temporal, prayed our Lord the King to do grace to the said Earl, having regard for the fact that he was of royal blood, and one of his uncles, and that it was the first time any such complaint had been made ... against him. (*Select Cases in Council*, pp. 77–81; see Baldwin 1981a, p. 49)

The king therefore pardoned him, though with a warning that he should not offend again.

However in *Piers Plowman* mercy is not obtained so easily. The king swears 'by Crist and by his crowne boþe' (that is to say by his duty to God and to his kingdom, 83) that Wrong should not go unpunished. Immediately the lawyers Wyseman and Witty, in a beautifully word-twisting piece of alliterative verbiage, suggest that both Peace and the king himself have more to gain from 'amendes'. They suggest 'maynprise', bail, a word which will come to have great significance in the poem:

> And he amendes mowe make, lat maynprise hym haue
> And be borȝ for his bale, and buggen hym boote,
> And amenden þat is mysdo, and eueremoore þe bettre. (88–90)
>
> maynprise: bail; borȝ: surety; bale: wrong, damage; boote, amenden:
> remedy; eueremoore þw bettre: better all round

Naturally it is merciful Meed, daughter of Amendes, who offers to pay the 'mainprise' and also to give a present to Peace – who peaceably begins to plead for his enemy. The king resists this idea and,

like Conscience at the beginning of the Passus, puts himself under
the guidance of reason of justice and truth:

> But Reson haue ruþe on hym, he shal reste in my stokkes (108)
> ruþe: pity; stokkes: foot manacles used in prison as well as in the
> street

Since the king has given authority to Reason many of the councillors
now turn to ask Reason to have mercy on Wrong, as they had asked
Richard II in 1389 to have mercy on the Earl of Devonshire.
However as we have seen repeatedly in Passus 2–4, mercy is a much
more slippery commodity on earth than in heaven, and we shall now
see Reason confirm the king's desire for impartial justice.

The (impossible?) reign of Reason 110–148

Reason now continues Conscience's Passus 3 prophecy about his
reign by describing the conditions which would allow him to be
merciful – that evil-doers will not take advantage of such mercy. He
recounts what Rupert Taylor (pp. 65–7) calls a 'paradoxical political
prophecy', which describes the corruptions of today as though they
were characteristic of some remote future. The Prologue of *Wynnere
and Wastoure* is in this style, as is 'When Rome is removed' (1389?)
which looks "forward" to a time:

> When pryde is most in price, ande wyt is in covetyse
> Lychery is ryffe and theffis has haldin þar lyff. (Robbins, 118)
> When we take pride only in expense, and find covetousnes clever; lechery is everywhere
> and thieves are unpunished

Reason's version is put the other way around, not an impossible
future made a setting for a real present, but the real present contrasted with an impossible future when Pride will be replaced by
Truth, the clergy will cease to be covetous, and children will be
appropriately punished (116–119). He adds the more relevant hope
(or is this an equally impossible dream?) for a time when 'þe Kynges

counseil be þe commune profit (123), and gives a version of
Conscience's prophecy that the bribes and oppressions of contemporary law, like weapons of war of *Isaiah* 2:4 – will be transformed into
the tools of cultivation (300) so that:

> Lawe shal ben a laborer and lede afeld donge,
> And Loue shal lede þi lond as þe leef likeþ. (147–148)

lede afelde donge: take manure to the fields; leef likeþ: would desire

He ends with a specific attack on Meed which continues
Conscience's attack in Passus 3 and his prophecy of a reign of
Reason:

> That I were kyng with coroune to kepen a reaume,
> Sholde neuere Wrong in þis world þat I wite my3te
> Ben vnpunysshed in my power, for peril of my soule,
> Ne gete my grace þoru3 giftes, so me God saue! (138–141)

That: If; kepen: protect: gete my grace: get into my favour through gifts; so me God
saue: so God help me!

He puts the same point in Latin: *Nullum malum inpunitum, nullum
bonum irremuneratum* – no evil should go unpunished, no good go
unrewarded (143–144, quoted again by Jesus, 18.391). But is such
an uncompromising principle of justice either possible on the horizontal axis of social life, or desirable on the vertical axis of salvation
where it would consign all sinners to Hell? How does Jesus use the
same Latin tag in 18.391?

The downfall of Lady Meed 149–195

Although the lawyers try to put a favourable gloss on Reason's
uncompromising insistence that all evil should be punished
(4.87–93), they are in a minority. Reason has the support not only
of the people present but also the qualities of Kynde Wit, Love and
Leaute who helped found the ideal kingdom (see Prol. 118–122,
and compare 3.284 and 4.161):

> Wit acorded þerwiþ and comendede hise wordes,
> And þe mooste peple in þe halle and manye of þe grete,
> And leten Mekenesse a maister and Mede a mansed shrewe
> Love leet of hir liȝt, and leaute yet lesse (157–161)

Kynde Wit: Natural Reason, teaching Natural Law(?); comendede: praised; þe grete:
nobility; leten: considered; maister: master; mansed shrewe: cursed rogue; liȝte: worth
little; leaute: justice, loyalty

The king, who had sought to marry her to Conscience, now realises the danger she poses to law and order, and condemns not only her but Wrong and the lawyers to be punished as they have deserved, in accordance with Reason's dictum:

> 'I wole haue leaute in lawe, and lete be al youre ianglyng
> And as moost folk witnesseþ wel, Wrong shal be demed.' (180–181)

leaute: justice; lete be al youre ianglyng: despite all your clever words; demed: judged

Finally Conscience reminds the king of the importance of the Commons (the community, 182) who had helped put him on the throne in the Prologue. It seems than that his view of Meed as a dangerous 'hoore' (65; see interpretations 2 and 3 on p. 42) is triumphant. She is stripped of the moral ambiguity (interpretation 1) given her by Theology and even by Conscience himself when he said there were two kinds of Meed. But is the Meed who is now humiliated really the greatest enemy of love and leaute? And can the king really function without her? How seriously should we take his request at the end that both Reason and Conscience should become permanent members of his Council? His readers must have increasingly felt the irony of this, as Richard II became more and more entangled with "Meed", using his own retinue to intimidate his people, and raising money by undermining the law. But the Vision which has occupied the first four Passus of the poem seems to end on a positive note, and to have established beyond doubt the importance of justice to a realm. As we shall see, the ensuing Vision begins to undermine this certainty.

Further reading

On political prophecy, see Dean (in list pf primary texts); Taylor, 65–7. On Natural Law and Reason, see d'Entrèves, 42–9; Alford (1988a). On 'maintenance' in *Piers Plowman*, see Baldwin (1981a), Ch. 3 and (1988a), 81–3.

The Second Vision: Passus 5–7

Passus 5

Will's awakening and falling asleep acts as a marker to the beginning of a new Vision in which the hero of the whole poem, Piers Plowman, at last makes an appearance. This next Vision (5–7) turns from the way the kingdom should be governed, to the way individuals should govern themselves, in relation to each other and to God. It starts with a *sermon* by Reason, the character who had brought the previous Vision to a triumphant conclusion, now dressed as a prelate or bishop and carrying a cross. The rest of the Vision is structured on the Sacrament of Penance (see text-box on the latter, p. 89). This inspires his audience to *contrition* for their sins and they make their *confession* to a priest called Repentance who sets each one a *penance* of prayer, fasting or almsgiving, and then tells them all (plus a thousand more) to make a *pilgrimage* to a shrine which should offer a *pardon*. All Langland's readers were supposed to enact this process at least annually, though not many would have taken it as far as a pilgrimage. In the next Passus the pilgrimage is interrupted by Piers who wants the pilgrims to help him cultivate his half-acre strip, but this does not seem to matter, because in Passus 7 Piers' helpers are granted a pardon just as if they had gone on the pilgrimage after all. The pardon itself however is problematic, and provokes a new departure in the next part of the poem.

This is one of the most traditional parts of the poem. There was a plethora of doctrinal or "homiletic" (religious and didactic) texts designed for priests and pious laymen to examine sin. Those I will be referring to in this chapter are introduced in the text-box on Sermons and Religious Education on p. 78. These, like many other homiletic texts, are organised as lists of sins with many subdivisions (see Moral Lists, p. 93); Chaucer provides an example in *The Parson's Tale*, which is a translation of two Latin Handbooks. The "way to Truth" at the end of the Passus is of this kind, but the confession of the Seven Deadly Sins which takes up most of the Passus is incomparably livelier, for Langland's Sins are not so much *personifications* of sins as *representative examples* of sinners, and often change both profession and sex while remaining themselves. Nor is it clear if they could, or should, really repent of the sins which create their personalities. So although this is easily the longest Passus in the B-text, it is very readable and intriguing. It covers the following parts of the Sacrament of Penance:

Passus 5	
Introduction to the Second Vision	1–8
The Sermon of Reason	9–59
The Confession of the Sins	60–477
Pride and Lechery	62–74
Envy and Wrath	75–185
Covetousness and Robert the Robber	186–296, 462–477
Gluttony and Sloth	297–461
The prayer of Repentance	478–506
The pilgrimage to Truth	507–642

The sermon of Reason 9–59

Throughout *Piers* Plowman Reason is closely associated with justice see 4.143–144 and Who is Reason? on p. 63), and his *Sermon ad Status* addressed to the different *estates* or classes of men warns them about the imminence of the Last Judgement (20). Reason sees evidence of judgement now, in the 'pestilences' and 'south-west wynd on Saterday at euen' (probably referring to a hurricane on Saturday 15 January 1362), which combined to fell both people and trees and so to humble men's 'pruide'(14–15). In the same way a poem of

1382 was to see the recent earthquake, plague and even the Peasant's Revolt as warnings 'to be war':

> The rysyng of the comuynes in londe,
> The pestilens, and the eorthe-qwake,
> These threo thinges, I understonde,
> Beoth tokenes the grete vengaunce and wrake
> That schulde falle for synnes sake. (*Political Poems and Songs*, 252)

Reason's words recall his 'prophecy' in Passus 4 of an impossible time of justice when he might allow himself to be merciful (compare 4.113–148 with 5.13–59 and see how many verbal echoes you can find). He then seems to return us to the chaotic opening scene of the whole poem, and suggest how it might be reformed:

> He bad Wastour go werche what he best kouþe
> And wynnen his wastyng wiþ som maner crafte; (24–25)

kouþe: knew how to; wynnen his wastyng: earn what he spent; crafte: skill, craft

Typically he sees reformation achieved through submitting to justice and punishment in this world as the only way to avoid agony in the next. Those in any kind of authority (parents, husbands, employers like Bette, 32) should beat the sin out of those entrusted to them. They must moreover extirpate their own sins: if you are a cleric you should 'preue it on yowselue' (42) what you preach to the people or risk having your property taken away in punishment (46–47; this threat is spelt out in detail in C 5.146ff. in a passage which appears in B 10.292ff.); even the Pope should 'gouerne first hymselue' (51), and the king should treat his people properly or risk them refusing him financial support (48–49). In a nutshell they should all follow Holy Church's advice and 'Sekeþ Seynt Truþe, for he may saue yow alle' (57). Reason's sermon therefore reaffirms the standard of moral justice or Truth and suggests appropriate social sanctions. But these will need backing by a religious leader if they are to work. Repentance must take the place of Reason.

In the C-text the sermon is preceded by the very interesting "Autobiography" in which Reason attacks Will for being a kind of

Waster himself; it is discussed in Langland's Autobiography on p. 105.

Sermons and Religious Education

The education of the people

Following the Lambeth Constitutions of 1281, the English Church pushed forward a programme to educate the laity (non-clergy) and reform the slothful clergy.

To educate the priests themselves, and the more pious laymen, a good deal of homiletic material was produced, some of it in English. This included the following kinds of text, all types Langland uses in Passus 5:

- Sermon Handbooks, such as the *Fasciculus Morum* (Bundle of Behaviour) produced by an English friar in about 1300 and translated recently by Wenzel.

- Confessional Manuals such as the *Oculus Sacerdotis* (the Eye of the Priest) or one of its derivatives, like the *Pupilla Oculi* produced by the English priest William of Pagula in the 1320s.

- vernacular treatises typified by the *Book of Vices and Virtues*, which was a translation made about 1375 of a treatise by a French friar. Chaucer's *Parson's Tale*, though derived more from Latin treatises, is another example.

To educate the laity, the clergy were required teach from the pulpit the Creed or Articles of the Faith (as Repentance does in Passus 5), the Seven Sacraments, and most of the Moral Lists given in the text-box on p. 93. In addition they, or the friars would give sermons. Langland uses two types:

(a) the *sermones ad status* These are sermons to different classes of society. Such sermons sought to combat the sins of the world by denouncing the vices and follies which beset it on every level, often threatening apocalyptic punishments both now and hereafter to those who persist in their sins. This is the kind of sermon which Reason delivers in Passus 5, and as Owst shows in his seminal book *Literature and Pulpit* the connections between religious satire of this kind, and the literary satire we associate with Langland and Chaucer, are very close.

(b) the modern or university sermon   One of the main aims of the friars (see Monks and Friars, p. 197) was to preach the word of God, and as they were increasingly associated with Universities they developed a new, more organised kind of sermon. As they travelled the country friars could deliver sermons of this kind, to supplement the teaching by the priest, who might also develop some of the new techniques. Fourteenth-century sermons written in English for parish priests can show some of the following sections (from Ross, xliv):

- *protheme* or *antetheme*: a prayer
- the introduction of the *theme* (based on Biblical *text*)
- the *division* of the *theme* into subsections
- the *discussion* of each sub-division, often using allegories, images, fables, anecdotes, quotations from Church authorities etc to make the sermon entertaining
- the *conclusion*, returning to the *theme*

Does the sermon of Holy Church (1) or of Anima (15) seem to you to be of this type?

Bibliography

For examples of sermons, see *Fasciculi Morum*; Krochalis and Peters, Pt. 13; Ross; the genre is discussed by Owst; Wenzel. For examples of other homiletic material see *Summa Virtutum*; *Book of Vices and Virtues*; Krochalis and Peters, Pt. 18; the genre is discussed by Little, pp. 187–96; Pantin; Braswell; Wenzel.

The confession of the Sins 60–477

The next section of the poem is both one of the liveliest and best known, and a very original use of traditional material. Langland's "Confessional Handbook" is dramatised into a series of dialogues between Repentance, acting as a confessor who knows the kind of questions which excavated a full confession from a forgetful sinner, the Seven Deadly Sins. The Sins had been worked out in the early Middle Ages, and can be fitted to the promises made on behalf of every child at baptism to renounce the *Three Enemies* of the World, the Flesh and the Devil (see Moral Lists, p. 93). Langland groups them in the same way, beginning (after a cursory glance at Pride and Lechery) with two Sins of the Devil (Envy and Wrath), following these with the Sin of the World (Covetousness), and ending with two Sins of the Flesh (Gluttony and Sloth). In the case of the paired sins, he makes one a layman (Envy, Gluttony) and one a cleric (Wrath, Sloth). The process of confession and the priest's absolution was supposed to remove the *culpa* or guilt for their sins, but most of the dialogues end with Repentance setting a penance such as fasting and prayer, to pay the *poena* the sinner would otherwise suffer in Hell. In two cases (Covetousness and Sloth) he also tells the sinner to make restitution of ill-gotten gains (see The Sacrament of Penance, p. 89 for these terms). What is the most significant aspects of these Sins? Is it for example the "Sins of the Tongue" (like boasting, swearing, lying, and chiding: see the Confessional Handbook *Vices and Virtues*, pp. 54–68) which violate verbal Truth, or the 'unkyndeness' (269) which extinguishes Truth in the sense of Loyalty and Love? Who is most harmed by each Sin – the victim or the sinner himself? Does the allegory convey the inadequacies and moral disease of each Sin, or does it on the contrary make its character interesting and distinct, so that repentance is essentially a destructive process?

Pride and Lechery 62–74

Langland gives little space to these vices at this point, in spite of the fact that Pride was generally held to be the chief sin. In the C-text he expands this section, giving Pride the traditional characteristics of disobedience, contempt for others, but also making him a show-off (perhaps like Langland himself?):

> Lauhyng al aloude for lewede men sholde
> Wene Y were witty and wiser then another. (C 6.23–24)
>
> lewede: ignorant; Wene: believe

In the C-text Langland also adds to Pride's portrait some lines from Hawkyn's confession from B 13 (see below, p. 177). However he adds hardly anything to Lechery; is this because he thinks it scarcely a Sin, or because he will confront it later (for example, 911.1–32)?

Envy and Wrath 75–185

Envy and Wrath were closely related in lists of Sins, partly because both began with 'I' in Latin (*Invidia* and *Ira*), and partly because both were "Sins of the Devil" (see p. 94 on the Three Enemies). They are afflictions of the mind, and hurt themselves more than others. This is particularly clear with Envy; as the preacher's handbook, the *Fasciculus Morum,* succinctly puts it:

> Envy, then, is sadness about someone else's happiness and glee about someone else's ruin and adversity ... an envious wretch makes someone else's good into an evil for himself. (*Fasc. Mor.*, p. 149; see Simpson 1990, p. 65)

So Envy, pale and shaking with Schadenfreude, longs to 'wreke hymslef' (84) on the fortunate, and would

> I wolde be gladder, by God! Þat Gybbe hadde meschaunce
> Than þou3 I hadde þis wouke ywonne, a weye of Essex chese. (91–92)
>
> meschaunce: bad luck; wouke: week; weye: three hundredweight

The healthy appetite for cheese is replaced by an isolating sickness:

> 'And þus I lyue louelees like a luþer dogge (117)
>
> luþer: vicious

Like a rabid dog who in Langland's sources 'other dogs do not dare to come near' (*Fasc. Mor.*, p. 163). Wrath, who lives mainly in religious communities, is equally friendless and the causer of enmity between others.

However the main link between Wrath and Envy in *Piers Plowman* is their corruption of truth through verbal destructiveness. Both are pre-eminently 'backbiters', committing a Sin of the Tongue in which evil is reported of others (contravening the Ninth Commandment: see Moral Lists, p. 93). In the *Fasciculus Morum*, if Envy wants a neighbour's property, 'will he not go to the bailiffs or the hundred-court and accuse his neighbour of being a thief?' (p. 153; Owst, p. 450; Secular Law Courts, p. 65). Langland's Envy uses the same trick, though out of malice rather than greed (93–95).

Whereas Envy backbites because he enjoys the misery of others, Wrath backbites because it inflames others to fight, a process described by a contemporary preacher in terms of lighting a fire:

> And riht as fuyre caste furst up smoke and afterward bresteth up the leie, right so after ire and yvel will cometh stryf and debate. (Owst, 459)

bresteth up the leie: bursts out the flame

Chaucer's Parson sees Envy and Wrath in the Devil's furnace increasing each other's heat, and also focuses on Wrath's verbal power to 'quyken the fir of angre and of wratthe', and even to incite men to war (*Parson's Tale*, 628). But where his Wrath is himself the promoter of the evil deeds which follow wrathful words – homicide, rebellion, and the like – Langland's Wrath seems to go no further than inflammatory speech. Does this lessen his responsibility for evil?

It may be that Wrath's lack of action is due to his being placed firmly in a religious context. It appears that, for Langland, Wrath and backbiting are peculiarly characteristic of monks, friars and nuns. According to Wrath, nuns only concern themselves with scandal, and the friars quarrel with each other about who has the more perfect way of life:

> Thus þei speken of spiritualte, þat eiþer despiseþ ooþer,
> Til þei be boþe beggers and by spiritualte libben, (147–148)

spiritualte: voluntary poverty (147), air, spirit (148)

The Spirituals were a group of Franciscan friars who took literally Christ's injunction in *Luke* 10:1–20 that his followers should own nothing, wear only a single garment, and beg for their living (see

Clopper, p. 31; Monks and Friars, p. 000). But in Wrath's confession this perfectionism is simply an excuse for the Spirituals to despise other friars, till their quarrelling reduces them to *in*voluntary poverty. The friars' betrayal of their ideals for Envy becomes crucial for the health of the whole Church in Passus 20 (see p. 270).

Covetousness and Robert the Robber 186–296, 462–477

Covetise means the inordinate desire for wealth, and in lists of Sins sometimes appears as a separate Sin from Avarice, the desire to hoard wealth. St Paul described the love of money as 'the root of all evil' (*1 Timothy* 6:10), and some writers, including those in the *Book of Vices and Virtues* tradition, made this, not Pride, the chief sin (discussed Bloomfield 1952, pp. 69–76). This can be seen as reflecting the development of a money economy in the later Middle Ages, a development we also saw reflected in Langland's equally topical satire of Lady Meed. And Langland, although he puts Pride first numerically, devotes more space to this vice than to any other, and adds even more material in the C-text revision. Why is this? Is it because Covetousness is the only Sin of the World, and so the most damaging on the horizontal axis of economic relations, the moral face of Meed? Or is it the worst 'dedly synne' on the vertical axis, the opposite of the Truth which Holy Church defined as 'God is love' (1.85–86, 144)? Or is it because Covetousness has more victims in society than any other sin, and they are from the poor and helpless? Covetousness says with some glee:

> 'I haue as muche pite of pouere men as pedlere haþ of cattes,
> That wolde kille hem, if he cacche hem my3te, for coueitise of hir
> skynnes!' (254–255)

Covetise's boastful cataloguing of various scams takes up almost all the confession, and allows Langland to satirise London life in detail, giving a more individual emphasis to the borough corruption he described in 3.76–100. Preachers also detailed the tricks of retailers when discussing Covetousness and Avarice, and like Langland, insisted that deceiving 'symple folk that arn hys neyghbours and kan no wyles' was much worse (though presumably much easier) than deceiving sophisticated purchasers (Owst, p. 357; *Fasc. Mor.*, pp. 345–6). But Covetousness's portrait is also very up-to-date; one can find as many parallels in the borough court records as in the Homilists. Covetousness sells stretched cloth, keeps his best ale hidden in his bedroom, clips coin, and does all kinds of things with weights and measures. Repentance follows the confessional method (see The Sacrament of Penance, p. 000) and asks if he has discovered the additional "branches" of Avarice: theft and usury. This encourages Covetise to describe a range of tricks (also found in Sermon Manuals and Confessors' Handbooks, see Owst, pp. 360–1; *Fasc. Mor.*, pp. 346–55), used to evade the Church prohibition on usury. For example he "sells" and then repurchases worthless goods as a way of lending money to the upper classes, thus making 'many a kny3t boþe mercer and draper' (cloth-seller, 251).

All these scams have violated truth in the sense of love, for Covetousness is 'an vnkynde creature' (269), and also in the sense of honesty, for as the *Fasciculus Morum* says, such traders 'deceive their neighbours with their falsehood'(p. 345). Covetise's tricks have also violated Truth in the sense of justice, and so in his case the *poena* – the punishment – for sin must involve restitution. One of the most popular Confessors' Handbooks, the *Pupilla Oculi*, has eight pages on restitution, in which several similar mercantile tricks are discussed; those deceived are required to be recompensed. Without such restitution Covetousness will be living a life of debt to those whom he has wronged:

> *Non dimittitur peccatum donec restituatur ablatum* ...
> For þe good þat þow hast geten bigan al wiþ falshede,
> And as longe as þow lyuest þerwith, þow yeldest no3t but borwest.
> (273, 288–289)

> *Non dimittur* ... The sin is not forgiven until the stolen goods are returned;
> yeldest, borwst: produce / borrow

The quotation *Non dimittitur* from St Augustine will return at 17.306 where it will reinforce the centrality of God's justice. But here the difficulty of making such restitution to individuals nearly drives Covetousness to suicide, but Repentance allows him to pay this massive debt through the Church (290–293). As Stokes explains in her study of justice and mercy in the poem, the Church was not supposed to use ill-gotten gains to support its own institutions, but could act as a go-between in distributing such money to the poor (p. 169; see also Tentler, pp. 340–3). The principle of restitution as debt-repayment worked out here for Covetousness will return again and again in the poem, till it is instituted by Piers in Passus 19 and subverted by the friars in Passus 20. In the C-text Robert the Robber's confession comes at the end of Covetousness's, which is a more logical than at the end of Sloth's, where it in the B-text (because Sloth includes Despair). Robert like Covetousness is in despair about his inability to make restitution, and for him there is no time to work out a solution. Langland seems loth to let him off, and hints that he is not forgiven:

> What bifel of þis feloun I kan noȝt faire shewe. (472)
> bifel of: became of

As always Langland is concerned with justice as well as mercy.

Gluttony and Sloth 297–461

Gluttony and Sloth, the two important Sins of the Flesh, are related in their physicality and their association with the Tavern, often seen as a kind of anti-Church and given its own characteristic Sins (*Book of Vices and Virtues*, pp. 53–41; Owst, p. 438). Gluttony was on his way to Church when he was inveigled into the Tavern, where he 'pissed a potel in a *Paternoster*-while' (pissed a potful in the time taken to say the Lord's Prayer, 342). Gluttony spends Friday, a fasting day, drinking (361), and Sloth boasts he spends all of Lent with 'my lemman in myne armes' (411). Both are therefore guilty of neglecting their Christian duties, and it is this, rather than their actions, which Repentance encourages them to confess by his questions. Clearly this is more serious for Sloth, who is a priest (at least in the section after 406), but one who fails to visit 'feble men, ne fetred folke in puttes' (pits, that is, prisons, 406) and thinks of 'ydel tales at þe ale' (404) even when his body is in Church. As the popular prelate Richard Fitzralph (d. 1360) said, he has 'his tongue in the Church and his soul in the tavern' (Owst, p. 436; see also *Fasc. Mor.*, pp. 235, 401). As with Chaucer's Friar and Monk, sins which are almost acceptable in a layman like Gluttony are socially dangerous in a cleric. A slothful priest fails to heal and help his parishioners to heaven; and this one, who does not even know the service (390–391) is precisely the kind of priest against whom the Archbishops were waging their campaign of education (see Sermons and Religious Education, p. 78). The *Fasciculus Morum* has a whole section on slothful priests, and includes the example of a priest who was 'a glutton and a tavern-haunter' and too drunk to say the service properly (pp. 416–42).

Was Langland writing about himself here? Will is in at least minor orders and Sloth's faults of neglect, of an idle and misspent youth, of not wishing to do an honest day's work, are the faults which Reason accuses himself of in C 5 (see Langland's Autobiography, p. 105). Later in the C-text he even seems to adopt a new *persona* of Recklessness – carelessness – an ambiguous name but one that the *Book of Vices and Virtues* attacks as the sloth of worldly men who neglect their religion (p. 28). Langland always seems to be tormented by the thought that his writing, like the 'rymes of Robyn Hood' (396) preferred by Sloth, was itself a distraction from the deeds which really earned salvation.

It is also characteristic of the writer that he focuses on verbal sins. The Sins of the Tavern mentioned in both portraits include these from a sermon: 'synginge with many idil wordes … lessyiggis, bacbitungis and scoryngis' (Owst, p. 279). Langland seems most interested in what the *Book of Vices and Virtues* calls the two Sins of the Mouth: 'glotonye' and 'wikkede tonge' (p. 46). Ignoring the violent and murderous actions which other writers associate with drunkenness (Owst, pp. 425–34), Gluttony's tavern sins seem merely to consist in vomiting, swearing and in using words to cheat Clement the Cobbler in a bargaining game (333–334). Sloth's verbal sins seem more damaging: he vows to act rather than actually acting

(398), prays with his tongue rather than his heart (402), tells lies, laughs, backbites (408), and fails to thank others for their 'kyndenesse' (434–436). His misuse of words is also covetous: he will forget to pay wages or debts, and 'forsake' or deny such obligations 'wiþ oþes', and so harm 'trewe men' (424–429). Therefore, like Covetousness, he is called 'unkynde' (269, 431) by Repentance, a word that becomes increasingly important in the poem as Langland develops his doctrine of charity. Sloth, like Covetousness, is told to make restitution to his victims for the *poena* of his neglect, and like Gluttony he is also given the normal penance for the *culpa* of sins of the flesh – abstinence and attendance at the true Church rather than the Devil's Chapel.

The prayer of Repentance 478–506

The familiar (to medieval Christians) pattern of Sermon and Confession ends with a Prayer for Absolution which not only comforts the sinners but teaches them some of the Articles of the Faith (see Sermons and Religious Education p. 78), using a traditional image of Christ as a champion which we can also find in the *Fasciculus Morum*:

> Therefore, out of the great love he had for us, the Son of God came as our closest relative and took our nature upon himself without stain of sin ... He comes like a champion and strong knight to defend us against our spiritual enemies' (p. 257).

So Repentance encourages the sinners to ask mercy of one who is 'oure fader and oure broþer' (504) and who lived and died in 'in oure sute / secte' (a word which then, as now, means both a court case or a suit of clothing, 488, 491) and 'in oure armes' (501). The passage is one of the high points of the poem; in it Christ appears simultaneously as the supernatural champion of man, fighting against his enemies and feeding him with his blood, and as his homely natural brother, wearing his grubby clothes and – hopefully – having 'ruþe on þise ribaudes þat repenten hem soore' (505).

Repentance's prayer gives the sinners a new hope, and enables them to start the new life which Reason had set out before them at the beginning of the Passus:

> And ye þat seke Seynt Iames and seyntes of Rome,
> Sekeþ Seynt Truþe, for he may saue yow alle. (6–57)

A pilgrimage was in fact the best possible end to the process of contrition, confession and absolution, for it would normally be to a shrine that offered a pardon for the *poena* (punishment) of all one's sins in Purgatory. The church of St James at Compostella, to which Reason is referring, offered such a pardon, but Reason would prefer an inner pilgrimage that cultivated truth. As we have seen, all the Sins have violated verbal truth and many have violated justice as well. Holy Church, back in Passus 1, had taught that truth involved not only honesty and justice but also loyalty and love. A pilgrimage to the 'Truþe' who dwells in the 'tour vp þe toft' (1.12) would direct the sinners to do well so that they could participate in their own pardon.

The Sins find this kind of pilgrimage very difficult. They 'blustreden forþ as beestes ouer ba[ch]es and hilles' (514) until they meet a palmer, a professional pilgrim. Such a man could be employed to make a pilgrimage on a busy sinner's behalf, praying for his soul and bringing back the pardon for him. In a world where a high proportion of priests were employed saying prayers for the souls of the dead, such a system was quite acceptable. Only, in spite of being decked with souvenirs from shrines all over the world, including 'shelles of Galice' (521) from Compostella, this representative of the profession does not know the way to inner truth:

> "Knowestow auȝt a corsaint,' [quod þei], 'þat men calle Truþe?
> 'Nay, so me God helpe!' seide þe gome þanne.
> 'I seiȝ neuere palmere wiþ pyk ne wiþ scrippe
> Asken after hym er now in þis place.' (532–536)

This is the pilgrim whose illustration, complete with a hatful of ampules, bound staff (pyk) and bag (scrippe), provides my cover (see

Pearsall and Scott in primary sources, 1–12). His rejected role as guide is the first to be taken by Piers Plowman, and both Will and the reader are in a sense pilgrims on the road to Truth, making this book merely a Guidebook to a Guidebook.

The Sacrament of Penance

Once a year every Christian was supposed to perform an act of *Penance* at his local church. In the weeks leading up to Easter they were to feel *contrition* for their sins, *confess* them to the priest, and promise to perform *satisfaction* as a punishment. Satisfaction generally consisted in prayers, fasting or almsgiving (depending on what was most appropriate to the sins confessed) but could also include *restitution* (restoring ill-gotten gains). In return the priest would give *absolution* for the sins confessed, releasing the sinner from the *culpa* or guilt arising from their sin, and the *poena* or punishment they should suffer in Purgatory for it after death. Penitents were encouraged to perform the occasional *pilgrimage* to a shrine, which would generally issue a *pardon* to the pilgrims, also excusing them from p*oena et culpa* in return for the journey they had made and the alms they had given to the shrine. *Pardoners* were licensed by the Pope to give *indulgences* to armchair pilgrims in return for a donation to their charitable project, such as building St Peter's Church in Rome, or supporting the Roncevall Hospital in London as Chaucer's Pardoner claims to be doing. Such pardons or indulgences supposedly drew on the *Treasury of Merit* which Jesus and the saints had banked in Heaven. The sale of indulgences was the subject of a great deal of attack, particularly from followers of Wycliffe, but more generally too. Langland's Pardon Scene in Passus 7 can even be read as an attack on paper pardons.

The most embarrassing and difficult aspect of the process was probably the confession, as priests were advised to probe the sinner's conscience as a surgeon probes a wound, searching for further sins and asking questions to gauge the severity of those confessed (when? where? how often? etc.). Sinners tried to soften this process by confessing to friars instead, as these were visitors to the parish and could not keep an eye on their future conduct. Franciscans in particular were licensed to hear confession and ask alms for their convent as satisfaction for the sins confessed (see picture). This was also the subject of Wycliffite attack and Langland returns to it again and again; Meed confesses to a friar, who absolves her for a 'seem of whete' (horse-lead of wheat, 3.40), and Unite falls in Passus 20 because Conscience allows a Frere Flatterer to take responsibility for the Christians' confessions (20.314–389). Do Langland's attacks on the friars and on pardons indicate a Wycliffite approach to reform, or simply an unease with their dilution of the Sacrament of Penance?

Priest with whip hearing a confession
(after the Penancer's window, north aisle, York Minster, 14th century)

Bibliography
Palmer (1952); Pantin.

Who is Piers Plowman?

It is at this moment that Piers the Plowman makes his dramatic entrance into the poem. The effect here depends upon what he is *not*: He is not a priest like Repentance but a secular 'plowman', which could mean a professional ploughman, though I prefer to translate it as 'simple countryman' or 'Piers the tractor-driver', for all those who work on the land must plough it at one time or another. Nor is he an allegorical ideal, the mouthpiece of abstract truths, but a human individual with practical experience of serving Truth as a master. And he is satisfied with the service for a very practical reason:

> He is þe presteste paiere þat pouere men knoweþ (551).

prespreste: promptest

In fact throughout the Vision he is characterised in a very human way, and there is even some satire at his expense in the next Passus. But in the second half of the poem he becomes increasingly ide-alised, suggesting the spokesman of of charity (13.124), and its incarnation in the Good Samaritan (18.10) and the human nature of Jesus (18.22, 19.6), before appearing for the last time as the first Pope (19.184). You should collect all these appearances and refer-ences and decide for yourself what he means for Langland, particu-larly in the context of his teaching on God as Love, and the pre-eminence of the law of charity. But it should never be forgotten that he is a ploughman, and so has as great an affinity with the ordi-nary man as he has with God. It is certainly as an ordinary man that he is characterised here and in the next Passus.

The pilgrimage to Truth 507–642

Since Piers has served Truth well, he naturally knows the way to reach him, However in spite of his 'common man' credentials, he suddenly starts talking in abstractions like Reason or Repentance, or indeed like a section from a very abbreviated *Book of Vices and*

Virtues. Not only does he list and organise moral qualities rather than exploring and personalising them, but also uses – rather casually – a variety of allegories: the landscape on the journey to Truth's Castle, the.Castle itself, and its various inhabitants. This excursion into homiletic methods and illustrations is quickly replaced (in the next Passus) by a programme of practical activity. Is this because his pilgrims are not capable of such a direct ascent on the "vertical" moral axis of salvation, and need something which will help them in their "horizontal" social lives? Or does Langland want to draw attention to the inadequacies of the genre he is imitating?

The text-box on Moral Lists (p. 93) should help you follow the passage, and indicate how Langland has selected only some of the available material. The journey begins with the *Virtues* (Meekness and Obedience, parts of Prudence, 561, 566) and ends with the *Seven Remedies* (the castle porters who include Abstinence, Humility and Chastity) which will help the Seven Deadly Sins to start a new life. It proceeds through some of the *Ten Commandments*, and you might find it useful to ask which of the Sins we have just met would benefit by observing the following:

- 'Swere-noȝt' (570 – Third Commandment)
- 'Coueite-noȝt (573 – Tenth Commandment)
- 'Stele-noȝt' (577 – Eighth Commandment)
- 'hold wel þyn haliday' (579 – Fourth Commandment)
- 'Bere-no-fals-witnesse (580 – Ninth Commandment)

The 'court' of Truth is mainly built out of the *parts of penance*: Belief, Prayer, Penance and (with the same prominence as in the confession of Avarice) 'Amende-yow' (596) or Satisfaction. If these are fulfilled the treasure of Christ's grace will be opened to the sinner and he will discover Truth as God within himself:

> And if Grace graunte þee to go in in þis wise,
> Thow shalt see in þiselue Truþe sitte in þyn herte
> In a cheyne of charite, as þow a child were,
> To suffren hym and segge noȝt ayein þi sires wille. (605–608)

The grammar here is a little unclear, but it must be 'Thow', the sinner, who is tied in the chain of charity as a child used to be roped to a chair, listening and not answering back to his father, Truth. Here then is the end of all those Sins of the Tongue which played so large a part in the confessions. For Langland, the poet and wordsmith, sin is shown above all in language and ended by silence.

As the only sinners who reject this account of the pilgrimage are the riff-raff of society – a cut-purse, a waferer, a pardoner and a prostitute, we may conclude that the 'thousand' (510) who listened to Repentance's Sermon are prepared to try it. And yet the next Passus offers a much less introspective and formulaic 'pilgrimage at plow'. What is the relation between the Commandments, Virtues and Remedies, seen as necessary in this pilgrimage, and the "alternative" programme of work organised by Piers in the next Passus?

Further reading

On Sins in general, see Bloomfield (1952), pp. 69–76; Braswell; Tentler. On the Sins in Piers Plowman, see Burrow (1965); Cooper (1991); Owst; Stokes. On the nature of Piers Plowman, see Goldsmith; Hewett-Smith; Godden (1990); Troyer.

Moral Lists

The Ten Commandments

1 You shall have no other God to set against me.
2 You shall not make a carved image for yourself.
3 You shall not make wrong use of the name of the Lord.
4 Keep the Sabbath day holy.
5 Honour your father and mother.
6 You shall not commit murder.

7 You shall not commit adultery.
8 You shall not steal.
9 You shall not give false evidence.
10 You shall not covet your neighbour's property.

(from *Exodus* 20, using *New English Bible*)

The Seven Deadly Sins and Remedies

Seven Deadly Sins	Seven Remedies
Pride	Humility (Meekness)
Wrath	Patience / Peace
Envy	Charity
Avarice	Mercy /Pity/ Generosity
Sloth	Strength /Holy activity
Gluttony	Abstinence
Lechery	Continence

The Seven Virtues

Theological Virtues	Cardinal Virtues
Faith	Prudence (Wisdom)
Hope	Temperance (Continence)
Charity	Fortitude (Strength)
	Justice (Equity)

The Three Enemies and Three Temptations

Three Enemies	Corresponding Sins	Three Temptations
World	Covetousness	Lust of the Eyes
Flesh	Lust, Sloth, Gluttony	Lust of the Flesh
Devil	Pride, Envy, Wrath	Pride of Life

The Seven Works of Mercy

Feeding the hungry	*Matthew* 25:35
Giving drink to the thirsty	*Matthew* 25:35
Giving shelter to the stranger	*Matthew* 25:35
Clothing the naked	*Matthew* 25:36
Visiting the sick	*Matthew* 25:36
Visiting the prisoners	*Matthew* 25:36
Burying the dead	Book of Tobit

Passus 6

At the end of Passus 5 the Sins decided to make a pilgrimage in 'satisfaction' of their sins, and Piers appears to direct them on a difficult moral allegorical journey through the Commandments, Remedies and Virtues to St Truth. Now at the beginning of Passus 6 Piers apparently offers an easier alternative pilgrimage, but one which is just as unlike a "real" pilgrimage as that allegorical one had been. It too is to be performed at home, and will include *everyone* – both winners like Piers himself, and wasters like the cut-purse and apeward (5.630–631) who did not fancy the allegorical pilgrimage of the last Passus. It is to be a 'pilgrymage atte plow' (6.102), at first presented as a preliminary to the allegorical pilgrimage, but soon taking its place as a life of obedience to the Commandments and a Remedy for the Seven Deadly Sins. "Work hard and shame the Devil" would appear to be Piers' message. But does the very inclusiveness of the pilgrimage not defeat its moral purpose, giving it the more worldly purpose of earning one's daily bread? And how ideal is this glimpse of peasant life, considering how much it reveals of the real problems of fourteenth-century farming? Just as in Passus 2–4 the justice in truth was undermined by contemporary misuse of money and power, so here loyalty in truth is undermined by contemporary changes in the relation between master and servant; so how can this be the route to St Truth? And yet somehow, in the next Passus, Truth himself will dispense pardon to both Piers and 'alle þat holpen hym to erye' (helped him to plough, 7.6). So Passus 6 confronts the question of whether one can live an active life in the world and still avoid sin.

In spite of some allegorical sections the Passus has a simple narrative structure and focuses on the essentially human figure of Piers:

Passus 6

Piers gives tasks to the different estates 1–56

In the spirit of inclusiveness which was so much a part of the Confession of the Sins, Piers begins this pilgrimage by giving occupations to everyone. Some will help work the land; others, like the women and the knight, are too weak or ignorant to help (though the knight seems keen to learn (23). The tasks Piers finds for these groups (sewing food-sacks, hunting vermin) gesture towards a common enterprise of food production. More importantly, he indicates how the upper classes could avoid sin in their daily lives by taking a responsible and not an exploitative attitude towards their dependent communities:

> Loke ye tene no tenaunt but Truþe wole assente ...
> And mysbede noȝt þi bondeman – þe bettre may þow spede (38, 45)

tene: trouble; but: unless; mysbede: injure; spede: prosper

Both the new communities of "tenants", and the old communities of "bondsmen" (see discussion below) are to be protected. There is nothing very new about the advice given here – it is typical of the *Sermons to the Estates* (see Sermons and Religious Education, p. 78) and of religious education to ask the powerful to show restraint to the weak (see for examples Owst, Ch. 6). But what is unusual here is that it is a ploughman, not a priest, who is giving the advice, and that his leadership of the pilgrimage gives him power even over the knight.

The allegorical pilgrimage of ploughing 57–104

In the next section Piers clarifies the bargain he is making with the sinners. If they will help him to sow his wheat ('bred corn') he will make the pilgrimage on their behalf, which is what palmers undertook to do (for a consideration):

> For I wol sowe it myself, and siþenes wol I wende
> To pilgrymage, as palmers doon, pardon for to haue. (63–64)

sythenes: then; palmers: professional pilgrims

> At heiȝ prime Piers let þe plouȝ stonde
> To ouerseen hem hymself, whoso best wroȝte
> He sholde be hired þerafter whan heruest tyme come. (112–114)

heiȝ prime: nine o'clock; whoso ... He: whoever ... should

The servants available for hire – the 'dycheres and delvers' (ditch-makers and diggers) and 'other werkemen' mentioned a few lines earlier (107, 109), were generally landless labourers without families who lodged with their masters or with local cottagers. But paid employees cannot be controlled as serfs could, particularly in a situation of relative prosperity, with fewer mouths to feed and rising wages. Piers' workers had started well enough, working eagerly and trying to please their master (109, 111), but by mid-morning some have already taken a break:

> And þanne seten somme and songe atte nale
> And holpen to ere his half-acre wiþ 'how trolly lolly' (115–116)

atte nale: over a drink of ale; holpen to ere: helped to plough [ironic]

Even more difficult to manage than such "slackers" were those who became beggars, parasites on the higher wages of their fellow workers. The 'Wasters' of the Prologue of the poem return as the 'faitours' or frauds of Passus 6, who pretend to be disabled (121), or like the 'Britoner' (a demobilised soldier from the Brittany campaign), demand food with menaces:

> A Bretoner, a braggere, abosted Pers als
> And bad hym go pissen with his plow3, ...
> 'Wiltow, or neltow, we wol have oure wille
> And of þi flour and of þi flesche' ... (154–157)

braggere: braggart; abosted: boastingly defied; Wiltow, or neltow: whether you will or not

Later in the Passus these 'Wasters' leave Piers' estate and wander the country in search of better conditions:

> And þo wolde Wastour no3t werche but wandren aboute
> Ne no beggere ete breed þat benes inne were (301–302)

(Bread made with beans was used for cattle food)

Lords put into the position in which Piers finds himself had for some time been complaining through their representatives in the House of Commons that servants were not keeping to their contracts but were wandering in search of better wages and conditions, or refusing to work at all:

> As soon as their masters accuse them of bad service ... they take flight and ... are taken into service immediately at new places at such dear wages that example is afforded ... to all servants ... to go from master to master ... And let it be known to the said King and his Parliament that many of the said wandering labourers have become mendicant beggars in order to lead an idle life ... although they are able bodied and might well ease the commons by living on their labour and services, if they were willing to serve ... and have become "staff-strikers" and lead an idle life, commonly robbing poor people in simple villages. (*Rot. Parl. II*, 340–1, transl. Dobson, pp. 73–4)

Indeed the comedy in this scene, with its continued innuendos on a dirty meaning for a plough, suggests that Langland half sympathised with the uppity Wasters. The comedy even increases when Piers tries to meet his contemporary problem with a contemporary 'solution'.

Controlling the Wasters 152–360

Parliament's answer to such social problems was always to institute new laws or reinforce old ones, often in the teeth of social trends. From 1349, the year after the first onslaught of the Black Death, it passed Ordinances and Statutes which tried to restore the stability which had once automatically governed medieval employment: stable (and low) prices, stable (and long) terms of service, and a stable (and local) pool of labour. To borrow Marxist terminology for a moment, the Statutes of Labourers clearly reflected the interests of the capitalists as against those of the working class, who were rejoicing in – as well as abusing – their new freedoms and improved earning power. Yet Langland seems at first to suggest that these laws promote the principles of truth which Holy Church had established in Passus 1, the principles of justice and loyalty. But is it is because they oppose Truth (the objective of this 'pilgrimage at plough') that Piers now attacks these Wasters? Or because they have been the enemies of ploughmen since the very beginning of the poem (Prol. 22)?

> Ye wasten þat men wynnen wiþ trauaile and wiþ tene
> Ac Truþe shal teche yow his teme to dryue (133–134)
>
> trauaile: effort; tene: suffering; teme: plough-team

Just as in Passus 1, Holy Church gave the knights the duty to 'taken transgressors and tyen hem faste / Til Treuþe termyned hire trespas to the ende (1.96–97), so now Piers reminds the knight of his promise to keep Piers 'fro Wastours and wikkede men' (28). This suggests that Langland expected his knights to be Justices of the Peace – the local magistrates who tried local criminal cases and who had, from 1362, the additional responsibility of enforcing the Statutes of Labourers:

> Thanne Piers þe plowman pleyned hym to þe kny3te
> To kepen hym as couenaunt was fro cursede sherewes
> And fro þise wastours wolueskynnes þat makeþ þis world deere
> (159–161)
>
> kepen: protect; shreewes: scoundrels; wolueskynnes: wolf-kind

As discussed in Langland's Autobiography on p. 000, Reason himself seems to use the Statutes of Labourers as a stick to beat Will in C 6. Is the poem simply endorsing the Statutes of Labourers?

Though to some extent it does seem to do so, as the narrative develops Langland exposes some of the weaknesses in using legislation to enforce truth. To begin with, the knight's sanction of the stocks, a common punishment for offenders against the Statutes of Labourers, does not scare the Britoner, who 'sette Piers at a pese and his plow3 bo3e' (considered Piers and his plough not worth a pea, 169). Piers then tries another sanction suggested by the Statutes, refusing them 'pity or alms ... so that thereby they may be compelled to labour for their necessary living' (*23 Edw. III* c.7). This sanction of starving men into work seems more effective:

> Hunger in haste þoo hente Wastour by þe mawe ...
> Faitours for fere herof flowen into bernes
> And flapten on wiþ flailes fro morwe til euen (174–184).

hente: seized; mawe: stomach; Faitours: hypocrites; bernes: barns; flapten: threshed

Piers himself tries to counteract the power he has invoked by some food handouts and renewed offers of employment (186–190). He is however ashamed of using hunger as a lever as the Statutes demanded, and voices his unease at their flagrant contradiction of God's law of charity:

> And for defaute of hire foode þis folk is at my wille
> And it are my blody breþeren for God bou3te vs alle (206–207)

defaute: want; blody breþeren: brothers in Christ's blood

Hunger's reply, like the Statutes again, involves a distinction between the deserving and the undeserving poor (a distinction which Langland develops in C 10; see Langland, Wycliffe and the Peasants' Revolt, p. 137), but unlike the Statutes he also commends Piers' "safety-net" of minimal almsgiving to even the undeserving poor – albeit of food normally prepared for animals to eat:

> Wiþ houndes breed and horse breed hoold vp hir hertes (214).

Hunger reinforces his liberal interpretation of the Laws by making an impassioned plea for charity to the genuinely unfortunate, and in any case he is a victim of his own success, for once the labourers have worked enough to drive Hunger away they again offend against Truth in honest work contracts in precisely the ways that the Statutes were trying to control:

> By that it neʒed neer heruest and newe corn cam to chepyng
> Thanne was folk fayn ... and garte Hunger go slepe.
> And þo wolde Wastour noʒt werche but wandren aboute ...
> (298–301)
>
> chepyng: market; fayn: pleased

It seems then that although Langland felt the new employment situation was dangerous both to Truth and to society, he did not see the Statutes of Labourers as either a wholly effective or a wholly moral way of enforcing those principles.

Do the final scenes of the Passus show Langland's contempt for the Statues or his dependence on their success? Referring to them directly he at first seems to be voicing the exasperation of the employers. From the first the Statutes of Labour always controlled wages:

> No-one moreover shall ... promise to pay to anyone more wages, liveries meed or salary than was accustomed ... nor shall anyone in any other manner demand them. (*Stat. Realm 25 Edw.III*, 1349, transl. Krochalis and Peters, p. 79)

So Piers' labourers demand perks instead and ape the life-style of their betters:

> Labourers þat haue no land to lyue on but here handes
> Deyned noʒt to dine aday nyʒt-old wortes;
> But it be fresh flesh ouþer fisshe ... else wolde noon of hem chide
> (306–317).
>
> handes: their hands are their only source of income; Deyned: deigned;
> nyʒt -old wortes: yesterday's vegetables; chide: complain

Putnam quotes the case of a Lincolnshire ploughman who 'refused to serve except by the day and unless he has fresh meat instead of salt, and finally leaves the town because no-one dares engage him on these terms' (p. 91). This seems to bear out her conclusion that the statutes were moderately successful in controlling wage inflation. Langland implies that they are effective enough to make the labourers grumble:

> He greueþ hym ageyn God and gruccheþ ageyn Reson,
> And þanne corseþ he þe Kyng and al his Counseil after
> Swiche lawes to loke, laborers to greue. (314–316)
>
> grucchep: grumbles

Moreover Langland adds an apocalyptic passage to the end of the Passus (319–329) which refers to the widespread (though unjustified, as it turned out) fear that a universal famine was the inevitable consequence of this modern rejection of honest work and loyal service:

> Ac I warne yow werkmen wynneth whil ye mowe
> For Hunger hiderward hasteþ hym faste! (319–320)
>
> hiderwode: towards here; hien: comes

This all seems to support the employers' position against the demands of the labourers.

On the other hand the verse itself points up the contrast between the condition of labourers who have 'no lond to lyue on but their hands' (landless casual workers, 306) and their glee at eating French-style for the first time in their lives:

> And that chaud and plus chaud for chillying of their mawe (310)
>
> chaud, plus chaud: hot, hotter; for: to prevent; mawe: stomach

Even if the narrator finds this 'ageyns Reson', would Piers himself not be more liberal? After all he is praised in the last Passus for his generosity, and how could generosity operate if everyone was a Winner:

> Ryght so Piers þe Plowman peyneþ hym to tilye
> As wel for a wastour and wenches of þe stewes
> As for himself and hise seruants, saue they are first yserued
> (19.438–440)

tilie: cultivate; wenche ate stewes: prostitute; saue: except

Indeed we can see from the use made of the poem in 1381 that it was hardly thought of as an employers' manifesto (see Langland, Wycliffe and the Peasants' Revolt, p. 137). As Aers argues (1994, 62–3), the critic should respond to the complexity of Langland's position, which itself reflects the complexity of the problems facing fourteenth-century society.

The attitude to the recalcitrant Wasters in this Passus is therefore quite ambiguous, encouraging at different points in the story our indulgence laughter, our righteous indignation, and our cynical acceptance of human behaviour. If the Labour Laws are a paradigm for the principles of truth, then all who disobey them must be condemned as sinners. But if they are shown to be ineffective and often misguided, what can be found to replace them? Since the ploughing has been offered as an allegory of the pilgrimage to Truth, should we take an equally ambiguous attitude to the sinners who are supposedly reforming their lives by working with Piers? It seems that, having offered all too realistic a picture of what contemporary farming was like, Langland has landed himself with a problem for the next Passus where the allegory must be decoded and only the Winners saved. But to judge by Passus 6, few have earned either their daily bread or their pardon from God.

Further reading

On Langland and labour laws, see Aers (1980); Baldwin (1981a), pp. 56–62); Dobson; Hanna (1997); Justice (1994); Middleton (1997). Texts of various Statutes of Labourers can be found in *Stat. Realm*; Krochalis and Peters; Dobson; Hanna (1993).

Langland's Autobiography

In the C-text Langland adds a passage to the beginning of Passus 5 in which Reason interrogates Will about his own attitude to work:

'Can thow serven' he sayde 'or syngen in a churche ...
Or eny other kynes craft þat to þe comune nedeth?' (C.5, 12, 20).

canstow: can you; kynes: kind

Will replies, very unconvincingly, that he is 'to wayke to worche with sykel or with sythe' (23), but this simply sets Reason onto another tack:

'Thenne hastow londes to lyue by,' quod Resoun, 'or lynage ryche
That fynde the thy fode? For an ydel man þow semest' (C.5.26–27).

lynage: relatives

In fact Will's position is not just irresponsible; it is downright illegal. After the Black Death labour was in such short supply that Parliament tried to legislate against idleness. As explained in this chapter , the Statutes of Labourers of 1349 required that 'Every man and woman ... able in body and ... not having of his own whereof he may live' (*Stat. Realm 23 Edw. III* c.1) should support himself by his service or profession'. A more detailed Statute against vagrancy and idleness was brought out in 1388, and as Middleton (1997) pointed out, its wording seems to have influenced the C-text directly. For example, this later Statute specifically exempted from work men of religion and licensed hermits, but not the able-bodied idler or those who avoided work 'under colour of pilgrimage' (*12 Rich. II* c.7). Will seems to know this, for he protests that 'Men sholde constreyne no clerke to knaven werkes' (men should not force clerks to do knaves' work, 54), and spends some time explaining that he really *is* a clerk, in spite of the fact that he is married and has a child. After all, he dresses like a clerk in 'this longe clothes' (41) – quite unsuited to manual labour – and is not so much idle as performing a different kind of labour:

The lomes þat y labore with and lyflode deserue
Is *Pater-noster* and my prymer, *Placebo* and *Dirige*, ... '
This y segge for here soules of suche as me helpeth (C.5.45–48)

lomes: limbs; lyflode: livelihood; *Pater-noster*: Lord's Prayer; *Placebo*, *Dirige*: psalms in service for the dead; segge: say

He is presumably a clerk in 'minor orders', that is to say trained to perform part, but by no means all, of a priest's duties. Donaldson calls him a kind of itinerant spiritual 'odd-job man' (Donaldson, pp. 218–19) – saying prayers in the houses he visits every month or so. These 'labours' of course, by implication, include his labour of writing poetry, which seems to have continued all his life. But do they justify his dependence on others to 'fynde him fode' (49) to his own Conscience and Reason, or are we to consider him another Waster, a parasite on the half-acre of the world, and condemned by the hero of his own poem?

Bibliography

Donaldson; Fowler; Hanna (1997); Middleton (1997). The Statute itself is reprinted in Hanna (1993), pp. 31–2.

Passus 7

The last Passus in the Second Vision clarifies the structure of penance and pardon which has been used since Repentance's sermon in Passus 5, and returns to the form of *estates satire* which had introduced the poem. It therefore seems to offer a resolution to the whole Vision. Truth sends a pardon for sin to those who work honestly in the world, helping Piers to feed Mankind. Their 'pilgrymage atte plow' seems now to be not so much a penance which pays for sin, as a way of life which will avoid sin altogether. But there are two problems with this scheme, and it is a mark of Langland's intriguing genius that he confronts both problems and risks undermining the "message" of the poem so far. The first problem we have already encountered: not everyone who worked on the half-acre followed the principles of truth. Truth's pardon includes not only agricultural workers but the other mestiers (crafts, 7) of the world, including those introduced in the Prologue and the Vision of Meed; ways of life are even more open to sinfulness than farming. Langland extends the problem even further by a discussion of beggars (expanded in the C-text), who do not work at all. The second problem is dramatically revealed when Piers reads the terms of the pardon itself, for it does not seem to offer what Piers had promised to his co-workers after all. He had said that they could earn pardon as they earned their daily bread, but this pardon offers only judgment for doing – or not doing – well. Piers is appalled at its inadequacy, tears it in half, and starts a new pilgrimage which Will will perform for him in the second part of the poem. This problematic conclusion not only questions whether worldly occupations can ever be a life of "Do *well*", but also whether obedience to the principles of Truth is either possible or sufficient for salvation. Can one keep the Ten Commandments simply by obeying the laws which govern employer and employee, and avoiding the 'meed mesureless' that Reason had attacked in Passus 4? And even if one can, is Truth to one's fellow men enough for the pardon of St Truth? By suggesting such question this Passus leads into the debate about the law and grace which preoccupies the next Vision.

The structure is as follows:

Passus 7	
Truth offers pardon to all Winners	1–64
Nobility	9–12
Bishops	13–17
Merchants	18–38
Men of law	39–59
The workers on the land	60–63
The beggars	64–104
The reading of the Pardon	105–138
The conclusion to the Vision and Introduction to Dowel	144–201

Truth offers pardon to all Winners 1–64

As Keen explains in her interesting study of the various documents in *Piers Plowman,* Truth's pardon has elements of both a papal indulgence and a royal grant. It offers release '*a pena et a culpa*' (from the punishment and the guilt, 3) of an individual's actual sins, as if Piers has 'purchased þis bulle' (sealed document, 38) from a pardoner or a pilgrimage shrine for his followers – who have, as required, already confessed their sins to a priest. But like a feudal document it grants a privilege not only to Piers but to' hise heires' (4), adds clauses 'in þe margyne' (18) and, in the C-text, some under Truth's 'secrete seal' (9.27, 138) or Signet which the king used when he wanted to exercise his prerogative to over-ride the law. We can judge the effect of this mixture after we have looked at the terms under which it is given.

The terms of Truth's pardon recapitulate the principles of truth enacted in the poem so far. There is a stress on truth as justice which was characteristic of Passus 2–4: the nobility must protect the

Church and rule 'riȝtfully' (10); the bishops should be expert in 'boþe lawes' (Canon and Civil; see Church Courts, p. 43). Those supposedly most responsible for justice, the lawyers, are treated more cautiously than any other group. Langland refers here to the old and thoroughly impractical proverb that that knowledge, like the elements of air, water and fire, 'is a gift of God and cannot be sold' (Yunck in Alford 1988c, p. 146):

> Ac to bugge water, ne wynd, ne wit, ne fir þe ferþe –
> Thise foure þe Fader of Heuene made to þis foold in commune: (52–53)

bugge: buy; wit: intelligence; foold: Earth

Only if lawyers dispense Truth's treasure of justice freely (by the kind of legal aid described, 46–50) will Truth pardon their normal professional ways.

Even more space is given to the merchants and other retail traders, who were among the closest followers of Lady Meed in Passus 3 and used Covetousness in Passus 5 (see above pp. 54, 83–5). These traders might seem to have little chance of living a life of Truth, but we must remember that Meed was once herself betrothed to Truth (2.120). Truth promises to suspend judgment on the merchants if they are honest and will use their profits for good works. Are we to approve this over-riding of the principle of justice, which in the C-text appears under the rather questionable 'secrete seal' (9.27), whose frequent use was said in 1377, to be 'to the great grievance of the people' (Baldwin 1981a, p. 152)? We may remember that in Passus 5 Covetousness could not give sufficient alms to compensate for his sin of getting wealth unjustly, fell into despair, and was advised to leave merchandise altogether (5.279–285). The merchants here are expected to feel the same despair ('wanhope', 35); indeed some penitential books suggested that this was one of the occupations which could hardly be performed without sin (Tentler, p. 163). Langland seems more charitable, and we may share their surprised relief (37) that their way of life is not condemned outright. Does their presence indicate Langland's realism, or does it anticipate Piers' rejection of the whole document?

Finally we come to the archetypal Winners and Wasters – the farmers and the beggars. The farmers seem to include the two groups of Passus 6: the husbandmen (7.6–7) and their employees, the labourers (60–63). As on Piers' half-acre, only those who 'treweliche wynnen' (61) will be pardoned. As for beggars, those who are too old or weak to earn their bread, deserve our charity whether or not they actually beg, and (in keeping with a principle of some Confessional Handbooks, see p. 182) their patient suffering can count as penance:

> For love of hir lowe hertes, Oure Lord haþ hem graunted
> Hir penaunce and here purgatorie vpon þis pure erþe (103–104)

Other beggars are not so privileged. Using a metaphor which will become increasingly important in the poem (see for example, 10.470–474, 14.106, both discussed on p. 142 and p. 182), Langland identifies those whose begging puts them in debt. False beggars not only defraud the needy (67) but, like Covetousness (5.289) they increase their own debt to God and man:

> And he þat biddeþ, borweþ, and bryngeþ hymself in dette. (79)

But Langland seems uncertain of his ground, and like Piers wants to supply all beggars with alms, 'For wite ye neuere who is worþi' (76), though the undeserving beggar may not receive Truth's pardon. In the C-text this discussion of the deserving and unde-serving beggar is much expanded, and includes a moving descrip-tion of the life of the poor, and several references to so-called 'lollars' (see Langland, Wycliffe and the Peasants' Revolt, p. 137). And in all three texts the correspondences between beggars raise another question: will God condemn all those who have failed to earn their pardon as he appears to condemn the able-bodied beggar, or will his knowledge of 'who haþ nede' (76) make him merciful to spiritual beggars?

The reading of the pardon 105–138

When Piers finally opens and reads his Pardon to a priest, we are surprised to find that it encapsulates only Truth's principle of honest earning, and not his principle of love and loyalty. Perhaps his meaning is being deliberately narrowed, for when Truth is next personified in Passus 18 it will be as the spokeswoman for Justice alone. The Pardon quotes the Athenasian Creed, which includes a long account of the Last Judgment and the works of mercy which will set one among the blessed (so that, according to Schmidt, 1995b p. 436, 'it does no more than ratify Holy Church's teaching at 1.128–133). A priest makes the obvious comment that it judges rather than pardons the pilgrims. Piers tears the pardon in half in anger – a controversial gesture which is removed in the C-text:

> 'Peter!' quod þe preest þoo, 'I kan no pardon fynde
> But "Do wel and haue wel, and God shal haue þi soule,"
> And "Do yuel and haue yuel, and hope þow noon ooþer
> That after þi deeþ day þe deuel shal haue þi soule!"'
> And Piers for pure tene pulled it atweyne (111–114)

tene: anger, trouble

Much has been written on this famous scene (a useful summary can be found in Marshall, pp. 63–70) and you should see whether you agree with any of the following interpretations. The first two demonstrate the ambiguity of the document itself (is it papal or royal?):

- It is a 'paper pardon' or papal indulgence and in tearing it Langland repudiates all such pardons, for in spite of his cautious disclaimer (7.177–182) the whole Passus suggests the Wycliffite scorn of pardons and their moral effects (see Frank, p. 28; Godden 1990, pp. 51–9; and Langland, Wycliffe and the Peasants' Revolt, p. 000). Unlike the Wycliffites Langland honours the sacraments, particularly Penance, though in a way that avoids a superstitious emphasis on signs (see Aers 2002).

- The words of the pardon sum up the Old Testament justice of the King of Heaven, so that in tearing it Piers cancels that justice. The torn pardon can thus be seen as an allegory of the Crucifixion, on the lines of the Charters of Christ that will be referred to on p. 216 (see Keen). In this way the pardon reveals the 'radical incapacity' (Simpson 1990, p. 83) of man to reach Truth by his own efforts, and so shows his need for grace.
- The poem so far has shown the ideals of truth working on the horizontal and the vertical axis at the same time, but the uncompromising pardon shows that they do not fit – that we cannot earn bread and pardon simultaneously. Piers' personal, angry reaction is to tear it and start an individual search for Dowel which will be continued by Will in the second half of the poem. Thus so far from showing man's need for grace, the tearing of the pardon indicates the necessity of individual good works, which are essentially incompatible with a life of work in the world.

These last two interpretations introduce the debate in the next two Passus between "salvation by works" and "salvation by grace" which preoccupies the next two Visions. But we must also try to relate the tearing of the pardon to what has gone before it. Throughout the Second Vision, and particularly in Passus 6 and 7, Langland has implied that the Winners who earn the bread will share it with the Wasters, including himself as an "idle" poet, and probably most of the Church and nobility as well. In some ways this is unjust, but in other ways it fits with the theory of the estates, by which different groups in society have different roles and connect "horizontally" with one another. This mutual dependence was a point forcibly made in the poem *Wynnere and Wastoure* which perhaps lies behind Langland's economic terminology in Passus 6 and 7, when it sums up the mutual dependence of production and consumption:

Whoso wele schal wyn, a wastour moste he fynde (390)

If these Passus are however read "vertically", as an allegory for the earning of spiritual reward, should we not expect that Christ will be as generous as the earthly winners, that like Piers Plowman he will 'tilie / As wel for a waster ... As for himself and his servants (19.439–440)? Christ should reward the morally strong but should he not also pardon the morally weak? We were glad when the king in Passus 4 refused to pardon Wrong, but before Christ's tribunal, are not all men in his position? We were glad when Piers used Hunger to get Waster to work, but also surely when he fed him with 'horse breed' (6.214)? The contemporary Commons might have mistrusted the earthly king's use of his secret seal to pardon offenders, but surely Langland's readers also hope that they, like the merchants, will have a special dispensation from Hell? Why then does the Pardon Scene suggest that sin will only be condemned? If this is the right reading, then it follows that we must focus less on work in the world, and more on being righteous. This indeed seems to be Piers' conclusion, for although he comes from the estate of literal workers, he will now use his limbs figuratively, like a cleric:

> 'I shal cessen of my sowyng,' quod Piers, 'and swynke noȝt so harde
> Ne aboute my bely ioye so bisy be na moore;
> Of preieres and of penaunce my plouȝ shal ben herafter' (118–120).

cessen: leave off; swynke: labour; bely ioye: appetite

So far from growing food Piers now intends to live like the birds of *Luke* 12:22 (125–130), relying on God to provide for him like the various hermits and "wise fools" of history. He quotes a tag from *Matthew* 6:25, 'ne solicitis sitis' ('Take no thought', that is, for your livelihood, 127) which will become a motif for the life of patient poverty celebrated in the Fourth Vision. This rejection of the needs of the community in favour of the needs of his own soul seems to put Piers into the uneasy position of Will in C 5; he also claimed that

> The lomes þat Y labore with and lyflode deserue
> Is *Pater-noster* and my prymer, *Placebo* and *Dirige*, (C 5.45–46)

lomes: limbs; deserue: earn; *Pater-noster*: The Lord's Prayer; *Placebo, Dirige*: offices said for the dead

Indeed this very human Piers seems to merge into Will at this point, for it is Will who now begins the search for Dowel which will occupy the rest of the poem.

The conclusion to the Vision and introduction to Dowel 139–201

At the end of Passus 7 Will awakes and thinks over what he has dreamed, placing himself once again in the Malvern Hills. At the same time he distances himself a little from the dream itself, quoting Biblical examples to show (as Freud did) that dreams must be read symbolically. It was common for writers of political advice literature (see Introduction, p. 14) to stress the fact that all their social criticism came from an unreliable dream – though generally such poems were rather more cryptic than Langland's (see Taylor). Will seems particularly uneasy about the way that the movement of this Second Vision has culminated in a non-pardon:

> And how þe preest preued no pardon to Dowel,
> And demed þat Dowel indulgences passed, (169–170)

> preued: proved; demed: thought; passed: surpassed

Perhaps he fears the reader may align this summary with the Wycliffite contempt for indulgences, as expressed in a near-contemporary sermon:

> Per corneþ no pdon but of god for good lyuynge & endyn in charite, & þis schal not be bou3t ne solde as prelatis chafferen þes dayes; for who … kepeþ wel þe hestis of god shal haue pardon & þe blisss of heueue (*English Works of Wyclif*, p. 238).

> chafferen: do business; hestis: commands

Will first back-tracks and then reinforces the offensive sentiments:

> And so I leue leelly (Lordes forbode ellis!)
> That pardon and penaunce and preieres doon saue
> Ac to truste to þise triennals – trewely, me þynkeþ,

It is noȝt so siker for þe soule, certes, as is Dowel … .
I sette youre patentes and youre pardon at one pies hele! (177–195)

doon: do; triennals: Masses said for the dead for the first three years; siker: sure; certes:
certainly; I sette: I put; patentes: letters patent (that is, indulgences); pies hele: piecrust

The Wycliffites attacked "superstitious" practices (like saying trien-
nial masses for the dead intended to spare the dead from Purgatory),
in a world where 'more and more of the Church's efforts were
devoted to teaching the living what they could do for the dead'
Rosenthal, p. 11). Though Langland himself may have earned
money in this way (see Donaldson, pp. 208–9), Will seems all too
Wycliffite in this outburst. Wycliffite ideas were blamed for the
Peasants' Revolt in 1381 (see Langland, Wycliffe and the Peasants'
Revolt, p. 137), and it may have been for this reason that Langland
cut the tearing of the pardon from this Passus in the C-text, and also
added a long section in which he dissociated himself from 'lollars'
(wandering beggars, if not actually Lollards). Perhaps we should
think of the Will who is about to begin his quest for Dowel as an
incipient Wycliffite, who will have to learn, through failure and suffering, that he needs grace as well as the good works of Dowel, and
so recover trust in the priesthood and sacraments of the Catholic
Church which are the channels of that grace.

Further reading

On pardons, see Rosenthal; Keen. On the Pardon Scene, see Aers
(1975); Carruthers; Frank; Godden (1990); Marshall; Simpson
(1990); Smith; and see Pearsall (1990, Bibliography), 280–7.

The Third Vision: Passus 8–12

Passus 8–9

Passus 8 introduces the long second half of the poem, known in some manuscripts as the *Vita*. From now on the narrator places himself at the centre of his visions, and only returns to his original role of reporter for the last three Passus. The journey Will makes is the search for Dowel begun by Piers at the end of Passus 7 because nothing else will apparently earn the pardon of Truth. Will does not explain why he is taking over Piers' pilgrimage, but after an initial waking encounter with two friars, begins his Third Vision (Passus 8–12). This is constructed, like a traditional *somnium*, a dream-vision including speeches by authoritative allegorical figures (see Introduction, p. 12). These encounters lend themselves more to *debate* and *sermon* than to dramatic visions, but they are brought to life not only by modern preaching techniques (anecdotes, allegorical pictures, Bible stories and the like), but by Will's confrontational attitude to them, his disagreements and downright rudeness. Perhaps it is because the characters Will encounters here are from inside his own head or from his educational experience, that he feels free to question and oppose them. But his revelation of the ambiguity and humanity of these unauthoritative authority-figures make the Third Vision an original, almost post-modern use of the *somnium* genre, and it is an intriguing task to sort out the relationships between the figures and the reliability of their always passionate declarations. Will's own *persona*, as explained in the Introduction, p. 4–5, is that both of William Langland and of the human will. In Passus 8 and 9 he encounters Thought and Wit, traditional opposites of human wilfulness. These Passus are joined together (as Passus 10) in the C-text and I will treat them in the same way. They are structured like this:

Passus 8	
Will's waking encounter with two friars	8.1–60
Will's encounter with Thought	8.61–113

Passus 9	
Will encounters Will and Wit	
The allegory of the Castle of Kynde	9.1–57
The failure to be governed by Inwit and the discussion	
of marriage	9.58–199
Wit defines Dowel	9.200–207

Will's waking encounter with two friars 8.1–60

For readers of C-text Passus 5 Will has already introduced himself to us as a kind of 'waster' (see Langland's Autobiography, p. 105) who lives on the charity of others, and this negative characterisation may be confirmed by the brief introduction to Passus 8:

> Thus yrobed in russet I romed aboute
> Al a somer seson for to seke Dowel (8.1–2)
>
> yrobed: dressed; Al a: throughout

Russet was a rough woollen cloth (the equivalent of the modern denim) associated with beggars and hermits. It was to develop a suspicious image after the Peasants' Revolt of 1381, for it was claimed in Parliament in 1382 that the followers of John Ball, clad in russet, had 'romed about' disseminating aspirations of equality and freedom (see Langland, Wycliffe and the Peasants' Revolt, p. 137). Even though the A-text, in which russet is also mentioned, was written much earlier than this, Langland's later readers may have seen Will here as an itinerant Wycliffite, who had expressed his hostility to the venality of the Church and its system of selling pardons at the end of the previous Passus.

This kind of itinerant life was also practised by the Wycliffites' arch-enemies, the friars, who modelled themselves on the early apostles and wandered over the country supposedly without bags (*Luke* 22:35), preaching Christ's gospel and living on the charity of others. In meeting the friars Will is meeting the social group who seem to be most like him both in their ideal of teaching the poor and their itinerant way of life. Perhaps William Langland was once a member of their Order (see Monks and Friars, p. 197; Clopper, pp. 69–72, 325–33)? As Clopper points out, his longest waking encounters are either with friars or spent discussing their way of life. So it may be autobiographical that Will now rejects their inviting claim that Dowel dwells with them:

> 'Amonges vs' quod þe Menours 'þat man [Dowel] is dwellynge ... '
> '*Contra!*' quod I as a clerc ... (18–20)
>
> Menours: Franciscans (Friars Minor); *Contra!*: On the contrary!

Will's contradiction (ironically fraternal in its method) introduces a dispute and an allegory – the characteristic narrative structures of the *Vita*. This particular allegory of the boat (31ff.), like most of Langland's allegories, is not altogether clear. Does it suggest that when a man becomes a friar he commits himself to a captain (Charity / Dowel) who can steer the boat of his body through the sea of worldly temptation, as Noah steers the Ark (= the Church) through the flood (= the world; in the picture on p. 120):

> Ac dedly synne doþ he noȝt, for Dowel hym kepeþ,
> And þat is charite þe champion, chief help ayein synne (45–46)
>
> ayein: against

But Will does not seem to believe in this rather reductive notion of Doing Well only by living within the little ark of the Friars' community, and prefers direct exposure to the 'wynde' and 'water' of experience where he may learn how to live:

> 'I haue no kynde knowyng,' quod I, 'to conceyue alle þi wordes,
> Ac if I may lyue and loke, I shal go lerne bettre.' (57–58)
>
> kynde knowing: natural knowledge (see below); loke: look about

Noah's Ark
(after a window in the north choir aisle, Canterbury Cathedral, 12th century)

In this Vision it appears that he looks for kynde knowyng (see Kynde, Kynde Knowyng and Kynde Wit, p. 153) by asking the various aspects of himself what Dowel, Dobet and Dobest might mean. Middleton (1982b) sees the discontinuous narrative of the poem as based on a series of conflicts, first verbal battles with himself, and then at the end of the poem, more literal conflicts with the Devil; Burrow (1993) on the other hand sees the narrative circling around the truth. As you read the Third Vision, ask yourself how, if at all, it seems to progress.

Will's encounter with Thought 8.61–113

To dramatise this search Will must fall asleep, and Langland reverts to the dream-vision trope of a beguiling landscape with birdsong (see Introduction, p. 10), to lull him into a new Vision. He now meets two allegorical characters who are both 'lyk to myselve' (70). The first of these is Thought.

Who is Thought?

As tentatively suggested in the text-box on Langland's Psychology on p. 123, Thought seems to be a natural, practical faculty, but precisely which one it is depends on how we judge him. If we see him as moderately wise, we can say that his is the kind of thinking exclusive to human beings, perhaps the *intellectus agens* or active intellect, which reasons and generalises from experience (rather than from God-given understanding as Reason can do). If we find him unhelpful, then we can translate him as one of the Inner Wits, *estimative* perhaps, the faculty which even animals possess in a limited degree, and which enables them to judge more or less by instinct, or *incognatio*, which processes visual images. We can even see him as Simpson does (1990, p. 100) as *fantasia* (an aspect of *imaginativa*) producing the 'ydle thoughts' and 'fantasies' of the Dreamer in Chaucer's *Book of the Duchess*, 1–29. Do you find what he has to say true, or limited, or even absurd?

Thought offers Will the first of the many 'triads' of Dowel, Dobet and Dobest which he elicits from the characters he meets. This one seems to refer back to the standards of the first two Visions and its divines set the pattern for many of the future triads. Dowel is the honest labourer, who is 'trewe of his tunge and of his two handes' (80). Dobet is socially superior for he has the power to be charitable, and 'helpeþ alle men after þat hem nedeþ' (86). Like the merchant in the Pardon Scene who built roads and bridges with his profits, Dobet 'wiþ Mammones moneie he haþ maad hym frendes' (has made friends with his ill-gotten money, as advised by Jesus himself in *Luke* 16:9: 89). Dobest bears a 'bisshopes croce' (95) with a crook at one end and a spike at the other:

> Is hoked on þat oon ende to halie men fro helle.
> A pik is on þat potente, to pulte adown þe wikked (96–97).

> halie: draw; pik: spike; potente: staff; pulte: thrust

This reminds us of Reason's double role in the Vision, directing the King to punish Wrong but also coming 'wiþ a cros' (B 5.12, cp. C 5.112) to direct the Sinners to Pardon. Should we compare Reason's dominant role in Passus 4–5 with his dominance here (though it is not clear whether the realm he rules is – the human heart):

> Thus Dowel and Dobet and Dobest þe þridde
> Crowned oon to be kyng to kepen hem alle
> And to rule þe reme by hire þre wittes (104–106)
>
> reme: realm; hire Pre wittes: the wisdom of all three

The way that this triad straddles the "horizontal" (social) and the "vertical" (moral) axes is typical of the slippery terminology of the triads in this Vision. The weight we give to this one relates to the weight we give to the personification Thought.

The verbal patternings of Thought certainly do not satisfy Will's hunger to really know Dowel, to savour (from *saporare*, to know) it through direct experience:

> Ac yet sauoreþ me noȝt þi seying, so me Crist helpe!
> For more kynde knowynge I coueite to lerne –
> How Dowel, Dobet and Dobest doon among þe peple. (109–111)
>
> sauereþ: appeals; kynde knowynge: natural knowledge

However Thought does not send him to look for practical charity among 'the peple', but, like the friars, directs him inwards to 'wit' (53). At this point Wit appears.

Langland's Psychology

English terms like 'Kynde Wit', 'Inwit', and 'Kynde Knowyng' proliferate in Langland's writing about the mind, and are confusingly intermingled with Latinate terms: 'Conscience', 'Reason' and 'Charity'. The psychological theory he would have studied at Oxford distinguished between the speculative functions of the mind, and the more practical ones which actually perceive the world and decide how to act. Its terminology derives from Aristotle, who did not really believe in the immortality of the individual soul, but most medieval theologians taught that the higher speculative functions were given by God's grace, and inherent in the immortal souls of all men (and to a lesser extent, all women). The practical functions however are natural and subject to sin, and should be guided and developed by the higher faculties. The most authoritative Christianiser of Aristotle's ideas, the thirteenth-century theologian St Thomas Aquinas, was determined to show that the soul, mind and body work together to form the whole person. Thus in the following table, based largely on Aquinas, the faculties on the left are in several cases higher forms of the faculties on the right to which they are linked. Langlandian terms are given in italics.

Bibliography

On medieval psychology, d'Entrèves, pp. 42–9; Harvey; Kaulbach; Kemp; Morgan; Potts. On Langland's allegory, Harwood and Smith; Quirk; Schmidt (1969); Simpson (2002).

Grace-given (in *Anima* or soul)	Natural (in mind and body)
Reason (teaching the Natural Law) *Perhaps Langland's Reason?*	**In human mind only** **Active intellect** (intellectus agens: reasoning and generalising powers) *Perhaps Langland's Inwit Kynde Wit/?*
Synderesis (higher Conscience, teaching the general principles of behaviour) *Perhaps Langland's Kynde Knowyng?*	**In human mind only** **Conscience** (attempting to make moral judgments, but fallible) **Will** (desiring or not desiring to love / obey Conscience / indulge the senses) *Perhaps Langand's Conscience and Will (and Concupiscencia Carnis etc.)?*
Memory *Perhaps Langland's Ymaginatif?*	**In humans and animals** **The inner senses of the brain** *Perhaps Langland's Thought / Wit / the Reason which governs beasts?* (i) sensus communis (perceiving objects) (ii) incognatio (recording visual images) (iii) imaginativa (creating new images) (iv) estimative (instinct / judgment possessed by animals) (v) memorialis (memory) *Perhaps Langland's Reason which governs the beasts*
	The outer senses of the body Sight Hearing Smell Taste Touch Touch *Perhaps Langland's Castle of Kynde?*

Who are Will and Wit?

In medieval poetry, as Simpson explains (1990, pp. 95–7), Wit was often seen in opposition to Will, as the spokesman of reason. In such contexts Will is selfish, heedless, concerned with bodily desire, while Wit is the wise counsellor who is above worldly passion. In the early fourteenth-century *Sayings of the Four Philosophers*, for example, the absence of Wit in the land has caused moral and political degeneration:

> Ffor wil is red, the lond is wreful
> Ffor wit is qued, the lond is wrongful (Robbins, *Historical Poems*, p. 142)
>
> red: counsel; wreful: full of revenge; wit is qued: wisdom is extinguished

Thought rubs in Wit's appropriateness as a teacher for Will by introducing him in a line which stresses the antithesis by its alliteration:

> Here is Wil wolde wite if Wit koude teche hym (126)
>
> koude: is able to

Wit is however surprisingly like Will; he is 'long and lene', 'of a softe speche', and takes 'no pride on his apparaill' (117–119). It will be remembered that Thought too was like Will ('a muche man … lik to myselue', 70). Should we begin to see William the dreamer as a composite of both the wilful and the wise in the human soul? Or should we see him as an unbalanced personality, relying on only that part of the psyche which desires heedlessly, without thought or reason? But this is to judge the Will very harshly; as can be seen from St Augustine's analysis of the Powers of Soul (see text-box on p. 192), Will, or *voluntas*, is the part of the human soul which corresponds to the Holy Spirit. Properly reformed the human Will can become more like God in its charity. Only Will's behaviour in the poem can help us decide what Langland means him to represent, and as we turn to the next Passus we see him becoming increasingly wilful, increasingly impatient with the authority figures of his own *somnium*.

The allegory of the Castle of Kynde 9.1–57

When Will asks Wit to define Dowel, he receives an answer which focuses on the body and its propensity to sin, particularly in sexual behaviour. This leads to a discussion of marriage. Since only the laity could get married (the clergy, such as Dobest the bishop mentioned at 8.95 and 9.14, were supposed to be virgins), it seems that at this early stage in his quest he is being taught about Dowel, for 'Triewe wedded libbynge folk in þis world is Dowel' (108). Wit's method is also appropriate for a sermon to the laity.

But before we embark on the discussion of marriage it would be as well to look briefly at Wit's rather puzzling allegory of the Castle of Kynde (see Kynde, Kynde Knowyng and Kynde Wit, p. 153). Here Kynde represents God 'creatour of alle kynnes thynges' (26) and the castle he has made out of the four elements is the body (2–5), complete with the five senses (22–24; touch is transformed into locomotion). The psyche within the body is seen as divided between higher and lower faculties, as in the text-box on Langland's Psychology on p. 123. The higher faculties are subsumed under *Anima*, the soul, and relate directly to Kynde, Anima's father, while the lower powers are directed by Constable Inwit whose power does not come from grace (59). Inwit may represent the *intellectus agens* or active intellect, which enables humans to reason and generalise on a natural level. Aquinas, who is the most significant figure in the Christianisation of this essentially Aristotelian scheme, was much exercised by how the higher speculative grace-given faculties related to the lower more practical and natural ones. Wit seems to do this by describing a marriage between *Anima*, daughter of Kynde and therefore of Divine origin, with Dowel (helped by Dobet and Dobest) who live in the body and are under the governance of Inwit. The allegory as a whole may therefore be an attempt to show how the well-directed individual can live in the world.

The proposed match between Anima and Dowel is Wit's first example of an ideal marriage, which in Christian teaching was one that reflected the love between Christ and his Church (*Ephesians* 5:25; this faithful love was for St Augustine a chief 'good' of marriage). Anima is also wooed by the Devil ('A proud prikere of

Fraunce, *Princeps huius mundi* : a proud French knight, the Prince of this World, 9). But as Tavormina has explained in her illuminating discussion of the Passus (pp. 48–102), such a disparaging match would violate the principle of pairing *like with like*, which Kynde himself instituted when he made both Adam and Eve in His own image:

> Ac he made man moost lik to hymself,
> And Eue of his ryb bon withouten any mene. (33–34)

bon: bone; mene: intermediary

Their marriage in Paradise before the Fall is Wit's second example of ideal marriage, and later he praises the political and social effects of such faithful unions (in people whose Anima is presumably wedded to Dowel):

> Trewe wedded libbynge folk in this world is Dowel
> For þei mote werche and wynne and þe world sustene. (108–109)

As Tavormina puts it: 'Langland conceives of ideal human marriage as being deeply in tune with nature in general and with ideal human nature in particular' (p. 80).

The failure to be governed by Inwit and the discussion of marriage 9.58–207

Wit develops his account of the dual nature of man into an indictment on those who fail to follow Inwit and so lose control of their bodies:

> Muche wo worþ that wiȝt þat mysruleþ his Inwit (60).

This will be developed in the next Vision, where Will leaves his Inwit to follow Passion and Appetite. The chief 'woe' which Wit discusses here is ill-matched marriages, but he precedes this by giving examples of those who fail to be regulated by Inwit: fools (67), ill-

governed children (75–81), and those who indulge in gluttony
(61–65) and other 'sins of the mouth' (97–104; see above, p. 000)
can disrupt society. Such lack of personal self-control harms society
for it makes people selfish and 'vnkynde til anoþer' (84). Wit tries to
shame his own society by contrasting it unfavourably with the
Jewish community, where 'Eyþer helpeþ oother' (86). With a side-
glance at true poets whose speech is a 'game of heuene'(102), Wit
turns to his principal theme: the contrasting of good and bad marriages.

Wit uses the principle of *like with like*, which was established in
God's creation of Adam and Eve, to judge the validity of human
marriages. In the first place they should be desired not only by the
relatives, but also by bride and groom. This principle was really protected by the Church, which from the twelfth century had insisted
on asking the consent of both groom and bride:

> First by þe fadres wille and the frendes conseille,
> And siþenes by assent of hemself, as þei two myghte accorde;
> And þus was wedlok ywroȝt, and God hymself it made; (115–117)

Secondly the marriage partners should have some similitude, and
marriages not be made between people of grossly divergent ages or
class, which (he claims) are as bad as illegitimate unions, however
legitimate in Church law. Inappropriate matches were still a
common occurrence in the higher social class; Richard II for
example at the age of 28 was espoused to a seven-year-old princess
in 1395 (see Lucas, p. 90). This was condemned by preachers and
parodied by storytellers (like Chaucer in the *Merchant's Tale*, but
Langland is remarkable in calling such loveless matches illegitimate:

> For goode sholde wedde goode, þouȝ þei no good hadde; ...
> For no londes, but for love, loke ye be wedded,
> And þanne gete ye the grace of God, and good ynouȝ to liue wiþ.
> (160, 177–178)

goode: good (morals/money); loke ye: be sure; good ynouȝ: enough money

The pun on 'goods' here underlines the contrast between the two kinds of marriage: those between the good and leading to grace, and those made for goods, which are likely to be sterile, and have 'no children but cheese and choppes hem bitwene' (fighting and blows, 169). Here Wit seems thoroughly humane.

Wit's words become darker when he begins to discuss marriages where the body is not controlled by Inwit. Confessors asked penitents the most intimate details of their sex lives, and required sexual relations to be suspended during times of penance or preparation for feast days (or female menstruation). Wit asserts children conceived out of wedlock, or from ill-sorted unions, or even from sex at the wrong time, are 'wastours and wrecches' (120). His evidence is from the Old Testament. Cain's wickedness was to be expected, as he was conceived at a forbidden time of penance (121; see Lucas, p. 111). And the Flood was sent to 'clene awey' the 'corsed blood' (136) of a misalliance: the "disparagement" by Cain's descendants of the nobler 'kynde' of Seth (128–142; see Ravishment and Disparagement, p. 000). The Ark preserved 'of ech kynde a couple (141) – good marriages to repopulate the earth. (This sequence of ideas is so close to that in *Cleanness* as to suggest that Langland knew this earlier alliterative poem.) That the children should bear the 'belsires giltes' (ancestors' guilt, 143) does strike Wit as being unfair, but he seems to have observed from his own experience that a 'sherewe' or wicked man can only beget another sherewe (148), either because 'kynde follows kynde', or because the children are not taught to obey their Inwit and follow Dowel. Such offspring 'wandren and wasten' and will be damned if God does not 'gyve hem grace ... to amende' (199). Should we see this a thoroughly uncharitable sentiment, and an indictment of Wit himself, or perhaps as Langland expressing a fear about his own moral standing?

Wit defines Dowel 9.200–207

It is hardly surprising that Wit, whose speech has been so preoccupied with the control of the body, should also be preoccupied with concupiscence – the natural tendency that fallen man has to sin, or as he puts it, to disobey Inwit. When he eventually gets round to defining Dowel it is in terms of obedience, suffering and control of his traditional opponent, Will:

> 'And þus Dowel is to drede God, and Dobet to suffre,
> And so comeþ Dobest of boþe, and bryngeþ adoun þe mody –
> And þat is wikked wille þat many werk shendeþ (204–206)

suffre: endure; mody: proud one (Will); shendeþ: harms

Is Wit trapped in an Old Testament world where God is punitive and children are born sinful? Has Will been discouraged by his attacks into believing that he cannot Do Well unaided? Or does Wit show us that we can Do Well in the world when supported by a true and loving marriage? He will be roundly attacked in the next Passus by an angry wife, proving that even allegorical marriages are fraught with problems.

Further reading

On women and marriage in *Piers Plowman* see articles by Pearsall, Cole, Aers and Somerset in *YLS* 17 (2003) which is devoted to Langland's treatment of women; Cooper (1990); Tavormina. On women in the period, see Lucas; Tentler. For Wit and Will, see Burrow (1993); Davenport; Simpson (1990), pp. 93–102. On Will's journey, see Carruthers, pp. 101–5.

Passus 10

The next Passus continues in the same genre of a "*somnium* with questionable authorities". Reversing the usual expectation that a husband is more learned than his wife, Wit's wife Study seems to represent Will's attempt to get beyond his own native wits by application to books. After lecturing Will on the proper use of learning, Study passes him on to two characters who seem even more external to his mind: Clergy and his wife Scripture. They are however both relations of Study: Clergy is her cousin and is married to Scripture. Thus they are all related to Wit, who is surely an aspect of Will himself; it is as if Will's learning from others is also a part of his own intelligence. Their discussion occupies Passus 10 and 11, and is commented on in Passus 12 by a third more clearly "inward" character, Ymaginatif. These figures, who are both internal and external, discuss not only the nature but also the importance of Dowel, and so extend the reference from what Will should do as an individual to be saved, to whether mankind as a whole (including non-Christians) can expect salvation. Study and Clergy are concerned about the backsliding of those who claim to follow them, and Clergy even goes against his own kind and threatens all churchmen, and particularly the monks and friars, with disendowment. Scripture then asserts that men are saved only for following Christ's law of love, but Will vigorously opposes this "salvation by works" suggestion and insists that the unlearned and poor are saved by grace alone. This debate puts onto the vertical axis of salvation the conflict between justice and mercy which had so occupied the Vision.

The Passus proceeds in the following way:

Passus 10	
Study attacks false study and hypocrisy	1–158
Study directs Will to Clergy	159–218
Giving him good work habits	159–169
Teaching him School and University subjects	170–181
Love the aim of learning	182–218
Will greets Clergy and Scripture	219–229
Clergy attacks clergymen and threatens them with disendowment	230–327
Scripture and Will debate salvation	328–472

Who is Study?

In an illuminating section on the Third Vision (1990, pp. 104–10) Simpson suggests that Will's move from Study to Clergy and Scripture parallels Langland's own move from school, where the texts *studied* need not be entirely religious, to university, where only the *Clergy* (living or dead) comment on *Scripture*. Study herself says she does not understand Theology: in acknowledging this incapacity, Study conforms to a standard educational structure, whereby students move from preliminary learning to theological study (1990, p. 106).

This interpretation fits particularly well with 10.159–217, in which Study describes the allegorical journey Will should make from school texts like Cato's *Distiches* (see Krochalis and Peters, Pt. 19), to the seven liberal arts (including logic, grammar, music and astronomy) taught during the first years of university, to the study of Theology under Clergy rather than Study.

Alternatively we can see Study not so much representing "school" as "the ideal of scholarship", and that she prepares for the more authoritative lectures of Clergy and Scripture by attacking those who use religious learning in the wrong way. Her ideal of scholarship is indeed self-subverting, for she sees all learning which does not lead to love as useless.

The speech of Study 1–218

In spite of her praise of love in general, Study seems to know little of love in particular, for she is a caricature of a nagging wife, and her first remarks are to attack her own husband for speaking to anyone as crazy as a poet (seen as 'fooles þat frenetike ben of wittes', 6). Most of her speech is directed against those who use her, Study, in altogether the wrong way. Such men include the whole tribe of hypocrites, be they self-important clerics, intellectually pretentious lords, or in particular the lying poets and entertainers with whom she associates Will, 'iaperis and iogelours and iangleris of gestes' (31; see Minstrels and Poets, p. 175). These supposedly 'feynen hem foolis' so as to deceive the lords who employ them. Should we take this attack as evidence that William Langland felt that he himself was forsaking the true principles of scholarship by writing poetry?

Study then reveals her focus on love as the main aim of study. The learned, *studied* talk at table encourages men to be 'unkynde to the commune' by directing their minds to the surface 'taste' of Scripture rather than its often uncomfortable meaning. There is more dramatic word-play about eating in her attack on the hypocrisy of clerical table-talk (a favourite Langlandian theme):

> Thus þei dryuele at hir deys þe deitee to knowe,
> And gnawen God wiþ þe gorge whanne hir guttes fullen.
> Ac þe carefulle may crie and carpen at þe yate,
> Boþe afyngred and afurst, and for chele quake (56–59).

> dryuele: drivel; deys: dias; gnawen: eat/revile; careful: troubled; afy gred: hungry; chele: chill

She includes special mention of the friars, notable teachers at the Universities and at the public pulpit at St Paul's, where she says (as Conscience will find in Passus 20) they argue for a greater share in the clergy's wealth 'for pure enuye of clerkes' (73; see below, p. 000). The evil results of this hypocrisy will be the general degeneration of the world and even the alienation of God (78). But these apocalyptic warnings are mixed with her mundane attack on the modern invention of 'parlours' (98–102) reminiscent of Joseph's sneer at them in *Wuthering Heights*, Ch. 13. This brings her back to the clever clerks who misuse her learning, and 'wilneþ to wite þe whyes of God almyȝty' (124). Her plea for humility (103–131) seems particularly pointed towards Will and his insistent questioning, and she correctly predicts that he will be reproved by Ymaginatif (117; compare 12.216). Does such an attack on the cut and thrust of debate, like her attack on poetry, diminish her real authority? Should we see her as genuinely wanting study to be used in the service of love, to 'prepare the soul for the reception of virtue' as Seneca was supposed to have said (Simpson 1986b, p. 53)? Or should we see her as a caricature of the elderly schoolteacher, fulminating against poets and clever dinner guests, issuing vague threats and lamenting the good old days?

Study directs Will to Clergy 159–218

Taking up Study's praise of humility, Wit vividly gestures to Will at this point to ask her, most humbly, to show him the way to Dowel. She directs him at once to Clergy, who, like Wit, has a wife more authoritative than himself: Scripture. They will teach him religion, and presumably he is to make this, rather than that unreliable poetry, his pursuit. She gives him her blessing (and 'tokenes', 218) and describes a journey which appears to be an autobiographical progress through school and University. First Will, like many another student, is advised to avoid excessive spending, drinking and speaking – keeping his will in control until he finds Clergy, and Scripture. They were once her pupils, for she has taught all the Arts subjects such as Logic, Law, Music, and Grammar, which made up the first part of an undergraduate course, though she later warns Will off astronomy and magic (209–215). She has also taught all the crafts. However she has not taught theology, which was a more advanced study, and one she cannot understand as she understands the practical wisdom of Cato (a schoolbook of proverbs):

> Ac Theologie haþ tened me ten score tymes:
> The moore I muse þerinne, þe mystier it semeþ, ...
> A ful leþi þyng it were if þat loue [þerinne] nere; (182–186)

> tened: annoyed; muse: think; leþi: empty; nere: is not

She may *say* that her disciplines cannot encompass theology, but this summary of the purpose of theology is no different from her own summary of the purpose of study: both should lead to love. She even hints that obeying the law of love will bring grace (and perhaps pardon?), a line of thought which will become crucial in the next two Passus. It remains to be seen if the characters Clergy and Scripture do indeed teach this true Christian doctrine, or whether the very violence of the debate into which Will will plunge with these two new characters indicates that the academics of the Church did not practice what they preached.

Who are Clergy and Scripture?

'Clergy' means both learning and the religious profession who had a monopoly on it. These professionals include both the *secular* clergy (bishops and priests) and the *religious* or *regular* clergy (monks, nuns, friars, and canons) who live in enclosed communities (see Monks and Friars, p. 197). However Clergy does not speak for this large group, but attacks it, in particular for its wealth and its misuse of learning and other privileges. He must therefore personify some ideal of learning and the religious life.

'Scripture' means the Bible, which was read not by itself but with a gloss or commentary which referred to the long tradition of learning that had accrued to every verse. Will can also quote the Bible, and uses the Fathers like St Augustine and St Ambrose to argue with Scripture. So Scripture too must personify an idea of Biblical scholarship as well as the text itself, and indeed she does summarise its message as the law of love (354–372), which for her (though not for Will) is the essential route to salvation.

The speech of Clergy 219–327

Like Study, Clergy seems to represent the invisible ideal from which those who profess to follow him have slipped. Will's question about Dowel, Dobet and Dobest seems to remind him of the Trinity, which is seen here as throughout the poem as the foundation of Christian belief. Dowel is to believe in it, Dobet is to suffer the difficulty of enacting such belief ('werche it in werk þat þi word sheweþ' or "practise what you preach", 254); and Dobest is to teach it and to be 'boold to blame þe gilty' (258). Clergy clearly takes this last duty to himself, and proceeds to blame the guilty clergy whose lives show they neither believe nor suffer Christian principles. The faithlessness and sinfulness of the laity should be on their consciences, for they 'preche sholde and teche / Alle maner men to amenden (improve, 267–268). Having attacked 'mansede preestes' (wicked, 278) for their covetousness, Clergy turns his attention to the 'religious' (291) by which he means the 'regular' communities of monks and friars. In a passage which repays close comparison with the Monk in Chaucer's *General Prologue*, 183–7, Clergy describes how monks leave the cloister to ride with horses and hounds and acts as arbitrators for out-of-court settlements (louedayes), implying that bribes can help them purchase more land:

> Ac now is Religion a rydere, a romere by stretes,
> A ledere of louedayes and a lond buggere,
> A prikere vpon a palfrey fro manere to manere,
> An heep of houndes at his ers as he a lord were (305–308).

> romere by streetes: wanderer on the roads; lovuedayes: arbitrations; buggere: purchaser; prikere: rider; palfrey: quality horse; manere: manor; at his ers: behind him

Such a monk, like Sloth in Passus 5, certainly neither suffers nor teaches the Christian life.

Clergy suggests the Church would be rid of such hypocrites if lords did not bequeath further lands to them in 'endowments' (gifts, 309–310), and if a reforming king stripped them of the endowments they already had:

> 'Ac þer shal come a kyng and confesse yow religiouses,
> And bete yow, as þe Bible telleþ, for brekynge of youre rule,
> And amende monyals, monkes and chanons,
> And puten hem to hir penaunce – *Ad pristinum statum ire*, (316–319)

> amende: improve; monyals: nuns; chanons: canons (another type of monk); *Ad ... ire*: to reform to their original state

The suggestion that it is the secular lords' responsibility to restore the clergy 'to their original state' by disendowing it of its lands is also made by John Wycliffe in 1378 in *De Officio Regis (Of the Duties of Kings)*. Wycliffe also argued that the king should have the right to tax all his people, including the monks. During the war with France, where the Pope himself was living until 1378, many agreed with him, and steps had been taken to tax and control the income of French monastic foundations, some of which had actually been disendowed in 1383 (see Statutes in Krochalis and Peters, pp. 71–5; Alford 1988c, p. 74). These provided precedents for later requests for the king to disendow the English Church (a step eventually taken by Henry VIII in 1532; see Langland, Wycliffe and the Peasants' Revolt, below). But while some wanted the state to reform the Church, others demanded that Christian principles should be used to reform the state (see Justice 1994, pp. 192–3). Is Langland shifting from the second, more traditional, position to the first, more radical one? Or, at the end of this "prophecy" does he draw back from the specifically political, and locate his reforming king at the end of the world?

Langland, Wycliffe and the Peasants' Revolt

John Wycliffe was a colourful and very significant figure in the middle of the fourteenth century. Although a priest and an academic theologian he developed ideas about the role of the Church that were very radical, and published them through public sermons as well as numerous books in the 1370s and 1380s. He also advocated translating the Bible into English so that the laity could read it, and followed Richard Fitzralph in his hostility to the friars (see p. 187; Lambert, pp. 225–42; Szttya, pp. 152–60). In the 1370s, when the B-text was being written, there was considerable open debate about such issues, and Langland participated in this debate in some of the following areas:

- Wycliffe argued that to have dominion (power and wealth) entailed a responsibility to be in a state of grace. He used this argument to attack the wealth of the clergy (saying that Jesus' words on the perfect Christian life in *Matthew* 19:21 applied to *all* clergy), and threatened them with disendowment by the laity. Langland gives similar warnings (10.317ff., 15.541ff.).

- Wycliffe condemned some papal practices such as raising money by selling indulgences and pursuing wars. Langland condemns such practices too (Prol. 81, 107, 7.187, 19:432–433, etc.; see pp. 115, 254).

- Both Wycliffe and Langland (notably in Passus 20) are highly critical of friars for failing to follow their high ideals.

In the 1380s Wycliffe's views were increasingly seen as dangerous. In particular it was said that his sermons had inspired the leaders of the Peasants' Revolt of 1381, and he was condemned by state and Church in 1382. Fascinatingly *Piers Plowman* was itself drawn into the area of suspicion, because the half-crazy priest John Ball, said (erroneously) to have been a pupil of Wycliffe for two years, seems to have used the poem in his coded messages to rebel groups in East Anglia. Some of these alleged letters were included verbatim in two of the Chronicles which describe the uprising. For example, in Walsingham's version we read: 'Iohn Shep ... biddeth Peres Plouȝman go to his werke ... and chastise wel Hobbe the Robbere' ... 'and do wel and betre.' This may mean that John Ball urges the ploughmen of England to punish Robert Hales, the Treasurer. Knighton quotes from another letter: 'John Ball ... hath rungen youre belle ... Nowe is tyme.' Astell suggests that he means it is now time to 'bell the cat' of Langland's Prologue, John of Gaunt (see above, p. 28). As Anne Hudson remarks, 'it seems impossible to avoid the conclusion that *Piers Plowman* had by 1381 gained sufficient fame amongst those likely to favour the Revolt to act as a rallying cry' (1988, 252).

Whether either Wycliffe or Langland meant to inspire revolt is of course quite another story. It seems most unlikely that either of them wanted bloodshed, and some critics argue that Langland revised his text from B to C partly as an attempt to distance it from the Revolt (see p. 137). However others (including Aers 1980, and Astell) suggest that Langland was deliberately ambiguous in his allegory, and that the poem is politically subversive. It is certainly true that Wycliffe's later followers, the Wycliffites or 'Lollards', continued to use *Piers Plowman* both as a literary model, and as an inspiration for their way of life as lay preachers, whose criticisms of the established Church were eventually condemned as heretical. Do you find rebellion and heresy incipient in the poem?

■ **Bibliography**

For Wycliffite texts to compare with Langland, see Hudson; Krochalis and Peters Pt. 14; Wyclif. On Langland and Wycliffites, see Astell, pp. 44–72; Cole; Galloway (2001); Godden (1990); Justice (1994), p. 193; Hudson (1988, 2003); Scase. *YLS* 17 (2003) is devoted to this topic.

Scripture and Will debate salvation 328–472

Will tries to sum up what he has heard from Clergy ('þanne is Dowel and Dobet,' quod I, *'dominus* and kny3thode?', 330), a misunderstanding which provokes Scripture into entering the argument. Her contribution, which is supported by both scriptural and non-scriptural authority, introduces a theme which will dominate the next Vision: the praise of patient poverty. She paraphrases two texts which Will will constantly return to: *Luke* 6: 20: 'Blessed be the poor, for yours is the Kingdom of God', and *James* 2:5: 'Hath not God chosen the poor of this world and rich in faith and heirs of the kingdom?', both of which condemn riches:

> And patriarkes and prophetes and poetes boþe
> Writen to wissen vs to wilne no richesse,
> And preiseden pouerte with pacience; þe Apostles berep witnesse
> þat þei han eritage in heuene – and by trewe ri3te,
> þer riche men no ri3t may cleyme, but of ruþe and grace. (338–342)

> written: wrote; wissen: counsel; wilme: desire; eritage: inheritance; ruþe: mercy

This leads to her central claim that all men should try to obey the law of love, which is the summation of both the Old and New Testaments (following *Luke* 10:27):

> That whoso wolde and wilneþ wiþ Crist to arise …
> He sholde louye and lene and þe lawe fulfille.
> That is, loue þi Lord God leuest aboue alle,
> And after, alle Cristene creatures in commune, ech man ooþer;

> And þus bilongeþ to louye, þat leueþ to be saued … .
> For euery Cristene creature sholde be kynde til ooþer (353–362)
>
> lene: leand; leueþ: believes

Will objects with scholastic gusto (*Contra!*, 343) to these suggestions that Christians must (at least partly) earn their salvation by suffering or by acts of charity, and insists that *any* baptised Christian has a passport into Heaven, whether or not he has suffered:

> þat is baptized beþ saaf, be he riche or pouere.' (345)
>
> saaf: saved

This is a very crude and unorthodox statement of the saving power of the 'sacramental character' conferred on Christians at baptism. He goes on to insist that only those who are predestined for salvation by being written into the 'legende of lif' (375) can escape the fires of Hell, in which are already burning those unbaptised heathens who preached obedience to God's law. Note the way the alliteration links the principles he despises (werkes, wit, wynne):

> And if I sholde werche by hir werkes to wynne me heuene,
> þat for hir werkes and wit now wonyeþ in pyne –
> þanne wrou3te I vnwisly, whatsoeuere ye preche! (386–388)
>
> wynne: earn; wonyeþ: dwell; pyne: peain

This dispute between Scripture and Will is really a continuation of the argument between the priest and Piers at the end of the Second Vision, on the issue of whether men can be saved if they fail to Do Well. The issue had been hotly debated in Oxford in the 1340s and 1350s (when Langland might well have participated) in the wake of a celebrated treatise *On the Cause of God against Pelagius* by Thomas Bradwardine (who died Archbishop of Canterbury in 1349; Pelagius is discussed below, p. 161). Scripture's position is that of "salvation by works": for her, Christians must obey Christ's law. Will on the other hand expounds a rigidly literal interpretation of the "justification by faith" position worked out by St Paul in the *Epistle to the Romans*.

> Therefore by the deeds of the law here shall no flesh be justified in
> [God's] sight, ... But now the righteousness of God without the law
> is manifested ... which is by faith in Jesus Christ. (3.20, 22)

Will gives this doctrine a deterministic interpretation which, like
Bradwardine, he probably drew directly from the later writings of
St Augustine. In *On the Spirit and the Letter* for example Augustine
insists (following St Paul) that as men cannot keep the Old
Testament law, God saves those whom he has predestined to have
faith in Christ ('for it is God who gives us even to believe', Ch.
54):

> The law indeed, by issuing its commands and threats,, and by justi-
> fying no man, sufficiently shows that it is by God's gift, through the
> help of the Spirit, that a man is justified ... in a word, not by the law
> of works, but by the law of faith (Ch. 15, 22).

However Augustine goes on to say that the Spirit or 'finger' of God
(*Exodus* 31:18) helps men to obey this new law of faith through
their love for one another – a sentiment much closer to Scripture's
position than to Will's:

> When love itself is shed abroad in the hearts of believers, then we
> have the law of faith, and the Sprit which gives life to him that loves.
> (Ch. 29)

Ignoring what Augustine or St Paul (or Scripture and Study) have to
say about man's obligation to try to keep the law of love, Will piles
up examples of those non-Christians who may be damned despite
their obedience to God's law (as they saw it), and Christians apparently saved by their faith in spite of their sinfulness. He uses Noah's
ark as a symbol of the Church 'þat herberwe is and Goddes hous to
saue' (405; see picture on p. 120), and cites the preferential treatment given to faithful sinners like the crucified thief or King David
over good men like the classical author Aristotle who 'writen manye
bokes / Of wit and of wisedom' (426). He even seems to conclude
that as salvation is in God's hands, we might as well accept human
imperfection:

> Forþi lyue we forþ wiþ liþere men – I leue fewe ben goode – ...
> And he þat may al amende, have mercy on vs alle! (437–439)

Forþi: therefore; liþere: evil; amende: cure

Such arguments almost undermine themselves. Is Langland deliberately giving Will a belief in "salvation by grace alone" which is so
much more determinist than St Paul's "justification by faith" as to
drive the reader back to Scripture's "salvation by works alone"? Will
finally turns his attack on to Clergy himself at 441, for did not
Augustine claim that there are foolish men in heaven and wise men
in Hell (455)?, which he interprets to mean that to know too much
Christian learning is a positive hindrance to salvation:

> Arn none raþer yrauysshed fro þe riȝte bileue
> Than are þise konnynge clerkes þat knowe manye bokes,
> Ne none sonner ysaued, ne sadder of bileue
> Than plowmen and pastours and pouere commune laborers.
> (457–460)

Will then uses the potent metaphor of debt (see Passus 5 above
and 14, 19 below) to express the moral responsibility that Clergy
bears. A lord's serf or servant does not get into debt in the way
that his reeve, who has to keep the accounts for the estate, generally does; it was indeed true that reeve-rolls begin with the word
'arerage' or debt (see *Walter of Henley*, 218–21 and Alford 1988a,
p. 10). In the same way the very ignorance and poverty of these
'plowmen', their incapacity, protects them from the 'arerage'
(debt) of sin which the more fortunate and educated clergy
cannot avoid:

> That seruauntȝ þat seruen lordes selde fallen in arerage
> But þo þat kepen þe lordes catel – clerkes and reues.
> Right so lewed men and of litel kunnyng
> Selden falle so foule and so fer in synne
> As clerkes of Holy Kirke þat kepen Cristes tresor (470–474).

Selde: seldom; arerage: arrears; catel: possessions; reues: reeves; lewed: ignorant;;
kunnyng: skill; fer: far.

It is attractive to suggest God should compensate the poor for their ignorance, but does not this line of thought reduce the importance of obeying the law of love? In Passus 6 the 'plowmen and pastours and pouere commune laborers' found that work on the half-acre by no means excused them from the need to Do Well.

Should Langland's readers, privileged as they must be with some learning, take seriously Will's claim that this very learning is a disadvantage when it comes to salvation? In questioning learning, Will is attacking not only Clergy but Study, whose path to understanding he seemed so ready to take in the middle of the Passus, and Scripture, whose Law must be the very foundation of his faith.

The Passus therefore dramatises the conflict about how men should Do Well as a debate between three characters who seem to represent mental and cultural resources (Study, Clergy and Scripture) and one who represents a natural power of the soul (Will). The intellectual abstractions recommend obedience to the law of love and the ideals of the Church, and they attack not so much Will as those who profess such ideals without keeping them. Will on the other hand, although at first compliant with these teachers, becomes increasingly hostile to them, not because he has failed to obey their ideals (he does not seem to have tried), but because he claims such a difficult obedience is unnecessary and almost self-defeating. Why worry about one's failure to keep Christ's law when one can rely on the Bible's apparent promise to save baptised sinners, especially poor and suffering ones (see for example *Galatians* 3:27, *1 Peter* 2:20, 3:21, though his interpretation is controversial)? He speaks as one might imagine the human Will would speak, and seems finally to be recklessly reliant on the grace which seems predetermined to the poor and ignorant, though he himself is neither poor nor ignorant. His position (which in the C-text is detached from Will and given to the disreputable Recklessness), is summed up by Burrow:

> In Passus 10 Will suddenly cuts loose, with a fierce tirade in which he casts doubt on the fundamental assumption that God does indeed reward those who do well, as Truth's pardon promised ... Virtue and intelligence, he objects, are *not* always rewarded with eternal life, for

is not Aristotle among the damned? Nor are stupidity and vice always punished, for did not Christ promise salvation to the thief on the cross? So, what price Dowel? (1993, p. 21)

Will's determinism will need to be answered in the next Passus.

Further reading

On Study and Clergy, see Bishop; Simpson (1990), pp. 104–7; Johnson.

Passus 11

At the end of Passus 10 Will seemed ready to let determinism and a reliance on baptism replace free will and moral responsibility, and at the beginning of Passus 11 we see the practical results of this intellectual decision. He falls asleep within his dream, and as if the two dream-states cancel each other out, he is returned to the experience of life (or did Langland simply forget that he had not awakened Will at the end of the previous Passus?). At any rate the 'inner dream' which occupies this Passus involves Will in experience as well as in intellectual debate. For 40 years he abandons the quest for Dowel and follows Fortune instead, and is only brought back to his quest by Elde (old age) and the imminence of Death. Having been let down by the friars, on whose pardon he had relied, he is once again harangued by Scripture about the importance of obeying the law of love. It is the same message she gave in Passus 10, but this time Will (apparently made wiser by the years of experience) does not respond with an irresponsible reliance on predestination, but with his own sermon on the efficacy of a grace-given baptism. The sudden appearance of Trajan from Heaven however seems to refute both Will's reliance on baptism and Scripture's reliance on obedience to the written law. Will takes the floor again, and seems to reveal a new acceptance of the power of both grace and works together. Using some passages from Scripture, read in the light of his own (disastrous) experience, Will claims Christ's brotherly mercy, but also confirms the need to Dowel through charity and patient poverty. An encounter with Kynde, who shows him the beauties of the natural world, and Reason, who advises him not to question God's providence, reinforces this belief that experience and 'suffrance' is the route to Dowel. The Dreamer "wakes" from his inner dream and meets Ymaginatif, who emphasises that this 'suffrance' is enacted patience: the willing acceptance of whatever experience one is asked to suffer. Thus the Passus which opened with Will plunging into the sea of experience ends with the lesson of experience: that, as Chekhov's *Seagull* Nina puts it: 'what really matters is not fame or glamour, but knowing how to endure things.'

The Passus follows the following scheme:

Passus 11	
Will falls into an 'inner dream'	
Will's reckless life: Fortune, the Three Temptations and the friars	1–107
The return to Dowel: grace vs works	108–229
Scripture on salvation by works	108–114
Will argues for salvation of all Christians	115–139
Trajan	140–229
Praise of patient poverty	230–329
The Vision of Kynde and Reason and the appearance of Ymaginatif	330–420

Will's reckless life: Fortune, the Three Temptations, and the friars 1–107

Passus 10 had ended with Will voicing his contempt for good works in the face of God's predestination. Scripture's response now is to quote a put-down ascribed to St Bernard: 'Many know many things but do not know themselves'(3). Will is so struck by the force of this that he falls asleep and sees himself and his life as if in a mirror. His experiences are described as an enactment of St John's words in his *First Epistle* 2:16:

> For all that is in the world, the lust of the flesh, and the lust of the eyes, and the pride of life, is not of the Faith, but is of the World.

Langland allegorises this as an encounter between Will and Fortune with her three daughters in 'þe lond of longynge' (8):

Thanne hadde Fortune folwynge hire two faire damyseles:
Concupiscencia Carnis men called þe elder mayde,
And Coueitise of Eiȝes ycalled was þat ooþer.
Pride of Parfit Lyuynge pursued hem boþ,
And bad me for my contenaunce acounten Clergie liȝte. (12–16)

Concupiscencia Carnis: lust of the flesh; acounten ... liȝte: think little of

Much has been written about this fascinating passage: the mirror, the land of longing, the Three Temptations (see Howard, pp. 178–85; Carruthers, pp. 101–5). Is Will literally enjoying the good life with the ladies and avoiding Dowel? Or is he describing the shallow intellectual adventures of the previous two Passus in the style of St Augustine who described 'Lust of the Eyes' as:

> a kind of empty longing and curiosity which aims not at taking pleasure in the flesh but at acquiring experience through the flesh, and this empty curiosity is dignified by the names of learning and experience. (*Confessions* X.35, quoted Carruthers, p. 102)

Whatever the precise meaning of Fortune and her daughters, Will's experience of them is typical of such allegories from *The Ancrene Wisse* to *Everyman* – he is first flattered and later deserted by their false friendship (25). Having rejected the advice of Elde and Holiness, he accepts that of Recklessness, a character who will be enormously expanded in the C-text as an ambiguous *persona* for Will himself (see Donaldson, pp. 169–74). In the B-text Recklessness works with Plato and Fauntenelle (34–48) to encourage Will to live in the present, and Covetousness of Eyes (50) suggests he can always buy a pardon from the friars later. Relying on this promise, Will lives carelessly 'Til I foryat youþe and yarn into elde' (60), when he is unfortunately too poor to buy the friars' intercessions on his behalf (74). In criticising the friars' partial and self-interested intrusion into the 'cure of souls' (see Monks and Friars, p. 197), Will again voices the belief he expressed in the last Passus that baptism is the most important sacrament – though now it not all-sufficient:

> For a baptised man may, as maistres telleþ
> Thoruȝ contricion come to þe heiȝe heuene – (80–81)

Lewte (Honesty) appears suddenly and commends Will's outspokenness against the friars in a passage (87–106) which reflects Langland's uneasiness about his own satire – unless it is wholly ironic:

> Þyng þat al þe world woot, wherfore sholdestow spare
> To reden it in retorik to arate dedly synne? (101–102)

woot: knows; spare: refrain; redden in retorik: put ininpoetry; arate: reprove

But this attack on the friars only conceals the uncomfortable truth that Will has spent his life recklessly and urgently needs some way to repair the damage.

The return to Dowel: grace vs works 108–229

At this point Scripture returns to rub salt into the wound of Will's shame by reminding him of the parable of the Wedding Feast in *Matthew* 22:1–14. Having failed to attract any invited guests to his son's wedding, a king goes onto the highways and byways and gathers in whomever he can find, but is then angry with one guest who has come in (understandably) improperly dressed and has him bound and thrown into outer darkness, 'for many are called but few are chosen'. Scripture, who had advocated "salvation by works" in the previous Passus, evidently intends Will to despair because his reckless life suggests he is like this rejected guest. The parable could however be used to show the pre-eminence of God's saving grace, signified by the Divine Host's invitation to all, which only some accept (see Portalie, p. 201, citing Augustine's use of the parable in this way, and Pelikan, III, p. 273, showing Anselm and Aquinas in agreement on the doctrine). So, on further reflection, Will decides that his baptism means he is one of the impromptu guests welcomed to the feast from the highways and byways, who were generally seen as the Gentiles who accepted baptism when the Jews (the invited guests) refused it. The wedding garments which all need wear could be interpreted (as in the poem *Cleanness*; see Baldwin 1988c) as the baptismal robes which the priest put on the naked children after they were christened. If this is what the parable means then Will can look with some confidence to Holy Church, whose sacraments of baptism and the mass offer all Christians the nurturing qualities of Christ when he comes 'like a loving mother to nourish us' (*Fasc. Mor.*, p. 257):

> For Crist cleped vs alle, come if we wolde – ...
> And bad hem souke for synne saue at his breste
> And drynke boote for bale, brouke it whoso my3te.
> 'þanne may alle Cristene come,' quod I, 'and cleyme þere entree
> By þe blood þat he bou3te vs wiþ and þoru3 bapteme after: (119–125)
>
> cleped: called; bote for bale: remedy for evil; brouke: enjoy

It is through baptism and the mass that Christians are enabled to participate in the redeeming blood of Christ (see Atonement, p. 227). In particular, baptism gives the Christian the 'sacramental character' which was compared by Augustine to an indelible military brand (*On Baptism against the Donatists*, 1.5, quoted P. F. Palmer 1952, p. 125), and which Will had claimed in 10.345 gave all Christians a passport into Heaven (see above, p. 142). Now he seems to stress the obligations rather than the rights of the baptised. Like 'cherls' (bondsmen) they cannot leave their lord without running into 'arerage' or arrears, despite the fact that they own no property. This is because their very bodies belong to their lord, and in the same way we belong to God who will punish us in his manorial 'prison of purgatory' if we try to escape his law:

> And Conscience acounte wiþ hym and casten hym in arerage,
> And putten hym after in prison in purgatorie to brenne,
> For hise arerages rewarden hym þere ri3t to þe day of dome (132–134).
>
> arerage: arrears; dome: judgment

How does this relate to Will's metaphor in 10.466ff. of the unlearned Christian as a serf who cannot fall in debt, since it now appears that the baptised Christians can fall into debt, having duties as well as rights?

Will's renewed trust in his own baptism is however suddenly upset by the intervention of Trajan, a Roman judge who claims he has been saved for his well-doing, although he was never baptised, so that "salvation by works" is more reliable than "salvation by baptism and grace". The version of this story from the *Golden Legend* (pp. 98–9) which Langland cites (160) describes how St Gregory won from God salvation of this righteous heathen man by weeping bitter tears for his pain in Hell. In the similar story of St Erkenwald, the saint baptises a centuries-old pagan corpse to release it from Hell. Langland however has no saintly intercessor, and so, in Chambers' words, 'contradicts all known authorities in making Trajan's salvation depend solely upon his own virtues' (p. 66). After all, as Trajan says, it is God who writes the book of rules:

> 'Loue and leautee is a leel science,
> For þat is þe book blissed of blisse and of joye:
> God wrou3te it and wroot it wiþ his on fynger
> And took it Moises vpon þe mount, alle men to lere.
> Lawe wiþouten loue,' quod Troianus, 'Iey per a bene' (166–170)
>
> lautee: justice; leel: honest, loyal; wrou3te: made; tok: gave; lere: teach; ley þer a bene: isn't worth a bean

The merciful judge Trajan was saved not for his justice but his love, which as Augustine said, was written by the finger of God, on the tablets of stone for Moses, and in the fleshly hearts of men for Christians (*On the Spirit and the Letter*, 30, using *2 Corinthians* 3:3). Anachronistically quoting St John, Trajan seems to suggest that this law of love saves or damns all men, irrespective of their Christianity:

> For Seint Johan seide it, and soþe arn hise wordes ...
> Whoso loueþ no3t, leue me, he lyueþ in deeþ deyinge; ...
> And comaundeþ ech creature to conformen hym to louye
> And [principally] pouere peple, and hir enemyes after (175–181).
>
> Whoso loueth ... : 'He that loveth not abideth in death' (*John* 3:14); conformen: be willing; principally ... after: first the poor, then their enemies

Here we are not relying on Christ to save the poor, but saving them ourselves in imitation of Christ. The section therefore ends with a different version of the parable of the Wedding Feast, this time from *Luke* 14:12–14 rather than *Matthew* 22. Luke does not include the verse about 'many are called but few are chosen', and moreover here Jesus introduces the story by saying that the *Christian* (rather than God) should call 'the poor ... lame and blind' to his feasts. Trajan (if it is he still speaking) promises that Christ will repay his charity:

> Ac calleþ þe carefulle lerto, le croked and þe pouere; ...
> 'Ac for þe pouere I shal paie, and pure wel quyte hir trauaille
> That ȝyueþ hem mete or moneie and loueþ hem for my sake.' ...
> For alle are we Cristes creatures, and of his cofres riche,
> And breþeren as of oo blood, as wel beggeres as erles. (191–199)

Carefulle: distressed; croked: crippled; pure wel quyte: recompense thoroughly: travaile: trouble; ȝyueþ: gives; of his cofres: from his treasure-chests; oo: one; erles: earls

This welcome echoes Repentance's sermon (5.504) and prefigures Christ's words as he harrows Hell (18.396). It is the poet's fundamental message of reciprocal charity as worked out in Passus 17: man's obedience to the law of charity will enable God's grace to pardon his sin. Will's anxiety about whether he or any are saved, is therefore replaced by an anxiety about whether he will deserve this 'spiritual nobility' of God's 'blody breþeren' (see Simpson 1985) or whether his 'synne' will stifle God's love:

> No beggere ne boye amonges vs but if it synne made (203)

boye: knave; made: caused

It appears that Langland is arguing both for salvation by baptism and grace, and for salvation by works, simultaneously.

Praise of patient poverty 230–329

But what works can the poor and unlearned perform? Without the knowledge to be able to teach (Dobet), or the power to perform works of charity and provide leadership (Dobest), they can only Do Well by suffering his poverty with patience. Thus this debate ends by introducing the principal theme of the next (Fourth) Vision: the praise of patient poverty. Indeed the poor should not just be the object of our love (as they were in the previous section) but also the model for our way of life. This point is made by the paradoxical "walnut metaphor", for only through suffering can one learn patience:

> And alle þe wise þat euere were, by auȝt I kan aspye,
> Preisen pouerte for best lif, if pacience it folwe,
> And boþe bettre and blesseder by many fold þan richesse.
> Alþouȝ it be sour to suffre, þer comeþ swete after;
> As on a walnote wiþoute is a bitter barke,
> And after þat bitter bark, be þe shelle aweye,
> Is a kernel of confort kynde to restore. (254–260)

> auȝt: anything; fold: times; withoute: outside

The sweet kernel within poverty is its restoration of 'kynde' – maybe that elusive 'kynde knowyng' which reveals the wisdom in the kernel of the soul (see Kynde, Kynde Knowynge and Kynde Wit, p. 153). It must however be accepted with patience. The principle that the poor were able to use their patience in poverty (though not the poverty *per se*) as a penance for sin was expressed in some Confessional Handbooks; for example the popular *Pupilla Oculi*:

> As for the trials which God imposes on men in this life, if a man accepts them willingly and with patience, they become a form of satisfaction for the purgation of his sins. (f.31r, my translation)

Patience, the virtue which is accessible to the poorest man, transforms the intractable circumstances of life into both a part of a sacrament and a dependence on God. In fact the life of patient poverty is to be seen as one form of the perfect life, for as Christ himself said (though not in Middle English): 'Whoso wole be pure parfit moot possession forsake' (274, referring to *Matthew* 19.21). It could be argued that Langland is moving here towards the principles on which first the monks and then the friars were founded – where Christ's injunction here to sell one's possessions was turned by the early Church into a fellowship of poverty (*Acts* 2:45; see Monks and

Friars, p. 197). Langland seems to recognise this for he digresses into another attack on the wealth and corruption of the present Church, who do not keep these injunctions to poverty (285–316; compare 10.316–345). But his praise of patient poverty, to which he will return over the next four Passus, is wider than any praise of a particular religious order would be, for it is the essence of Dowel and can be practised by the laity as well as by monks and friars. It can even be practised inadvertently by people who have neither wealth nor learning but whose baptism – as the Passus so far has shown – will be enough to save them so long as they try to fulfil the law of love.

Kynde, Kynde Knowynge and Kynde Wit

In Middle English the noun *kynde* essentially means nature, either in an analytical sense (the qualities, disposition, constitution and form of person or animal: *MED*, noun, pp. 1–4), or in a more general and abstract sense, as the Universe or Creation (*MED*, noun, p. 7). It is in this latter sense that Chaucer personifies Nature (after Alain of Lille's 'Pleynt of Kynde') as the 'vicayre o the almighty lord' in his *Parliament of Fouyles* (316, 379). In Passus 9 Langland personifies Kynde in a similar way, as 'creatour of alle kynnes thynges' (26). But the Middle English noun also approaches the more modern sense of "kindness": natural and instinctive moral feelings (*MED*, noun, p. 5b), and the adjective *kynde* can mean 'benevolent, loving, affectionate' and 'generous' (*MED*, adj., pp. 5, 6). These moral feelings are still seen as "natural", however. Langland uses *kynde* as an adjective throughout the poem to suggest this natural moral feeling, which becomes virtually a synonym for the charity which obeys the Christian law of love. Its opposite, *unkyndenesse*, becomes the unforgivable sin in Passus 17. Langland also uses the adjective *kynde* and the adverb *kyndely* to mean learning naturally by experience, rather than artificially from books (5.538) and this often means learning through suffering, as Jesus does on the Cross (18.220).

Kynde knowynge is also significant term in the poem, closely associated with Love. Will tells Holy Church that he has no 'kynde knowynge' of Truth (1.142–143), and she responds by a sermon on 'God is love'. The phrase continues to reappear in various forms throughout the poem, charted illuminatingly by White, and Davlin (1971, 1981). Like *kynde* its meaning varies depending on context, sometimes suggesting the process by which Will learns wisdom through experience (as perhaps 8.57, 110), and sometimes the wisdom that he learns (as perhaps 1.142–143). In Langland's Psychology, p. 123, *kynde knowyng* is seen as given by God (*Kynde* in its higher sense) and tentatively equated with *synderesis*, which is the Greek word for Conscience, and used by Aquinas to refer to that authoritative aspect of the Conscience which teaches the general moral principles. One way of seeing Will's journey would then be that he (helped by grace) learns to recognise *kynde knowynge* in himself; if he then follows its teaching he will become reformed to the image of God in man, which is Piers Plowman. There is plenty of room for seeing *kynde knowyng* in other ways however.

Kynde Wit is more consistently seen as a natural quality, and defined by Ymaginatif as natural (visual) knowledge of the world (of *quod vidimus* comeþ kynde wit, 12.68; discussed below, p. 160). Perhaps it is, as Wit may be, another name for the *intellectus agens* (active intelligence) which a man or woman possesses naturally, rather than the Reason given them by grace (see Langland's Psychology, p. 123). It is criticised by Ymaginatif for facile cleverness, which would make it like Thought or even like the Coueitise of Eiʒes of 11.7. However in the Prologue it is given more dignity, working with – rather than against – Clergy to establish Natural Law 'ech lif to knowe his owene' (121–122), a concern with the right use of property confirmed by Holy Church (1.55).

Bibliography
The Middle English Dictionary (*MED*); Davlin (1971, 1981); Harwood; Morgan; Simpson (1986); White, pp. 41–59.

The vision of Kynde and Reason and the appearance of Ymaginatif 330–420

Just as Will was shown his own life at the beginning of the Passus, now he is shown the life of Nature at the end, in a passage that is both poetically attractive and hauntingly sad:

> I was fet forþ by ensaumples to knowe,
> Thoruʒ ech a creature, Kynde my creatour to louye.

I sei3 þe sonne and þe see and þe sond after,
And where þat briddes and beestes by hir make þei yeden, …
 Man and his make I my3te se boþe;
Pouerte and plentee, boþe pees and werre,
Blisse and bale – boþe I sei3 at ones,
And how men token Mede and Mercy refused. …
 Ac þat moost meued me and my mood chaunged –
That Reson rewarded and ruled alle beestes
Saue man and his make … (324–333, 368–370)

Kynde: God; make: mate; bale: harm; meued: disturbed

The natural world is presented not for its own sake but as an example to help Will to love God (325). In this extended celebration of the wonders of the natural world, look at how the alliteration links all the variety in creation into a mirror of God's goodness ('þe sonne and þe see and þe sond'), but divides human society into moral confusion ('pouerte and plentee', 'blisse and bale'). Animals even obey the sexual laws which Wit had shown broken by man in Passus 9 (336–343). Still driven perhaps by the 'lust of the Eyes' which Augustine said included 'the tendency to examine closely the hidden things of nature' (*Confessions* X.35), Will 'rebukede Reson' (372) for not governing man as he governs Nature. Reason explains that God too is patient, allowing man to survive in spite of his wicked ways (the lesson of the poem *Patience*) and so allowing time for repentance:

Who suffreþ moore þan God?' quod he; 'no gome, as I leeue.
He my3te amende in a minute while al þat mysstandeþ,
Ac he suffreþ for som mannes goode, and so is oure bettre. (379–381)

gome: man; minute while: moment; ystande: stands amiss

Reason develops the theme of 'suffraunce' (378), which is another name for patience, that is to say, the ability to allow the blows of fate, or the speeches and actions of others, or even the flaws in oneself. Its opposite was revenge or grudging (complaining) and Reason points out that Will should learn to suffer the teaching of his betters, and to acknowledge his own shortcomings, before he 'lakke my lif' (criticise, 386). Patience in this sense is a major theme in the

fourteenth century. We have now been introduced to it in three contexts, as the endurance of poverty, the endurance (by God) of
human wickedness, and the non-endurance (by Will) of authority.
Indeed Reason himself seems long-suffering, and speaks with charity
of man's sexual incontinence, for sex allows some 'murþe wiþ man
þat most wo þolieþ' (398). In fact it is well worth looking at Reason's
speech in some detail, because it analyses a concept which is at the
heart of Langland's poem; the patience of Dowel, the 'kynde
knowyng' of Dobet, and the charity of Dobest all express 'suffraunce' of one kind or another.

Stung by shame, the dreamer awakes – or at least lapses into his
first dreaming. If the "inner dream" he has been having throughout
the Passus represents his experience of "reality", then the following
meeting with Ymaginatif returns him to the *somnium* in which he
encountered the authority figures of Study, Clergy and Scripture
(though Will also met Scripture in his inner dream as well – maybe
Langland is simply confused). Ymaginatif, a faculty closer to our
idea of memory than to the creative Imagination of Coleridge, does
not introduce himself until the following Passus, but he does elicit
from Will a new, more contrite definition of Dowel in terms of
patience or suffraunce:

> To se muche and suffre moore, certes,' quod I, 'is Dowel.'
> 'Haddestow suffred,' he seide, 'slepynge þo þow were,
> Thow sholdest have knowen þat Clergie kan and conceyued
>   moore þoruȝ Reson' (410–412).
>
> certes: certainly; þat Clergy kan: what Clergy taught; conceyued: grasped

Indeed throughout the Passus there has been a tension between
knowing through listening (which Will still has to learn) and
knowing through experience (which Will has longed for since Passus
8 and has just tried out recklessly here). To a lesser or greater extent
all the authorities have taught him to love his fellow men and share
with them what he has – instructions best performed, as Scripture
has just explained, in a condition of patient poverty. Ymaginatif,
perhaps the most reliable of this series of authority figures, provides
a bridge between the Third Vision, where these lessons are taught

primarily by the words of Study, Clergy and Scripture, and the Fourth Vision, where Patience himself is allegorised as a character and proves to 'knowe' more about the Christian life than the doctors of the Church.

Further reading

On the theology, see Adams (1988); Portalie; Palmer (1955). On the Three Temptations, see Howard, pp. 41–55. On the friars, see Szittya. On serfdom, see Hilton.

Passus 12

The vexed questions of whom God saves and how, questions which have dominated the poem since Passus 8, are now brought much closer to resolution by a new character, Ymaginatif. He appears abruptly and comments on the Third Vision with an authority unmatched by anyone since Holy Church in Passus 1 had commented on the Prologue. With a tidiness uncharacteristic of Langland, he reduces the previous three Passus as a debate between Clergy (representing learning, Christianity, sacramental grace) and Kynde Wit (representing reason, experience, the natural and heathen worlds). It is perhaps unsurprising that he prefers Clergy as a route to salvation, and scolds Will for having (in Passus 11) rejected that in favour of Kynde Wit. According to Ymaginatif, Clergy empowers both the learned and those in their care to withstand sin; indeed Christ himself both sanctioned and used it. Above all, Clergy gives us the sacraments which are essential for the salvation of both learned and ignorant. This prompts Will to raise again the question of the righteous heathen, who died before the establishment of the sacraments, or die now without knowledge of them. Ymaginatif here seems to waver a little in his defence of Christian knowledge, for he allows the heathen salvation by their own law, and in a famous passage which concludes the Passus, offers us a belief in the salvation of all righteous which is remarkable in its tolerance and openness.

The Passus is divisible into several parts, which are shown in the following table; the chapter will deal with them all together.

Who is Ymaginatif?

To the modern reader, "imagination" is a personal and creative faculty, but in the Middle Ages *imaginatio* is best translated as that part of the memory which collects images. The classical philosopher Aristotle placed *imaginatio* between the senses and reason, as the faculty which collects images in the memory, so that reason could work on them, for 'without imagination reason may not know' (Richard of St Victor quoted H. Jones, p. 586). As you will see from the table in Langland's Psychology, p. 123, it is a complex faculty. In the mind of men and animals it appears both as a collector of images (*imaginatio*) and as a creator of new images (*cognitiva*, but also called *imaginative*). In the soul of humans alone it appears as *vis imaginativa*, the power to reason with images in order to approach divine truths, and in some cases the power to prophesy and have visions (see Kaulbach 1985). Thus at B 13.14 Will claims it was 'with the aid of his Ymaginativa that he had a 'dremel' (dream) of Reason in Passus 11.

We can also use the older psychological analysis of St Augustine (see The Powers of Soul, p. 192) to understand the authority which Ymaginatif is given in the poem. Augustine compared the human memory with God the Father, and placed it above his other two divisions of the mind, reason (compared to God the Son), and will (suggesting the Holy Spirit). Langland may be suggesting a similar hierarchy when Ymaginatif, the faculty which remembers and organises images, takes control in Passus 12, and tells Will to turn from Kynde Wit (a kind of reason) to Clergy (revealed religious knowledge). But is Ymaginatif turning Will from experience to authority, as Simpson argues (1990, pp. 136–8), or is he directing him towards the suffering of direct experience (Hanna 2002, 93)?

Ymaginatif admonishes Will and discusses works and grace 1–63

As if to underscore his difference from the modern imagination, Ymaginatif begins his speech by attacking Will's hobby: 'þow medlest þee wiþ makynge' (you meddle with poetry, 16) – the very sin which John But claims at the end of this Passus, in the A-text, brought him to an early grave (A 12.109). Will replies that everyone needs a bit of light relief sometimes, and, presumably to get Ymaginatif off his case, asks him to define Dowel. Ymaginatif replies in terms of the three Theological Virtues (see Moral Lists, p. 000), and suggesting that Dowel is Faith (lewte):

> Feiþ, hope and charitee – alle ben goode,
> And sauen men sondry tymes, ac noon so soone as charite.
> For he dooþ wel, wiþouten doute, þat dooþ as lewte techeþ. (30–32)
>
> sondry: several; soone: quickly; lewte: faithfulness, obedience.

As Ymaginatif develops his account of this life we recognise it is like Scripture's and Trajan's life of patient poverty, the life lived in obedience to the law of justice and charity. Ymaginatif tells Will to 'lyue forþ as lawe wole þe while ye lyuen boþe' (34) and claims that not only 'catel' (possessions) but 'kynde wit' are enemies to this kind of obedience:

catel and kynde wit acombreþ ful manye (5)

catel: possessions; kynde wit: reason; acombreþ: hinder, trouble

So far we are on familiar ground. These had been Scripture's arguments in favour of "salvation by works" (obeying the law of charity),
when Will had argued that man was "saved by grace" either through
his baptism or simply through God's choice – arguments which discouraged a moral life. Then Ymaginatif begins to restore the balance
between works and grace. He does this by an analogy of grace as a
plant which can only grow in the ground of a holy life:

> Ac grace is a gras þerfore, þo greuaunces to abate.
> Ac grace ne groweþ noȝt but amonges [gomes] lowe:
> Pacience and pouerte þe place is þer it groweþ,
> And in lele lyuynge men and in lif holy,
> And þoruȝ þe gifte of þe Holy Goost (59–63).

gras: healing herb; abate: reduce, end; gomes lowe: humble people; lele: faithful

It is not that men need to Do Well in order to be saved, for that
would damn nearly everyone, but that they need to try to Do Well
in order to attract God's saving grace. This is the position which
Adams, in a detailed and persuasive article in 1983, refers to by the
(early modern) term 'semi-Pelagianism', because it goes some way,
but crucially not all the way, towards the heresy ascribed to Pelagius,
and vigorously attacked by St Augustine, that men are saved by their
own good works without the need for God's grace. It is a compro-
mise position between the two, 'by which 'God was covenanted to
reward with grace those who do their very best' (Adams 1983, p.
375; see also 1988). A kind of semi-Pelagianism was advocated by
many mainstream fourteenth-century theologians (for example,
William of Ockham and Robert Holcot), and indeed Thomas
Bradwardine said he was prompted to write his celebrated treatise
The Cause of God against Pelagius because 'almost the whole world is
inclining to Pelagius' errors' (quoted in Pelikan, IV, 18). Although
Will had seemed in Passus 10 to be taking Augustine and
Bradwardine's determinist position (see above, p. 141), that salvation
depends solely on God's grace, the poem as a whole tends to the

semi-Pelagian position described by Adams (1983, 1988), by which man needs to obey the law of charity *in order to* receive God's saving grace. Here, by describing grace as a healing herb which can only grow in those who try to Do Well, Ymaginatif shows Will how to resolve his agonising fear of being damned either by his lack of good works, or by God's determination not to give him grace: it is by patience and obedience to the law of charity that he will be enabled to *receive* the grace which God freely offers to all. This idea will underlie the next Vision too, and be explained even more vividly in Passus 17 when the metaphor for the Holy Spirit or grace is that of a torch whose wax can only 'melteþ to mercy' (17.231) when first lit by the by the charity of Christians towards their fellow men.

Clergy and Kynde Wit 64–187

Before Ymaginatif turns to the saving merits of non-Christians, he spends a good deal of time explaining to Will how Christians like himself can be saved. The main thrust of his argument is to demonstrate the necessity for Clergy (Christian learning), and to rebuke Will's 'Kynde Wit' for attacking Clergy's representatives in Passus 10 and 11. Kynde Wit means Natural Reason; see Kynde, Kynde Knowynge and Kynde Wit, p. 153). And although it is also 'to comende' (70), it is below Clergy in eminence; Kynde Wit only interprets what it sees naturally, while Clergy derives from heavenly revelation in the Bible:

> Of *quod scimus* comeþ clergie, a konnynge of heuene,
> And of *quod vidimus* comeþ kynde wit, of siȝte of diuerse peple.
> (67–68)
>
> of *quod scimus*: from what we know; konynge: skill, knowledge; *quod vidimus*: what we have seen; of siȝte: from the visual experience

Ymaginatif continues to show evidence for the pre-eminence of Clergy by referring to the story of the woman taken in adultery from *Matthew* 7 – or rather to the mystery play version. It was by writing ('clergie') that Jesus saved her from stoning, for he supposedly wrote the sins of her persecutors on the ground and so shamed them into creeping away. More significantly, Ymaginatif returns to Will's own faith in the efficacy of baptism in Passus 10 and 11 (see above, pp. 143, 148–51), and points out that it is only by 'Clergy' that the sacraments carry God's grace at all:

> 'For Goddes body myȝte noȝt ben of breed wiþouten clergie,
> The which body is boþe boote to þe riȝtfulle,
> And deeþ and dampnacion to hem pat deyeþ yuele. (85–87)
>
> boote to þe riȝtfulle: remedy to the virtuous

Ymaginatif puts this even more strongly a few lines later, distinguishing between the unconverted (but rational) heathen, and Christians with access to God's Treasury of Merit:

> Na moore kan a kynde-witted man, but clerkes hym teche,
> Come, for al his kynde wit, to Cristendom and be saued –
> Which is þe cofre of Cristes tresor, and clerkes kepe þe keyes.
>
> (107–109)
>
> kynde-witted: naturally reasonable (that is, not a Christian); but: unless

This invisible Treasury in Heaven, which was made up of the Passion of Christ and his saints, is opposed throughout the poem to the material possessions which have 'poisoned' the Church (see 15.560–564). At other points in the poem (10.316, 15.320) Langland suggests that the problem of an imperfect human Clergy (the Church on earth) administering the perfection of God's Clergy (the divine knowledge and sacraments) would be remedied by confiscating most of the Church's property. But Ymaginatif does not rebuke Clergy at all; instead he offers a series of sermon *exempla* to show how the laity can use Clergy to help them reform their own sinful lives. If Reason gives people intellectual weapons then Clergy gives them the sight to use them effectively (104). The untaught person despairs while the person with clerical instruction learns to hope (107–108). These analogies include one or two passages of inspired poetry. In one, Ymaginatif acknowledges the interdependence of Clergy and Kynde Wit as mirrors of the soul (rather as memory, reason and will mirrored the Trinity to St Augustine). How is this mirror different from the mirrors of fortune or Kynde which Will had looked into in the previous Passus?

> Forþi I counseille þee for Cristes sake, clergie þat þow louye,
> For kynde wit is of his kyn and neiȝe cosynes boþe
> To Oure Lord, leue me – forþi loue hem, I rede.
> For boþe [as mirours ben] to amenden oure defautes. (92–95)
>
> neiȝe: near; rede: advise; amende: cure; defautes: defects, sins.

Augustine saw the third element of the Trinity, the Holy Spirit, in the will, and in a kind of reprise of 1.53–58, Ymaginatif prophesies that it will be the virginal Clergy (equated here with 'clennesse' as in the poem of that name) who will receive the Holy Spirit:

> 'For þe heiȝe Holy Goost heuene shal tocleue,
> And loue shal lepe out after into þis lowe erþe,
> And clennesse shal cacchen it and clerkes shullen it fynde: (140–142)
>
> tocleue: cleave asunder; clennesse: virginity, purity

Here Ymaginatif is truly the prophetic *imaginativa* of the human soul.

Salvation of non-Christians 188–215, 264–295

After his praise of Clergy, Ymaginatif returns to the question of works and grace and explains his understanding of the salvation of non-Christians. He does this by presuming a hierarchy in Heaven, and also God's freedom to give grace to whomever he will. The crucified thief to whom Christ promised heaven apparently without Clergy (either in knowledge or in sacraments) will not have the 'worship' in heaven that is accorded to the saints and martyrs:

> So it fareþ by þat felon þat a Good Friday was saued:
> He sit neiþer wiþ Seint Iohan, ne Symond ne Iude, ...
> But by hymself as a soleyn, and serued on þe erþe. (201–204)
>
> felon: thief; as a soleyn: solitary; erþe: ground.

The image of the dinner here is taken from the parable of the Wedding Feast which Scripture and Will both used in the last Passus. Here Will's Ymaginativa does indeed seem to be using Biblical images to apprehend divine mysteries! Then, after a digression on Kynde (see below), he is equally dogmatic about Trajan, placing him 'in þe loweste of heuene' (211). As he will later joke, 'Yes he was saved– but only just!' (*vix*, scarcely, 278). He also mentions Aristotle, whose damnation had been used in 10.382 by Will to prove the unimportance of obeying the Law. Ymaginatif thinks he, too, like other virtuous pagans, must have been saved by God 'for his grace' (because of, 272) given as a reward for his virtue (and as Adams says, for having done his very best). When further questioned by Will, Ymaginatif affirms that Trajan too was obedient to the Law (his Law, that is) and that this obedience was a kind of baptism of the fire of the Spirit (from *Matthew* 3:11), equivalent to the baptism of blood suffered by martyrs:

> Ac þer is fullynge of font and fullynge in blood shedyng,
> And þoruȝ fir is fullyng, and þat is ferme bileue:
> *Aduenit ignis diuinus, non comburens set illuminans* ...
> Ac truþe þat trespased neuere ne trauersed ayeins his lawe,
> But lyuede as his lawe tauȝte and leueþ þer be no bettre,
> (And if þer were, he wolde amende) and in swich wille deieþ
> Ne wolde neuere trewe God but trewe truþe were allowed. (282–287)

fullynge: baptism; lyuede: believed; allowed: approved, accepted *Adenuit ... illuminans*: There came a divine fire, not burning but illuminating (*Acts* 2:3)

The word 'allowed' here seems to mean God's 'acceptance' of meritorious works as sufficient for salvation, as seen by the Ockhamists; indeed Adams comments that 'No episode in the poem marks Langland more clearly as a semi-Pelagian than this one' (1983, p. 375). But note how Will has changed since Passus 11. God's 'allowance' of Trajan's unchristian 'faith' is at the opposite extreme from his supposed welcome of 'plowmen and pastours and pouere commune laborers' whom Will asserted 'passen ... Into þe blisse of paradis for hir pure bileue (10.459–461). Will has now learned that belief must bear the fruit of Dowel, that Clergy can help it to do so, and that it is the Doing Well and not simply ignorance and poverty which attracts God's grace.

Ymaginatif comments on Reason and Kynde 216–263

Finally Ymaginatif comments on the Vision of Kynde which had been part of Will's inner dream in Passus 11. In a long digression in the commentary on the salvation of the unbaptised, he discusses the moral laws which can be drawn from nature. Just as he had turned Will from questioning Clergy to using it to reveal his own life, so now he turns him from a futile envy of a rational natural world, to seeing in that very world examples of his own weaknesses. So far from being perfect, the peacocks suggest 'proude riche men' (239) who will be damned for their failure to obey the law of charity. The lark, on the other hand, suggests 'lowe libbynge men', presumably living in patient poverty. Do you find Ymaginatif's moralising of the natural world answers the questions Will put to Reason in the previous Passus?

So rather abruptly we come to the end of the Passus and Ymaginatif's disappearance. What are we to make of him? Should we see him as only one psychological faculty among many, or does he have the persuasive power of the poet himself? The Passus seems to end on a note of certainty, with Will chastised for his earlier doubt of Clergy, and ready to accept that he must subdue his 'kynde wit' and accept the faith. From now on he will not be confronting his own intellectual faculties, but will look to moral ideals like conscience, patience and charity, to find a 'kynde knowynge' of Dowel. The Passus has also shown us a way to resolve the conflict between "salvation by works" and "salvation by grace". But all its praise of Clergy cannot hide the corruption of the individual clergymen who are supposed to administer the treasure of God's grace, and once Langland has shown Will that to Dowel he will have to return to this insoluble problem.

Further reading

On Ymaginatif, see Hanna (2002); Adams (1983, 1988); Simpson (2002).

The Fourth Vision: Passus 13–14

Passus 13

The Fourth Vision is a relief after the long speeches of the Third. Once again we see a dramatic vision, an allegory where the personified characters act as well as speak, and where actions and props add significance to their words. Clergy is now incarnated as an academic doctor dining at Conscience's house with the learned Friar, and Will and Patience are lowly pilgrims accepting his charity at a side-table. This allows Langland opportunity for much comic *satire* which somewhat undermines the authority of Clergy after the panegyrics of Ymaginatif. Their *debate* moves the search for Dowel from the intellectual discussions of the Third Vision to a more *affective* or experienced 'kynde knowyng'. Piers Plowman himself is invoked as an authority, and Patience develops his advice to "love your enemies" into a programme of "patient politics" which could end all wars. Like the programme of social justice which he develops in the next Passus, these utopias have something in common with the *political prophecies* of the *Visio*, but there is an important difference. Instead of starting with the social institutions of his time and trying to make them more moral, working as it were from the outside inwards, Langland starts with the moral faculty of Conscience and the virtue of Patience and works outwards to the kind of society they would create, which leads to original and radical thinking.

The feast ends with the host, Conscience, leaving with the two pilgrims, as if Will were saying goodbye to the intellectual search for Dowel, and beginning a search through "doing". Patience and Conscience's first act is indeed one of moral practice, for it is to convert Hawkyn, an active man stained by sin. His confession takes us back to the material of Passus 5, though as Hawkyn is a part-time minstrel, it also includes some discussion of bad poetry. Hawkyn is given the penance of patient poverty in the next Passus.

Passus 13	
Introduction and recapitulation of turning points in Third Vision	1–21
Feast of Clergy	
Will impatiently watches the Friar (Doctor) eat	22–110
Friar, Clergy and Patience define Dowel	111–179
Conscience, Patience and Will set off as pilgrims	180–220
Encounter with Hawkyn	221–460
Hawkyn introduces himself	220–270
Allegory of Hawkyn's sins as the filth on his coat	271–421
Digression on minstrels	422–457

Who is Patience?

The dominating character in the next two Passus is Patience, a personification of a quality which has been often been used in the poem to alliterate with penance or poverty. The word did not have the modern meaning of "the ability to wait", but expressed an ideal attitude to life that derives from Greek Stoicism. Endurance, long-suffering (Langland's 'sufferance'), uncomplainingness are all part of it. But whereas the Greek Stoic tried not to feel the vicissitudes of fortune, the medieval Christian was expected to have his share of genuine suffering, and to patiently put up with it without complaining or losing faith in God's providence, in imitation of a God who patiently suffered on the Cross. This strength of mind is praised in much of the contemporary literature, and generally the exercise of patience (by Chaucer's Griselde or Custance; see discussion in Mann) overcomes the hero's or heroine's enemies, for *patientes vincunt* (the patient will overcome). Patience gives this principle a surprisingly broad application and then takes Will and Conscience on to the next stage of their journey. In Passus 14 Patience will explain more detail how Christ 'witnesses' the proverbial and paradoxical "triumph of patience" by defeating his enemies through his death. Patience will then appear not only a key quality of Christ, but also of Piers himself.

Feast of Clergy 22–219

The scene changes from the indeterminate space where intellectual faculties debate, to a specific interior, the 'court' or 'palace' (23, 29) of Conscience, the king's friend and advisor in Passus 4. Now he is entertaining Clergy, whose married status seems to have been forgotten, as he now appears a prominent cleric. These crucial characters from the First and Second Visions are brought together with a 'maister' or 'doctor' (University professor, 25, 61) who is a friar. Because of their preaching mission, friars had founded a network of excellent convent schools, which sent pupils on to their private college, the *stadium generale* at Oxford. Here they studied the Bible and its commentaries, Canon law, and Theology, generally starting at a higher level than students who were not friars, and expecting to take part in adult education back at their convent. But their presence was fiercely opposed by some, including an ex-Chancellor of the University, Richard Fitzralph, in 1359, when Langland might have been developing his anti-fraternal satire – or maybe even learning under the friars.

Will is not of the same social class as Clergy and the Friar, who sit with Conscience at the 'dees' (dais, 61) and is placed at a 'side borde ' (lower table, 36) , next to Patience, who seems to be another pilgrim or hermit begging for charity (30). The grandees are offered the food that only the learned could appreciate: the Latin writings of the Bible and the Church Fathers (Augustine and Ambrose, 38), though the Friar prefers mashed fare (potages, 41) – presumably a dig at his knowledge of commentaries. But at the same time they are also offered literal food, the 'Wombe cloutes and wilde brawen and egges yfryed with grece (tripe, brawn, 63), the kind of rich dishes which the learned even now tend to enjoy in their College Halls. In a similar mingling of allegory and satire, Will and Patience are fed with the 'sour loaf' of penance (48) and 'a dish of derne shrifte' (private confession, 54). Does Langland mean that because they are poor they are scarcely fed at all, and that this privation acts as a penance for their sins, provoking contrition (57) and confession (54)? If so, this kind of service is 'propre' (excellent, 51, 58) because it both *cleanses* them (in the French sense of *propre*), and is *appropriate* to the personality of Patience, well practised in putting up with hardship. Will is however lacking in this virtue, and

> mornede evere
> For this doctour on the heighe dees dranke wyn so faste (60–61)
> mornede: sulked; dees: dais, platform

Will is struck as so often in the poem by the hypocrisy of the friars (there is danger in false brethren, 70) because they do not practise the life of Christ, the life of pain and discomfort ('mischefe and malaise', 77) which their Order set out to follow (see Monks and Friars, p. 000). Patience reassures him that a penance of a stomach-ache will follow such gluttony, as it will follow pretentious religious talk, which he wittily parodies. Sure enough Conscience asks the Friar to define Dowel, Dobet and Dobest (which he does as a 'trinite', 115ff.), but Will interrupts with a surprisingly modern claim that the greed of the rich robs the poor, and this not only invalidates their moral authority to teach, but threatens social strife (maybe even in the Friar's Dickensian orphanage!):

> 'By þis day, sire doctour,' quod I, 'þanne be ye no3t in Dowel!
> For ye han harmed vs two in þat ye eten þe puddyng,
> Mortrews and ooþer mete – and we no morsel hadde.
> And if ye fare so in youre fermerye, ferly me þynkeþ
> But cheeste be þer charite sholde be, and yonge children dorste
> pleyne!' (106–110)

> mortrews: stews; fermerye: infirmary; strife; pleyne: complain

It is true that some of the preachers who supposedly encouraged the Peasants' Revolt were vehement in their attacks on the friars for (among other things) so often forsaking the ideal of poverty (see Langland, Wycliffe and the Peasants' Revolt, p. 137). But should we associate Langland with Will's angry threats?

Conscience struggles to keep his dinner-party going. He 'preynte' (winked, 113) at Patience to control Will, and asks first the Friar and then Clergy to define Dowel. The Friar, with dramatic irony, says that Dowel is to obey, Dobet is to teach, and that Dobest is to perform what you teach – exactly what Will said he was not doing. Clergy is more cautious, and introduces another authority, one who seems at first sight to be his complete opposite:

> For oon Piers þe Plowman haþ impugned vs alle,
> And set alle sciences at a sop saue loue one (124–125).
>
> impugned: refuted; sop: worthless morsel

Is Clergy denigrating his own contribution to human knowledge by pointing to the superior knowledge of a ploughman? This is the first mention of Piers since Passus 7, and he seems to have a new status. His definition of Dowel, as quoted by Clergy, is both authoritative and cryptic; Dowel, Dobet and Dobest are seen as 'infinites'; does this mean that they are found in an infinity of ways by different people acting in the world? Conscience does not want to pursue this without Piers' presence (indeed he makes a sudden appearance at this point in C-text 15.139–159) and suggests that Patience has a particular insight on Dowel:

> Pacience haþ be in many place, and paraunter knoweþ
> That no clerk ne kan, as Crist bereþ witnesse:
> *Pacientes vincunt* ... (134–135)
>
> paraunter: perhaps; *Pacientes vincunt:* the patient overcome

This introduction shows that the poem is moving away from the theoretical learning of academics towards a new kind of knowledge. Patience puts the principle of *patientes vincunt* (taken not from Christ but from a popular pseudo-Biblical text called *The Testament of Job*; see Besserman; Adams 1978) with Christ's injunction to 'Love your enemies' (*Matthew* 5:44), an insight derived not from books but from his 'lemman' (beloved, 140), Love herself. In loving our enemies we will obey Christ's law of love 'for þe Lordes loue of heuene' (143), and also defeat those very enemies and show the triumph of patience, as they 'bowe for þis betyng' (submit to this "attack", 147). Patience therefore brings together the Friar's and Clergy's definitions of Dowel, Dobet and Dobest, for this 'science of love' (124) does well, and loves, and teaches all at once, for to quote St Paul, 'Love suffereth long and is kind' (*1 Corinthians* 1.3:4).

I said at the beginning that in this part of the poem Langland seems to start with the moral virtues and work outwards to the kind of society they would create. This certainly seems to be what happens now, for Patience now claims that this formula of patient love can solve all the world's problems. He does this by means of a riddle, which he claims (158–172) makes both the individual and the nation invincible (discussed Baldwin 2002):

> Kynde loue coueiteþ noȝt no catel but speche.
> Wiþ half a laumpe lyne in Latyn, *Ex vi transicionis,*
> I bere þerinne aboute faste ybounde Dowel,
> In a signe of þe Saterday þat sette first þe kalender,
> And al þe wit of þe Wednesday of þe nexte wike after;
> The myddel of le moone is þe myght of boþe. (151–156)

laumpe: lamp; *Ex vi transitionis*: from the power of transition; wike: week

Following the contemporary practice of describing letters riddlingly as physical objects, Galloway (1995) sees both the 'half a lampe' and the 'myddel of a moone' as the letter C, suggesting the word *cor* (heart) as it also does in C-text 15.162 and in B-text 3.327. Here *cor* must mean love, particularly the love given one's enemies (144–145), which is made particularly relevant to current affairs, by the allusion to Saturday and a Wednesday. These *may* refer to Saturday 20 June 1377, which had been the last complete day in the life of Edward III; the next day began a new reign and so a new official calendar (medieval dating is by the years of the current king's reign, 149). The following Wednesday, 24 June, was the day on which the Treaty of Bruges, which had kept the peace between England and France since 1375, expired (see Saul, pp. 22–33). *Ex vi transitionis* could refer to the transition of royal power (*vis*) from Edward III to Richard II. The riddle therefore could mean that it would show 'wit' and 'myght' (155–156) to extend the expiring truce. This would be *cor*, love of one's enemies in France. Here Patience requires a policy of love and peace, which will not only obey Christ's commandment, but will save England from a war it was obviously losing (159–164). Writing after the event, for the treaty was not renewed, Langland may also be pointing out that peace would have been a better 'yemere' (guardian, 171) against the attacks which the French army repeatedly made on the south coast ports as soon as the treaty had expired. The solution to the riddle, a policy of love of one's enemies, would make England a freeman of the world:

> Ther nys neiþer emperour ne emperesse, erl, kyng ne baroun,
> Pope ne patriark, þat pure reson ne shal make þee
> Maister of alle þo men þru3 my3t of þis redels –
> *Pacientes vincunt.*' (166–172)

nys: is not; ne: not; redels: riddle

In this passage, then, Langland seems to be returning to contemporary political satire, and advising England to choose a peaceful foreign policy for pragmatic as well as moral reasons. He was not alone in wishing for peace, as J. Barnie demonstrates (pp. 122–38). But the passage has been interpreted in several other ways too (see Kaske 1963; Galloway 1995).

Clergy is not impressed by this utopian 'wit' which, he avers,

> Kan no3t [par]formen a pees bitwene le Pope and hise enemys,
> Ne bitwene two Cristene kynges kan no wi3t pees make
> Profitable to eiþer peple' – (175–177)

wi3t: man; pees: peace; Profitable: mutually profitable

He expects Conscience to agree, but to his amazement Conscience is inspired by Patience's speech to abandon Clergy, and all the social and academic distinction he stands for, and to throw in his lot with Patience and Will. Clergy's offer to teach Conscience 'to knowe' (187) by reading is met by another account of the new kind of learning, where his 'goode wil' learns 'to moorne for my synnes' (192–193). This moment should be compared with those in the First Vision when Piers began pilgrimages: in Passus 6 he left his penance to see if he could serve God 'atte plow' (6.102), only to leave the plough in Passus 7 to serve God by 'preieres and ... penaunce' (7.120). Now Conscience is leaving book-learning to become 'parfit' by the route of suffering, and seems to believe he can take the world along with him, making the extraordinary claim that:

> If Pacience be oure partyng felawe and pryue with vs boþe,
> Ther nys wo in þis world þat we ne sholde amende (207–208).

felawe: partner; pryue: intimate; amende: cure

While he goes off to realise Patience's ambition to 'conformen kynges to pees' (209–210), Clergy promises to 'confermen fauntekyns and ooþer folk ylered' (214) to the more perfect ways of Patience, who certainly seems to have triumphed at the dinner!

Who is Hawkyn?

Conscience and Patience (shadowed, we presume, by Will) now meet a new character, Hawkyn, who introduces himself as *Activa Vita* (Active Life, 225), that is to say, one who lives in the world rather than keeping himself apart from it as clerics or pilgrims do. He seems to have two professions, being both a 'mynstrall' and a 'wafrer' (225–227). As a minstrel he writes songs in a noble household, which is clearly a cut above the normal, and complains he does not get enough 'robes ... or furrede gownes' (228), because he is not as entertaining or low-brow as his lord's other minstrels (229–235; see Minstrels and Poets, p. 175). Waferers were of similar status to minstrels, being retainers rather than cooks, and given a fee and livery (Conscience will promise Hawkyn a new livery at 14.25). In return they made every day hundreds of wafers, which were a kind of round biscuit cooked between special iron plates, and then rolled into a pipe-shape while hot – the ancestors of French *galettes*. The medieval nobility were mad about them, and meals accompanied by music and wafers were the mark of social distinction:

... every gentleman with social pretensions had his bevy of minstrels, no matter how small, his trumpeter, drummers and pipers, his harper and his waferer. (Bullock-Davies, p. 50)

Hawkyn, then, who brags that 'Al Londoun, I leue, likeþ wel my wafres' (264), is both a Winner who provides bread for others, and a Waster, a member of a noble circle – a "Hawk's kin". He is lively and engaging, but are you convinced by his badinage? And what has he got in common with Will?

Minstrels and Poets

Minstrels and poets and are referred to in both approving and disapproving ways throughout the poem, and seem to be of the following kinds:

- Professional minstrels and jongleurs, scathingly referred to in the Prologue as 'iaperes and iangeleres, Iudas children' (jokers and liars, children of Judas, 35), in Passus 10 as 'iaperis and iogelours and iangleris of gestes' (jokers and jesters and tellers of tales, 31), and in Passus 13 as 'fool-sages, flatereris and lieris' (wise fools, flatterers and liars, 423). These were men retained by lords for entertainment, and had other functions as well; Hawkyn introduces himself as a mynstrall ... A wafrer ... and serue manye lordes (a minstrel and a waffle-maker, 13.225–227; see pp. 174). Will is not alone in finding that true poets are passed over in favour of comedians; the author of *Wynnere and Wastoure* for example complains he too is passed over in favour of those who 'jangle as a jaye and japes telle' (chatter like jays and tell jokes, 26).
- The genuine 'maker', a more literary figure than an entertainer, one who earns 'gold wiþ hire glee – synnelees, I leeue' (Prol. 34), though probably the gold was from the very lords who employed minstrels. Will does not discuss his role very much, but it seems that what distinguishes him from the comedians he condemns is the originality and importance of his material. The *Wynnere and Wastoure* author sees legitimate poets as 'makers of myrthes that matirs couthe fynde' (composers of verses with some real content, 20). In A 1.137 Holy Church tells Will that it is God's love he should 'preche ... in Þin harpe,' and in Passus 13 Will praises 'Goddes

minstrales', genuine beggars who can tell 'of Good Friday þe storye' (13.440, 447). Simpson suggests Langland means friars here, for they referred to themselves as 'God's jongleurs' (*ioculatores dei*) and sang hymns as they preached (1990, pp. 157ff.). But if Will includes himself as one of these poor men who can tell the story of Jesus, then, as Hanna has recently argued, he is creating 'an apostolic function both for himself and for his poetry' (1997, p. 48).

- In the C-text it is lunatics who are described as 'Godes munstrals' (C 9.136–139), 'fools for God' who are occasionally inspired to 'preach in play' (114, and see Clopper, 271–3 for this as what the friars called themselves). This positive evaluation of foolishness is inspired by *1 Corinthians* 1.18–25, which speaks of the 'foolishness of God' as wiser than men. In the B-text this could be a descriptor not only of the lunatic, but of the voluntary poor who are welcomed into Unite at B 20.61, and the poet whose foolish prattle can contain truths. In Passus 15 Will asserts his contempt for public opinion, demonstrated by being 'loth to reverence / Lordes or ladies (5–6) or to care if people think him a 'lorel' (waster, 5) or a 'fool' (10). Like Shakespeare's lunatic, lover and poet, he is 'of imagination all compact' (*Midsummer Night's Dream*, IV.1.71).

Bibliography

Bullock-Davies; Hanna (1997); Burrow (1993); Scattergood, Ch. 9.

Encounter with Hawkyn 221–460

Hawkyn seems at first to be self-assured, inclined to blame the pride of others rather than himself (260), and claiming to feed the 'trewe trauaillours' (240) like Piers Plowman with his wafers of bread. But we can also see him, as Godden does (1990, pp. 109–15), embodying the worst aspects of the world of the *Visio*. Like the sinners in Passus 5 he has a long confession to make, and is disillusioned with the available pardons (246–250). But those sinners were poor men who needed a pardon to allow them to focus on feeding society rather than their own souls. Hawkyn is far more of a mixture: his social estate is ambiguous his work can be seen as 'wholly peripheral ... to society's needs' (Godden 1990, p. 111), and he himself seems complacent as well as anxious about his soul. If Conscience and Patience can reform him they can reform anyone in secular society.

Conscience begins his reformation by pointing out that his 'coat of Cristendom', the allegorical coat which was given him clean at his baptism, is filthy (315; see above, p. 87). Hawkyn immediately identifies the stains, which include all the Seven Deadly Sins, beginning with Pride:

> He hadde a cote of Cristendom as Holy Kirke bileueþ;
> Ac it was moled in many places wiþ manye sondry plottes –
> Of pride here a plot, and þere a plot of vnbuxom speche (274–276)

moled: mired; plottes: stains, patches; vnbuxom: disobedient

The coat becomes a compendium of many of the sins associated with the active life in the world: Pride (276–313); Wrath and Envy (321–342); Lechery (344–354); Covetousness (356–399); Gluttony and Sloth (400–457: this includes the Sins of the Mouth described in Passus 5.328–336). Although Langland does end the Passus with a discussion of the sins of minstrels like Hawkyn (422–457; see Minstrels and Poets, p. 175) for the preceding shower of sin he seems to forget that the sins should be appropriate to a member of a lord's household, and makes him a representative simply of the sinfulness of life in the world. Indeed, as in Passus 5, he begins to turn the sins into different characters, and to adopt the language of the confessional (such as the 'braunches of Sloth'). The whole section belongs more naturally to the Confession of the Sins in the B-text of Passus 5, which is where Langland puts some of it in the C-text, reducing Hawkyn from a composite sinner to an impatient questioner of Patience (compare the two texts here for yourself). This representative figure is by his own admission hardened to sin, tending to laugh at those who advise him to repent. Can Conscience and Patience restore his coat so that it will be fit for Heaven? This will be the subject of the next Passus.

Further reading

On Patience, see Besserman; Hanna (1978); Mann (1991). On Patience's riddle, see Baldwin (2002); Galloway (1995); Kaske (1963). On Hawkyn, see Middleton (1997); Godden (1990).

Passus 14

This Passus concludes the Fourth Vision, and the experiment in practical Christianity which Conscience and Patience have been conducting on Hawkyn. Conscience has encouraged him in the last Passus to *confess* his sins, and Patience now takes him through the rest of the sacrament of penance. The *satisfaction* he imposes seems at first to be fasting, but soon is expounded as a life of patient poverty and dependence on God's grace. Hawkyn, who might have hoped to find a way to live righteously without altering his comfortable and prosperous occupations, finds he must change his life completely. Using *allegories* of debt and of the changing seasons Patience demonstrates that a life of patient poverty will fit him for God's saving grace. Patience spends the rest of the Passus explaining what is wrong with a life of prosperity, and why this life of poverty is not only the best life for the individual soul, but the best for society as a whole. Indeed it is one of the most radical indictments of wealth and celebrations of poverty written in the period. To adopt Patience's teaching would make society more just, more spiritually wealthy, but also universally poor.

The Passus is structured on the sacrament of penance:

Passus 14	
Hawkyn's penance	1–93
Patience offers to feed Hawkyn	31–68
Measure	69–81
Restitution: the duties of the rich towards the poor	82–180
Pardon	181–201
The life of patient poverty	202–319
Hawkyn reforms his life	320–332

Hawkyn's penance 1–93

Having confessed his sins in the previous Passus, Hawkyn is now led by Conscience through the sacrament of penance. This will clean the 'coat of Christendom' he was given at baptism, using the scraper of contrition, the wringer of confession, and the beater of satisfaction (1–28, 87–96; see The Sacrament of Penance, p. 89). Together these will lay up for Hawkyn treasure in Heaven, an incorruptible version of his earthly coat in a place where 'Shal neuere my[te] bymolen it, ne moþe after biten it' (23, see Alford 1974). The elements of penance are repeated at 82–93.

Any fleeting notion that *Activa Vita* can continue in his old life is immediately dispelled, when Patience gives him his 'penance' or 'satisfaction', which is fasting. He offers him some invisible bread (43–69) and the text which Piers had quoted in Passus 7 when he tore up his 'pardon' and began a life of pilgrimage: *Ne solicitis sitis* (*Matthew* 6:25):

> 'And I shal purueie þee paast,' quod Pacience, 'þouȝ no plouȝ erye,
> And flour to fede folk wiþ as best be for þe soule; ...
> We sholde noȝt be to bisy abouten oure liflode:
> *Ne soliciti sitis ... Volucres celi Deus pascit ...*
> *Pacientes vincunt ...* ' (29–34)

> purueie: provide; past: dough; erye: till; liflode: livelihood; *Ne soliciti ... vincunt*: Be not anxious for your life, what you shall eat ... consider the birds of the air; *Pacientes vincunt*: The patient triumph

Patience seems to want Hawkyn to give up his job, and transform his reliance on 'wafres' into reliance on the word of God. The bread is in fact 'a pece of þe *Paternoster* – *Fiat voluntas tua* (Thy will be done, 49, *Matthew* 6:10), words which are also used in 15.178 to suggest a total reliance on God's grace. Is he recommending a life of begging like that of the friars? Although Patience's examples of people who have lived on this airy diet, including Noah and the Seven Sleepers, are rather far-fetched (63–70), he follows them by a practical (if traditional) programme for the alleviation of poverty:

> And if men lyuede as mesure wolde, sholde neuere moore be defaute
> Amonges Cristene creatures, if Cristes wordes ben trewe.

Ac vnkyndenesse *caristia* makeþ amonges Cristes peple,
And ouer-plentee makeþ pryde amonges poore and riche; (70–73)

mesure: restraint; defaute: lack; *caristia*: dearth; ouer-plentee: superfluity

From the Sermon of Holy Church's onwards "living by mesure" has
been seen as a tantalisingly simple cure for social injustice. Here it is
fitted into Hawkyn's penance; if he gives away his possessions for a
life of comparative fasting, this will cure his personal pride and help
the condition of the poor around him. This section ends with a reca-
pitulation (82–93) of the parts of penance.

Restitution: the duties of the rich towards the poor
82–180

Hawkyn is not completely convinced that he must give up all his
possessions, and puts the question: could not a rich man who was
also a good man be saved?

'Wheiþer paciente poverty', quod Haukyn, 'be moore pleasaunt to
Oure Driȝte
Than richesse riȝtfulliche wonne?' (101–102)

Driȝte: Lord

In answer Patience address all rich and powerful men, and more
remarkably, God himself. The underlying metaphor is one of debt:
the debt which the rich owe to the poor in charity is a kind of restitution for their lives of pleasure and plenty, and the salvation which
God – it is hoped – owes to the poor is a restitution for their lives of
suffering. (The metaphor was first used in Passus 10, see p. 142, and
will be returned to with more inclusive force in Passus 19, see p.
247). Traditionally men were seen as stewards of the goods they had
enjoyed, whose accounts would be examined on Judgment Day (see
Kolve):

Of al þir gudes men byhoves
Yhelde acounte, als þe buke pruvwe,

> I drede many in arrirage mon falle,
> And ti] perpetuel prison gang
> For pai despended pa gudes wrang. (*Prikke of Conscience*, 159–60)
>
> byhoves: is appropriate; Yhelde: give; drede: fear; arrirage: arrears; mon: must gang: go

As usual Langland gives the metaphor a worryingly realistic twist and refers to the *Statute of Accompte* (Accounts). This century-old law threatened imprisonment to any corrupt steward who kept the estate income for himself while the estate ran into debt, but allowed him to appeal if he had kept back income to cover his expenses:

> It is agreed and ordained that when ... such servants ... are found in Arrerages – all things allowed which ought to be allowed – ... their bodies shall be ... delivered to the next Gaol ... until they have satisfied their Masters fully of the arerages. (*Statutes of the Realm, 13 Edw. I* c.11)

For Patience the rich man risks a similar imprisonment in Hell for his debt to God for the goods he enjoys and the sins he has committed, while the poor man can claim a reimbursement or 'allowaunce', further defined in the statute as 'Expenses, or reasonable Disbursements' – for the suffering he has endured:

> I wiste neuere renk pat riche was, þat when he rekene sholde,
> Whan he droȝ to his deeþ day, þat he ne dredde hym soore,
> And þat at þe rekenyng in arrerage fel, raþer þan out of dette,
> Ther þe poore dar plede, and preue by pure reson
> To have allowaunce of his lord; by þe lawe he it cleymeþ:
> Ioye, þat neuere ioye hadde, of riȝtful iugge he askeþ, (105–110)
>
> rekene: settle accounts; droȝ: drew near to; arerage: arrears; allowaunce: reimbursement

The poor man's sufferings can be set against what he owes God for his sins. This argument, though put in a very original way, does have parallels in contemporary writing about penance. John de Burgo for example argued, in his popular fourteenth-century handbook, the *Pupilla Oculi*, that the poor man need not fear God's judgment as much as rich men, for his whole life is a penance:

The trials which God imposes on men and women in this life, if accepted willingly and patiently for the purgation of their sins, then they will be as satisfaction. (31r; my translation)

In a more theological context, Robert Holcot was among those who argued that God allowed himself to owe man grace (Adams 1983, pp. 376, 401); this was normally for acceptable merit, but Langland is extending it to include patience in suffering. If the very poor actively accept their poverty, their patience can count as the Dowel which attracts God's grace. And so in a moving metaphor of the seasons, Patience prays that God will indeed accept the suffering poor into his Kingdom, and imagines them presenting their case to God:

> And seiþ, 'Lo! briddes and beestes, þat no blisse ne knoweþ,
> And wilde wormes in wodes, þoru3 wyntres þow hem greuest,
> And makest hem wel nei3 meke and mylde for defaute,
> And after þow sendest hem somer, þat is hir souereyn ioye,
> And blisse to alle þat ben, boþe wilde and tame.'
> 'Thanne may beggeris, as beetes, after boote waiten,
> That al hir lif han lyued in langour and in defaute.
> But God sente hem som tyme som manere ioye
> Ouþer here or elliswhere, kynde wolde it nere;
> For to wroþerhele was he wro3t þat neuere was ioye shapen!
>
> (111–120)

wormes: snakes; meke: tame; defaute: want; somer: summer; after boote waiten: expect recompense; languor: pain; elliswhere: in heaven; kynde wlde it nere: Nature would never wish that; wroþerhele: misfortune

In this dramatic opposition of 'joye' and 'wrotherhele' (misfortune) one feels Langland's own bitterness at the injustice of this world; one imagines that he spent much of his life crossing between home amidst the destitute of London, and the wealthy households who supported his literary ambitions. Are you convinced by his faith that the next world will be fairer, that the 'fader of kynde' will indeed be 'kind'? But where does this leave Dowel?

As for rich men, Patience does allow that some are saved for their charity to the poor (133–158), though by careful gradation and by grace or 'curteisie' (147) and not as of right (see Clopper, pp. 241–5). But on the whole they are like the rapacious servants we met in the Second Vision (6.311; see above, p. 102); they hope to be paid double for their work; having already enjoyed his life in this world, they looks forward to happiness in Heaven. This is possible, but rare:

> Ac it nys but selde yseien, as by holy seintes bokes,
> That God rewarded double reste to any riche wye. (155–156)

selde: seldom; wye: man

By line 172, then, Hawkyn is in a similar position to Piers at the end of Passus 7. To live in the world with measure and charity does not seem so 'siker for þe soule, certes, as is Dowel (safe, 7.181). Only a life of patient poverty can help Hawkyn to keep his coat clean and to find mercy in Heaven.

Pardon 181–201

Continuing his "reprise" of the *Visio*, Langland now introduces the pardon which Hawkyn has been waiting for (13.256–260). It is offered to an astonishing spread of sinners in the world ('to robberis ... to harlotes, to alle maner peple', 182–183) if they have taken the sacraments of baptism and penance. So far so orthodox, but Patience adds a more semi-Pelagian codicil which indicates the contribution that a life of patient poverty makes to the works of grace:

> Ac if þe pouke wolde plede herayein, and punysshe vs in conscience,
> He sholde take þe acquitaunce as quyk and to þe queed shewen it –
> *Pateat, &c: per passionem Domini*
> And putten of so þe pouke, and preuen vs vnder borwe. (189–190)

pouke, queed: devil; *Pateat ... Domini*: Let it be manifest ... through the Passion of our Lord

If his performance of and faith in the Church sacraments is insufficient to attract God's grace, Hawkyn and others who are 'pore of herte' (*Matthew* 5:3) can produce an 'acquitaunce', the document which must be shown for a debtor to be released (Alford 1988a, p. 8). Punning on *Pateat* / Patience, Patience says that it both 'shows' that the debt has been paid from the Treasury of Christ's Passion (grace), and represents Hawkyn's patient poverty (Dowel):

> Ac þe parchemyn of þis patente of pouerte be moste,
> And of pure pacience and parfit bileue … .
> And principalliche of alle peple, but þei be poore of herte. (192–195)

> patente: deed; but: unless

Patience's lesson is therefore that God's grace is available to all men who try to Dowel and perform charity, but that it is particularly accessible to the patient poor. Perhaps struck by the radicalism as well as the justice of this idea, or its similarity to Will's dangerous determinism in Passus 10.371ff., Langland cuts this metaphor from the C-text (after 16.36). On the other hand Langland's celebration of the value of patient poverty can be read as thoroughly traditional, a maintenance of the *status quo* and a 'pacified and deferential poor so pleasing to the pious' (Ares 1988, p. 43). How do you read it?

The life of patient poverty 202–319

Patience now modifies his argument (and this section is retained in the C-text) by showing how patience, when mingled with poverty, does in fact inhibit sin, and so like an act of penance, is more deserving of pardon. This is much more orthodox, and a similar line of thought is presented in the *Summa Virtutum de Remediis Animae* (*The Vices and Remedies of the Soul*) translated by Wenzel. He dramatises the vices as rich men, trying to dominate and marginalise the poor, who have little opportunity to sin in these ways. So in resisting the Pride, Wrath or Covetousness in himself, the poor man is also showing his superiority to the rich, who are governed by such passions. So for example the envious poor man is unlikely to succeed in court so keeps his grumbling to himself:

If Wraþe wrastle wiþ þe poore he haþ þe worse ende,
For if þei boþe pleyne, þe poore is but feble,
And if he chide or chatre, hym cheueþ þe worse. (225–227)

pleyne: complain; feble: weak; cheueþ: achieves

This is perhaps an over-optimistic view of the effect of poverty on
the individual psyche, but it is supported by a famous quotation
from Vincent of Beauvais, which is paraphrased as a riddling series
of paradoxes, the *distinctiones pauperitatis* (275–317). These claim
that poverty gives the individual a better quality of life, releasing him
from care because he has so much less to care about. Patience sums
up their message in the same text from *Mathew* 6:25: *ne solicitis sitis*
(Take no thought for your life, what ye shall eat, 306, 317) which
was used at the beginning of the Passus (34). Does the freedom and
faith expressed in this verse encapsulate the mind-set of patience, its
reliance on God transforming the physical hardships of poverty into
an inner peace available only to the 'poore of hearte'? The *Summa
Virtutum*, 206–214 is not alone in linking patience to peace. In a
pun on pain and the French for 'bread', Patience insists that suffering of this kind feeds the soul:

For pacience is payn for Pouerte hymselue (314)

Patience wants to solve the 'woes in the world' by eliminating not
poverty, but riches.

Hawkyn reforms his life 320–332

Hawkyn is not one of the 'pacified poor' since he is reasonably
wealthy, living in a lordly household. To become poor he must give
away his possessions *voluntarily*, like the rich man seeking perfection
in *Matthew* 19:21, and follow Christ. Godden argues that 'the word
"penance" is often used by Langland and his contemporaries to refer
to voluntary poverty, the ascetic life of hermits and others who
forsook the world to follow Christ (1984, p. 136; 1990, p. 54).
Patience recognises (261–272) that he is asking a lot of Hawkyn,

and will admit that very few choose poverty voluntarily. To accept this 'secte' (suit, 259) of Jesus would be an act of courage and sacrifice comparable to that of a woman who leaves a rich family to marry a poor but beloved man, but would give him a real advantage in asking for grace:

> Muche hardier may he asken, þat here myȝte have his wille
> In lond and in lordshipe and likynge of bodie,
> And for Goddes loue leueþ al and lyueþ as a beggere.
> And as a mayde for a mannes loue hire moder forsakeþ,
> Hir fader and alle hire frendes, and folweþ hir make – ...
> So it fareþ by ech a persone þat possession forsakeþ
> And put hym to be pacient, and pouerte weddeþ,
> The which is sib to God hymself, and so neiȝ is pouerte.' (262–273)
>
> hardier: more boldly; likynge: pleasure; make: spouse; sib: kinsman

The genders have been changed, but Patience is clearly referring to the story of St Francis' "love-affair" with Lady Poverty, for whom he left his wealthy family. The Franciscan Order (see Monks and Friars, p. 97) was the only religious order which still retained absolute poverty – an ideal to which all the monks and friars had originally aspired. The importance of this ideal for all religious men will be the subject of the next Passus, where the Franciscans are praised even more explicitly (15.325–330). Yet elsewhere in the poem the Friars are vilified for their hypocrisy, and their corruption of the ideal of poverty completely undermines the Church in Passus 20. This conundrum is discussed by Scase (pp. 55–59; see also Clopper 1997, pp. 72–83, 241–7), who shows that many of the texts quoted by Patience throughout this passage, including *Ne solicitis sitis* (be not anxious for your life) and *Beati pauperes, quoniam ipsorum est regnum celorum* ('Blessed are the poor, for theirs is the kingdom of Heaven', *Matthew* 5:3), had been used in his London sermons of 1359 by Richard Fitzralph to attack the friars for *not* following Christ's example of perfect poverty, for *not* espousing Lady Poverty but for owning considerable property (albeit communally) and performing some lucrative religious services. The debate we have been analysing can therefore be given a much wider context than the individual choice of Hawkyn, and his decision to embrace a life of patient poverty may imply that Langland wanted above all to purify the friars, and perhaps saw them as leading – or undermining – the religious and social reformation which the whole poem draws upon.

If Hawkyn follows Patience's advice he will, like Piers at the end of the *Visio*, be unable 'pouere men to fede' (10), and become socially dependent; he will however keep his coat clean, and be prepared for his pardon. We might find this a difficult choice, but for Hawkyn, Patience has won the argument. He repents that he had 'euere he hadde lond or lordshipe ... / Or maistrie ouer any man (327–328). He takes off his coat, symbol of his property and his sin, and walks out of the poem with Patience, naked save for his shame, like Adam re-entering Paradise.

Further reading

On Hawkyn, see end of previous chapter and Alford (1974). On debt, see Baldwin (1994). On Patient Poverty see Frank, pp. 75–6; Godden (1990), pp. 62–7; Pearsall (1988).

The Fifth Vision:
Passus 15–17

Passus 15

At the beginning of Passus 15 Will awakes and begins a life which many consider foolish (3, 10); presumably he is following the advice Patience gave to Hawkyn, and living as a mendicant beggar. However he quickly falls asleep again and has a vision which is more concerned with charity than patient poverty, though it shows many links between the two virtues. An early rubric (subtitle) denominates Passus 16–18 as 'Dobet' and 15 as a transitional Passus, marked '*finit dowel & incipit dobet*', which seems quite appropriate. Langland also leaves his discussion of the Active Life which was the concern of the Fourth Vision, and turns his attention to the life of the Church. In a new *somnium* a character called Anima (the soul) appears from nowhere and examines how far the life within the Church displays charity, particularly in those who supposedly live a life of patient poverty – the monks and friars. Like Clergy in Passus 10 he warns the monks that they risk losing their hereditary lands and wealth, and like Patience in Passus 14 he suggests a reformist policy involving peacekeeping and the redistribution of wealth. The writing is a mixture of *satire* and *sermon*, and develops the radicalism of the previous Vision. Where poverty heals the individual soul, charity heals society, but neither virtue will be adopted by the laity unless they are led by a reformed Church.

Anima's sermon is not clearly organised and I have had to abandon chronology for my last section, but the Passus can be roughly divided into the following sections:

Who is Anima?

The principal speaker of this Passus is the last of the great psychological personifications who have led Will since Passus 8. His name is Anima (Soul), and he defines himself by referring to a dictionary, which even Will seems to find rather funny (22–40). Simpson, using the Aristotelian model of the psyche we have referred to so far (see Langland's Psychology, p. 123), argues that Anima combines in his attributes both the characters derived from intellectual faculties of the Third Vision (*Mens* and *Ratio* are like Thought and Reason, or the Kynde Wit described by Ymaginatif in Passus 12), and the faculties derived from moral virtues in the Fourth Vision (*Conscience* and *Amor* are like Conscience and the charity praised by Patience). Thus 'he 'represents the achievement of a reintegrated soul' (Simpson 1990, p. 175).

However the faculties which lay behind Thought, Wit, Kynde Wit and even Conscience seemed to be more the natural faculties of the mind than the grace-given faculties of the soul, and it seems more likely that Langland is using a different model here. The analysis in Isidore's *Etymology*, though it includes some Classical attributes like *Sensus* and *Spiritus*, is based on Augustine's description of the three powers of the soul in the *De Trinitate* (see The Powers of Soul, p. 192): Memory (an image of God the Father), Reason (an image of the Son) and Will (which receives the gift of Love from the Holy Spirit). As the Trinity provides the structure for Passus 16–17 it may be that Anima represents the image of the Trinity in the human mind, which would explain why he is so concerned about those people in society who teach the faith and administer God's grace: the clergy.

Anima rebukes Will's pride 1–91

Almost immediately Anima starts to attack Will's pride, extending his criticism to those who have taught him his intellectual curiosity, the 'Friars and fele others maistres' who preach learned 'folies' (70–77). It may even be supposed that he studied at a (friars') convent school or even the *stadium generale* at Oxford, for friars called themselves '*idiota dei*' (fools of God), and Will has already described himself as a fool (3); in fact Anima remarks later that 'we ben Goddes foles' but he may only be referring to *1 Corinthians* 1:18–25 (see Clopper 1997, pp. 245–53; Minstrels and Poets, p. 175; Monks and Friars, p. 197). Indeed neither Will nor Anima need to be friars in order to attack intellectual pride; Ymaginatif had done as much in Passus 12. But it makes more sense of the following sermon if we see them both as clerics of some kind, for Anima's chief reason for attacking pride and avarice is that they above all obstruct charity in the Church.

The importance of charity for the Church 92–148

Anima's attack on the avarice and corruption of the whole Church is full of quotations, allegories and similes, and other teaching aids, in spite of his scorn for Will's intellectual pride. This again suggests he is a cleric, although his attack spares no part of the Church. Having finished – for the moment – his criticism of the friars (70–88), he moves on to 'curatours' (priests, 90–117), the 'inparfit preesthode' whose backslidings and failure to educate or support the laity have poisoned the whole of society:

> Right so persons and preestes and prechours of Holi Chirche
> Is þe roote of þe right feiþ to rule þe peple;
> Ac þer þe roote is roten, reson woot þe soþe,
> Shal neuere flour ne fruyt, ne fair leef be grene. (99–102)
>
> Right: orthodox; be grene: grow

This tree image is taken from pseudo-Chrysostom (see Allegorical Trees, p. 203); Langland cites the passage at length (117) because it is a kind of text for his whole sermon. The Church is crucial to the health of Christendom, and to the health of the wider world. It is the avarice of the priesthood (for which Anima gives a few choice examples, 128–149) which is the chief source of the corruption, the rottenness which has poisoned Christendom. He will go on to attack the monks as the chief sinners in avarice and lack of charity. But first he tells Will how to recognise charity.

The Powers of Soul

When looking at the allegorical figures of Passus 12–17 Aquinas' Aristotelian psychology (see p. 123) is less helpful than Augustine's more Platonic theory of the *attributed powers of the soul*. Augustine worked these out in *De Trinitate* (about 420) to which Langland frequently refers. Augustine's powers, in conjunction with some Classical faculties, are the basis for St Isidore's analysis of the soul in his seventh-century dictionary, which Langland quotes in Passus 15, and they eventually became a part of the theory expounded by Aquinas. The following table tentatively suggests some equivalents between these two anatomies of the soul and Langland's allegory. Augustine's powers are in bold.

Augustine	Isidore	Langland 12–17
Memory (an image of the Father)	**Memory**	Faith?
Reason or Intellect (an image of the Son)	**Reason** Mind/Thought Sensus (sense-perception) Conscience	**Reason**? Hope? Conscience?
Will / Love (an image of the Holy Spirit)	**Love** (Charity)	The Samaritan? Piers Plowman?
	Liberum arbitrium	Liberum arbitrium Will?
	Immortal Spirit	Anima?

What is charity? 149–194

Before he moves on to the failures of the Church in England and the world as a whole, Anima shows us the original ideal. Just as Hawkyn had asked Patience to define patient poverty, so now Will asks Anima to define charity. Anima begins his reply by saying that charity is a moral rather than an intellectual power, which resides in 'a fre liberal wil' (150, discussed Simpson 1990, pp. 184–6). The 'fool' Will evidently knows St Paul's wonderful chapter on charity in *1 Corinthians* 13, for he observes that he has never met a man who came up to this ideal save 'as myself in a mirour' (162). What can he mean by this enigmatic phrase? St Paul used the phrase to describe God (v.11); does he mean that God's love is reflected in the individual will, as Augustine explained in *De Trinitate*, where the Holy Spirit gives love to the human will? Anima paraphrases a considerable part of the same passage from *Corinthians* (165–175) and then gives more signs by which to recognise the charitable man (165–194).

Anima's lessons have much in common with Patience's. For example, charity 'Of rentes ne of richesse ne rekkeþ he neuere' (he cares nothing for riches, 177) but relies on *Fiat voluntas tua* (Thy will be done, 179). Like Hawkyn the charitable man washes his clothes, or his sins, in the 'lauendrye' of his soul (188), particularly removing all pride (189, 218). The signs of charity also include the works of mercy (183–185; see Moral Lists, p. 93). Returning to his point that charity is seen in the will (150), he warns Will against people who only seem to be charitable and patient but are actually proud-hearted with 'pepir in þe nose' (turn their nose up, 201–204) when they actually meet the poor. Only Piers Plowman can look into men's hearts and see 'þe wille' (200):

> Therfore by colour ne by clergie knowe shaltow hym neuere,
> Neiþer þoruȝ wordes ne werkes, but þoruȝ wil oone,
> And þat knoweþ no clerk ne creature on erþe
> But Piers þe Plowman – *Petrus, id est, Christus.* (209–212)

> colour: appearance; clergie: learning; oone: only; *Petrus ... Christus*: Peter the Rock, that is, Christ

Thus at the centre of the passage is Piers Plowman, here identified, for the first time, with Christ himself, '*Petrus, id est, Christus* (*petrus* means 'stone', and both Jesus and Peter were said to be the foundation stone of the Church (*Matthew* 16:18; *1 Corinthians* 10:4). From the next Passus we will be shown how both Piers and Christ exemplify charity.

Types of charitable people 195–317

But Anima, with a new optimism, then lists the unexpected variety of genuinely charitable people (216–334), found not only among the poor but in every station of life – the rhythm here underscoring the similarity of singers and runners:

> I have yseyen Charite also syngen and reden,
> Riden, and rennen in raggede wedes;
> Ac biddynge as beggeris biheld I hym neuere. (225–227)

> syngen and redden: sing and read as a priest; biddynge: begging

At first Anima seems to be distinguishing charity from patient poverty: charity cannot be a beggar, and was only a friar once, when St Francis gave away his property (351). He can be glimpsed 'in riche robes' (228) and 'in kynges court' (235). But Anima soon returns to those who, like Patience, can live without any solicitude (care for one's livelihood), like the hermits and saints of the early Church who lacked all, and were fed by birds, the method that Patience had recommended to Hawkyn (14.39–47) and appropriate for those who are so lacking in pride (306). Indeed charity shares many characteristics with patient poverty, for the 'liberal will' lacks solicitude and avarice, avoids pride, is mild and long-suffering, and is 'poore in herte'. Why should this be, and what implications do the coincidences have for Langland's ideal of social life?

The failure of charity in the Church 318– 611

It is because poverty of heart is at the centre of Christian virtue, that wealth has so corrupted the Church. For the rest of the Passus, Anima ranges through his experience of the contemporary Church, following on from where Clergy left off in Passus 10, and repeating his demand for disendowment. Considering the vast tradition of *venality satire* Anima has to draw on (see above, p. 40), he is remarkably restrained, focusing less on what is wrong than on how it can be changed. His ideas come under three main headings, and it is clearer to deal with each in turn than to try to work through the text chronologically.

The corruption of the clergy 319–385, 416–490, 569–580

The ideal poverty of the saints provides a model for the Church of Langland's day. Anima is convinced that it is the Church's 'endowments', the wealth bequeathed to it by secular lords, which are the source of her corruption (318–330), the infection which spreads from the root to infect the laity as well. As the clergy get financially wealthier, they get spiritually poorer, like light coin (348–354), and this makes the people weaker Christians too:

Ac þer is a defaute in þe folk þat þe feiþ kepeþ,
Wherfore folk is þe febler, and noȝt ferm of bileue.
As in lussheburwes is a luþer alay, and yet lokeþ he lik a sterlyng.
(346–348)

defaute: ack; lussheburwes: base Flemish coin

This devalued clergy have little learning or skill: astronomers no longer know how to predict the weather, 'guile is maister' (376) in the schools and we cannot rely on the orthodoxy of their teaching. Focusing at various points on the secular clergy (priests and bishops) who should guide the laity, he gives a fanciful revisiting of the Parable of the Wedding Feast (461–484; see *Matthew* 22) which has already appeared twice in the poem (11.108, 192). Anima asserts that the food the guests were given was all tame: poultry that followed the lord's whistling (!), calves' flesh, and milk. He allegorises this mild food as the 'loue and leaute' (467) which the clergy should give their flock by example and not mere words:

Riȝt so rude men þat litel reson konneþ
Louen and bileuen by lettred mennes doynges (475–476).
rude: ignorant, unlearned; lettred: learned

Indeed our distant forefathers were originally converted from paganism by the 'miracles' and 'werkes' of the saint-missionaries (437–457). He takes up the theme again in 569–580 when he attacks the failings of the bishops who are supposed to feed their flock (572) and teach them the faith.

He has similar strictures against the endowments of the regular clergy (monks and friars), who should set an example to the laity (see Monks and Friars, p. 000). Their 'possession' has distorted the ideals of the founding fathers, driven charity from the Church and so grace from the land:

Dominyk and Fraunceys,
Beneit and Bernard [boþe], þe whiche hem first tauȝte
To lyue by litel and in lowe houses by lele mennes fyndynge.
Grace sholde growe and be grene þoruȝ hir goode lyuynge, (420–423)

fyndynge: support, bequests

Once again it is the poorness of heart, the humility which is engendered by poverty, which is the ground in which charity grows and which wins grace (see 12.59–63). Suddenly reversing his previous criticisms, he suggests that the only clergy who really show charity to the poor, performing *Psalms* 111:9, are the Franciscans, some of whom still provided for themselves by begging:

> If any peple parfourne þat text, it are þise poore freres (326).
> þat text: He has distributed, he has given to the poor

Begging will however also be shown as problematic in Passus 20.

Monks and Friars

Monks

The most perfect Christian life was believed for more than a thousand years of Christian history to be lived by the monks, who followed various versions of the Rule of St Benedict and lived in stable and static communities. The three vows of poverty, chastity and obedience were made by all monks, but the four *Orders* differed in several ways: *Benedictines* shared to some extent in the life of the nobility; *Cistercians* lived on remote and often very extensive estates; *Augustinians* tended to be in towns, and *Carthusians* were silent contemplatives. Langland probably attended a monastic school, and Bloomfield argues (1962, pp. 59–67) that his various grades of perfection, such as Dowel–Dobet–Dobest, or marriage–widowhood–chastity, suggest a monastic approach to the Christian life. However few monks appear in the poem, and the longest passage about them threatens them with disendowment. *Canons* lived in smaller communities in towns and worked to assist their community.

Friars

Friars are mentioned constantly by Langland, and they make numerous and sometimes crucial appearances. Their foundation arose from the same impulse to recreate the perfect Christian life that gave birth to the monastic Orders, when Dominic and Francis of Assisi each tried, in the early thirteenth century, to reform the Church from within. The communities of friars (brothers) they set up tried to live like the Apostles after

Jesus' death described in *Acts*, and differed from the monks both by embracing real poverty and by mixing actively with the community, teaching the Christian life by word and example. Two much smaller Orders (the *Carmelites* and the *Austin Friars*) were founded later, but Langland's references are much easier to apply to the main Orders of the *Franciscans* and the *Dominicans*.

The Franciscans (also called Grey Friars, or Friars Minor, or Minorites) became the biggest Order, with about 500 houses or *convents* all over Europe. Their Rule emphasised poverty and renunciation; even their convents were the property of the Pope. They made their living by begging, following Jesus' brief outline of the 'perfect life' in *Matthew* 19:21. Some spent their time travelling, preaching and hearing confessions, while others stayed in convents where they had an active programme of education leading to university teaching. Langland shows how such a life is open to corruption, but also seems to admire it for its idealism, and its imitation not only of the Apostles' lives, but the lives of the ordinary working poor. A particularly fanatical group, the *Spirituals*, are discussed on pp. 82–3.

There were about half the number of Dominicans (also called Black Friars or Friars Preacher). These were founded in 1220 partly to confront heretics, and were more carefully organised than the Franciscans. They modified their Rule so that they could own property communally, which relieved them from the need to beg, so they could spend more time preaching and teaching. They also established an advanced educational system for their members, many of whom worked at Oxford as Masters or Doctors of Theology (perhaps a model for the friar in B-text 13?).

Was Langland himself ever a friar? His focus on a "patient poverty" which relies on God to provide might suggest that he was. The friars argued interminably about whether Christ and the Apostles owned property or relied on begging, and whether friars should be allowed to have money, or at least bags to save food. Does Langland's bitter castigation of their hypocrisy suggests that it is more significant than the failures of other Christians? On the other hand many critics insist that Langland ultimately exposes the falsity of the friars' position (discussion in Szittya, pp. 268ff., Clopper, pp. 69–72, 325–33). What do you think?

Bibliography

In history and literature: Jeffrey; Roest; Little; Szittya. In *Piers Plowman*: Clopper; Bloomfield (1962); Scase.

The Church in the wider world 386–415, 491–540, 581–612

Anima goes further in his exposure of an infected Church: it not only corrupts its mission in England, but in the wider world bishops are appointed to distant sees (like 'Bethleem and of Babiloigne', 509) so that they can fulfil profitable episcopal duties in England (528), whereas they should take these roles seriously and act as missionaries to the whole world:

> And siþ þat þise Sarzens, scribes and Iewes
> Han a lippe of oure bileue, þe lightloker, me þynkeþ,
> Thei sholde turne, whoso trauaile wolde and teche hem of þe Trinite
> (500–502).
>
> lippe: portion; lightloker: easier; trauaile: work

Langland may wish us to remember the salvation of Trajan as Anima paints a glowing picture of the mission to convert the Jews and pagans begun by Christ and continued by his disciples and saints, and now lost (503–524). Worst of all, Christians fight the people of other faiths in senseless Crusades that are only cloaks for further covetousness, the crowns and crosses engraved on coins rather than the Cross painted on their banners (compare the image at 350):

> And now is werre and wo, and whoso why askeþ –
> For coueitise after cros; þe croune stant in golde.
> Boþe riche and religious, þat roode þei honoure
> That in grotes is ygraue and in gold nobles. (541–544)
>
> cros: cross on coin / the Cross; roode: cross; grotes, nobles: coins

The C-text is even more explicit in its attack on crusading Popes, for Anima probably refers here to Urban VI's support of the Despenser Crusade in 1388, which was in fact nothing more than an extension of the Hundred Years War into Flanders (see Baldwin 2002).

> For were presthod more parfyt, that is the pope formost
> That with moneye meyneyneth men to werre vpon cristene
> Ayeyns the lore of oure lord, as seint luc witnesseth (C 17.233–235).

In contrast to this covetous policy, Anima advocates a peace-policy towards the Saracens which is a development of Conscience's policy in Passus 3 and Patience's in Passus 14. Since Moses and Jesus had converted the Jews by patience and peace (596–597), it would only take patient teaching 'litlum and litlum' (little by little, 607) to bring the Saracens to Christ.

Disendowment 541–568

The culmination of this line of thought is a radical programme for purifying the Church by taking away its landed possessions (549–567) – the 'disendowment' already threatened in 10.317–327. Anima uses the traditional idea (556–566) that the first such gift, the supposed 'donation' by Constantine in 315 granting land to the Pope, brought the poison of possession into the Church. Disendowment has been successfully used to purify the Knights Templar (562–563), and should now be used to decontaminate the whole Church:

> Takeþ hire landes, ye lordes, and let hem lyue by dymes;
> If possession be poison, and inparfite hem make,
> Good were to deschargen hem for Holy Chirches sake (563–565).

The French king's virtual confiscation of the lands of the Knights Templar in 1312 (referred to at 546) even gave a precedent for a possible disendowment of religious houses. As explained above (see p. 137), voicing this call does not mean that Langland was a heretic, for the Church's right to own property was an issue regularly raised and increasingly discussed.

Thus a demand for disendowment concludes Anima's sermon on charity, which had been prompted both by Will's question 'what is Charite?' at 15.149, and by Hawkyn's at 14.97. It is linked to the previous Vision by the importance given to patient poverty, from which charity is shown to grow, and with which it has much in common. But whereas the sermons of Patience were directed at Hawkyn, the active and secular man, Anima seems mostly to be addressing the clergy. So he defines charity by what it is not, listing the many ways in which the Church practises pride and avarice rather than charity, and suggesting that it should be reduced to the patient poverty it has lost. But perhaps his tone is itself impatient and uncharitable as he scolds and hectors the reader. At any rate Langland turns to a quite different, more 'poetic' and positive treatment of charity in the next Passus, where a Tree called Patience bears the fruit of charity, and where Piers Plowman and Christ – the figures who embody both patience and charity – reappear and join together.

Further reading

On corruption of the Church, see documents in Krochalis and Peters, Pts 6, 7; Hudson (primary texts); Lambert; Szittya.

Passus 16

Passus 16 feels in many ways like a new beginning, although it is still part of the Fifth Vision. Abandoning the hectoring tone of Anima's *sermon*, Langland now presents charity as a dramatic *vision*, which Will sees in another 'inner dream' where he actually speaks with Piers Plowman himself. The setting is at first a traditional *allegory*: a garden in which Piers cultivates the Tree of Charity. Will "wakes" into another vision, this time of the life of Christ. Both narratives refer to the allegory which will be crucial in the next Vision: the duel fought by a knight against the Devil for possession of the fruit fallen from the Tree. Will then meets Abraham, whose historical reality makes him unlike all the characters of the Third and Fourth Visions who were faculties of Will himself. Like Will he is on a quest. It transpires from his talk of the Trinity that both he and Piers might be looking for the same thing, Christ in Piers, God in man. Their discussion also looks forward to further discussions of the Trinity in the next Passus, and clarifies the Trinitarian divisions of the poem as a whole. Abraham is named as Faith, and so he is the first not only of the Biblical characters brought to life in the poem, but also the first of the seven Virtues which will be denominated in this and the Seventh Vision. If the early readers were right in seeing this Passus as the first of Dobet, which we have come to define as charity, then is it still man's charity towards his fellow men, or a new topic of God's charity towards man, which is the focus?

The Passus is divided as follows:

Passus 16	
The Tree of Charity	1–79
The Life of Christ	80–166
Will meets Faith (Abraham)	167–252
Will looks in Faith's lap	253–275

The Tree of Charity 1–79

Although Will thanks Anima politely on behalf of Hawkyn (is this because Anima's proposed reformation of the Church would help those who live the Active Life?), he still seems unclear about what charity actually is, and asks another of his flattening questions:

> Ac ʒit I am in a weer what charite is to mene. (3)
>
> weer: perplexity

Anima has already given Will a sermon, so now he changes genre and offers him a diagram, of the way charity grows in the individual heart. This image seems expanded from Ymaginatif's image of the plant of grace growing in 'lif holy' in 12.59–63 (see p. 161):

> 'It is a ful trie tree,' quod he, 'trewely to telle.
> Mercy is þe more þerof; þe myddul stok is ruþe;
> The leues ben lele wordes, þe lawe of Holy Chirche;
> The blosmes beþ buxom speche and benigne lokynge;
> Pacience hatte þe pure tree, and pore symple of herte,
> And so þoruʒ God and goode men groweþ þe fruyt Charite.' (4–9)
>
> trie: choice; more: root; stok: trunck; buxom: obedient; hatte: is called

---

Allegorical Trees

The tree was a favourite preaching *exemplum* (see picture on p. 204) which Langland uses several times: vices are seen with branches (13.410), priesthood as the diseased root of the Universal Church (15.99–102, 118), and grace as a plant that grows in 'pacience and pouerte' (12.60–61). His most important tree is Charity in Passus 16, which several critics (notably Smith, Dronke, Aers 1980, and Goldsmith) have analysed. It has its roots, so to speak, in the Bible; we could mention the Trees of Life and of Knowledge growing in the Garden of Eden (*Genesis* 2:9, 17), or the Tree of Jesse (*Isaiah* 11:1) which is the family tree of Jesus, or the fig tree of Jesus' parables of the good and bad fruit of human lives (*Matthew* 7:15, 24:32). These all offer inter-esting perspectives on Langland's tree, but Langland could also have drawn on the Fathers of the Church. Goldsmith cites St Augustine's *Tractatus on the First Epistle of John* where the apostolic farmer 'sees men's hearts as a field' but in what condition does he find them? He finds weeds; he roots them out. If he finds clean land, he plants. He wants to plant there the tree charity. And what weeds does he want to root out? Love of the world. Listen to him who roots out weeds' (p. 59). Augustine explains that these weeds are (from *1 John* 2:16): the Lust of the Flesh, Lust of the Eyes and the Pride of Life which Will encounters in Passus 11. Alteratively Langland could have used more contemporary sources. Smith cites several examples where the Virtues are located on the Tree of the Cross, including one by Lombard which places Perseverance on the upright, which seems quite close to Patience on the 'pure tre' (trunk; Smith, p. 59). And Lewis finds a treatise by Anselm where God and man co-operate to grow 'rectitude of spirit' from man's heart. Does this rich tradition make any difference to your understanding of Langland's tree?

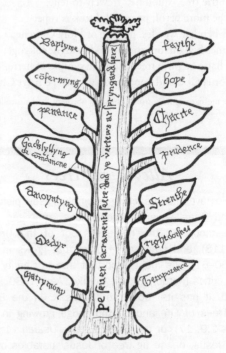

A Tree of Virtue

(after a Yorkshire Carthusian Miscellany, B.L.Add.37049, 14th century)

Bibliography

See Aers 1980; Dronke; Goldsmith; Lewis; Smith.

Patience, hero of the last Vision, is metamorphosed into a tree-trunk, and other remedies for sin which guide man's relationship with man – meekness, mercy, loyal speech – are leaves and blossoms. But just as Piers turned the diagrammatic way to Truth in Passus 6 into a dynamic life-path on the half-acre, so here does Piers suddenly appear to transform this schematic moral tree into a social and historical allegory.

The next section can be read as an 'inner dream', for when Will (who is supposedly already dreaming) hears Piers' name he 'swowned' for 'pure joye' and enters a 'loue-dreem' (19–20), though maybe Langland has forgotten that Will is already asleep. At any rate the poetry becomes suddenly much more dramatic and its meaning more inclusive. The tree is supported by the Trinity, seen (as St Augustine taught) in three aspects of the human soul, the power of the Father, the wisdom of the Son, and the free will of the Holy Spirit (see The Powers of Soul, p. 192). These Divinities are used respectively against the Three Enemies which a Christian abjured at his baptism, into which (according to the popular *Mirour of Lewed Men* (see Bloomfield 1952, pp. 141–63) all the Deadly Sins can be fitted: the World (Covetousness), the Flesh (Lust, Sloth and Greed) and the Devil (Pride, Wrath and Envy). Do you think these are the real enemies of charity, and that appropriate means are taken to resist them? *Liberum arbitrium* (Free Will) is given a particularly important role as Piers' 'assistant'; in the C-text he replaces Piers as gardener. This may be because of his name (*Arbitrium* suggests *arbre* or tree) or because for Langland, perhaps following Augustine's *On the Spirit and the Letter*, he expresses the function of the 'freed and healed will' (Goldsmith, p. 59).

In the B-text what has now become a comprehensive moral allegory is then given a new social dimension with the naming of the fruit as the three possible kinds of Christian life: 'Matrimoyne ... Continence ... Maidenhode'. This seems unexpected (though see Tavormina, pp. 114–21). Do the fruits suggest the grades of perfection of those who live in the world's way (marriage; see Lucas, p. 108); those who as laity try to live apart from the world (widowhood), and the clergy, monks, nuns and friars (virginity); and if so why do all three seem to fail in the poem? Or do they suggest Dowel (which was associated with Marriage in Passus 9), Dobet (the life of patient poverty and charity to which Will and Hawkyn have turned), and Dobest (the virgin life of the good clergy).

Langland does not linger on the names of the fruit for he now adds a historical level to the moral and social ones already in play. Will himself enters the story as Adam, asking for an apple from the Tree, and Piers acts as the owner of the fruit, shaking off the patriarchs and prophets only to see the Devil take them into Hell:

> For euere as þi dropped adoun þe deuel was redy,
> And gadrede hem alle togideres, boþe grete and smale –
> Adam and Abraham and Ysaye þe pophete, ...
> And made of holy men his hoord *in Limbo Inferni* (79–84).

hord: hoard; *Limbo Inferni*: verge of Hell

According to the legend of the Harrowing of Hell (see Atonement, p. 227, and picture on p. 235), the descendants of Adam had all been condemned to Hell for his sin, and those who had true faith in God (like Abraham and Isaiah) waited there in Limbo to be rescued by Jesus in the time between the Crucifixion and the Resurrection (see below, p. 211). This rescue will be described in Passus 18, and so this passage prepares the ground for that part of the story. Piers is angry that the Devil has robbed him of his fruit, and seizes the 'pil' (stake) of the Son in order to get it back – and that is the moment when God sends his Son to Mary's womb. Note that it was 'pure tene' which also made him tear the Pardon in 7.115; should we connect the two incidents?

> And Piers, for pure tene, þat a pil he lauȝte,
> And hitte after hym, happe how it myȝte,
> *Filius* by þe Faderes wille and frenesse of *Spiritus Sancti*,
> To go robbe þat rageman and reue De fruyt fro hym.
> And þanne spak *Spiritus Sanctus* in Gabrielis mouþe (86–90).

pure tene: sheer rage; pil: stake; lauþte: seized; hitte: went; *Filius*: the Son; frenesse: generosity/grace; *Spiritus Sancti*: Holy Spirit; rageman: coward; reue: take

The Life of Christ 80–166

The notion that Jesus will simply 'robbe' back his fruit is immediately transformed into the much more judicial metaphor of a trial by battle which will prove the rightful ownership of the fruit (see p. 000 below):

> That Piers fruyt floured and felle to be rype.
> And þanne sholde Iesus iuste þerfore, and bi iuggement of armes,
> Wheiþer sholde fonge þe fruyt – þe fend or hymselue. (94–96)
>
> felle: happened; iuste: joust; iuggement of armes: trial by battle; fonge: take

Langland now narrates Jesus' life in an abbreviated, poetic way, seeing him as the pupil of Piers Plowman who teaches him to use 'lechecraft' on sinners and sick (106–118), perhaps as Piers himself helped the sinners in Passus 7. He is therefore is ready for the death-blow of Satan, 'That þou3 he were wounded with his enemy, to warisshen hymselue; (cure, 105), so that he will rise again to become 'leche of lif, and lord of heigh heuene' (118; this allegorisation of Christ as the healer of Christians will continue in Passus 17 and 19, where Jesus both gives mankind an example of the law of charity, and offers them his charity through the sacraments, combining works and grace). The story of Jesus' life continues to focus on charity: Jesus' anger against the Jews' ingratitude at his, Christ's, kindness prefigures his judgment against Christians' ingratitude (121–129), and Judas' 'kissynge and fair countenaunce and vnkynde wille' (149) reminds us of Anima's warning against those who are only superficially charitable (15.201–204). The story ends with some lines which movingly express Christ's love for mankind:

> That on þe Friday folwynge for mankynde sake
> Iusted in Ierusalem, a ioye to vs alle.
> On cros vpon Caluarie Crist took þe bataille
> Ayeins deep and þe deuel, destruyed hir boþeres my3tes –
> Deide, and deep fordide, and day of ny3t made. (162–166)
>
> boþeres: both; fordide: destroyed

Even though at this point Langland is telling the literal story of

Christ's passion there is a sense of its transforming significance. What are the two sides in this conflict of opposites?

Will meets Faith (Abraham) 167–252

The vision of the Passion wakes Piers from his inner dream (though not from the Fifth Vision which began at 15.11). He finds himself, like Keats' knight-at-arms, 'Alone and palely loitering', and searching, if not for a fairy, then for the elusive Piers, in a subdued frame of mind and still looking like an 'ydiot' (170; see 15.3). He meets Faith who is also is searching for a manifestation of Piers, for the 'bold bacheler' (179) who is to fight the battle of the Passion, and rescue the fruit fallen from the Tree of Charity. Accustomed as we have become to the triad of Dowel, Dobet and Dobest, we will probably realise from the outset that a new character called Faith will be followed by others called Hope and Charity; these were known as the Theological Virtues and were a foundation of the moral teaching of the Church (see Moral Lists, p. 93). Like the Dowel triad they ascend in importance, according to St Paul's authoritative chapter on Charity:

> Now abideth Faith, Hope and Charity – these three, but the greatest of these is Charity. (*1 Corinthians* 13:13)

The poem sees to be returning to the earlier form, where Will wandered on a search for Dowel, and met characters who spoke for aspects of what he sought. However the characters which embody the Theological Virtues are, for the first time in Will's journey, historical figures. Faith is represented by Abraham, the first 'patriarch' or founding father of the Jewish faith, and he will be followed by Moses as Hope and Jesus (the Good Samaritan) as Charity in the next Passus. And when we relate them to the Dowel triad, it seems that both Faith and Hope represent Dowel, that Jesus will represent Dobet, and that it will be Piers Plowman himself who returns to represent Dobest in the Seventh Vision.

Abraham was often seen as a type of Faith, partly because he was prepared to sacrifice the life of his son Isaac, born after his legitimate wife had given up all hope of children, in obedience to God's demand (231–234; see *Genesis* 22). He presents himself as relying wholly on God:

> Myn affiaunce and my feiþ is ferme in þis bileue (238; see *Romans* 4:3)

Although he is called the 'þe foot of his feiþ' (245; founder of the Jewish faith; see 235–252; *Romans* 4:8–11), Abraham's faith seems now to be a Christian one, for the knight he is pursuing bears the Trinity as his 'blason'. Abraham was indeed linked to the Trinity, and describes how he entertained three angels one summer, an incident generally interpreted as a vision of the Trinity (225–230; see *Genesis* 18). He and his wife Sarah were also mentioned in the marriage service as an ideal of marriage. Langland uses these associations with Abraham to link the three Persons of the Trinity emblazoned on the knight with marriage, and so with the fruit of Piers' Tree:

> Thus in þre persones is parfitliche pure manhede –
> That is, man and his make and mulliere hir children, ...
> So is þe Fader forþ with þe Gome and Fre Wille of boþe ...
> Which is þe Holy Goost of alle, and alle is but o God. (220–224)

> pure manhede: the complete nature of man; make: mate; mulliere: woman (born);
> Gome: Son; of alle: born of both; but o: only one

Although of course Abraham is following Augustine in seeing the Holy Spirit as God's Free Will (see The Powers of Soul, p. 192), Augustine only uses the analogy of the Three Persons wit the family to dismiss it:

> It will be clear that I do not find the opinion very convincing which supposes that the Trinity ... may be composed of the union of male and female and their offspring (*De Trinitate* xii 5:324).

Clopper points out that the Franciscan Bonaventura did use the analogy of a generative Father who creates through the Word (the Son) and whose offspring is the Holy Spirit (pp. 112–21), and Galloway (1998) explores parallel examples of this feminising of

God in the period. Does Langland use this unusual image in order to distance Faith from the more patriarchal implications of the Old Testament law?

The tripartite structure of the poem as a whole

Faith has in effect introduced the next Passus, which is structured on one triad – the three Theological Virtues, and concerned with another – the three Persons of the Trinity. And in working out the meaning and relationship of these two triads, we are led considerably closer to understanding the structure not just of this section but of the poem as a whole. Frank is only the most notable of several critics who have seen Will's search for Dowel, Dobet and Dobest in terms of the Trinity in human history, as described by Joachim of Fiore in the thirteenth century in texts which continued to be very popular. Joachim saw the Old Testament as the Age of the Father which was lived according to the law, and we can see the Third and Fourth Visions of Langland's poem, which were called *Dowel* by an early reader, as concerned with life in the world lived by God's law. The Third Vision was dominated by Scripture and Clergy, and although their teaching was of love, it was always derivable from Biblical law. The Fourth was dominated by Patience, and he too taught obedience and acceptance of God's will. Joachim called the period of the New Testament the Age of the Son, and we can see the Fifth and Sixth Visions (called *Dobet* by the same reader) as centred on the life of Christ. Joachim's Third Age, that of the Spirit, was said in different places to begin at different times (such as with the founding of the monastic orders), but for Langland a new "Age" begins at Pentecost with the coming of the Holy Spirit to the Apostles. His Seventh and Eighth Visions are therefore concerned with the life of the Church, and called *Dobest*.

In exploring the structure of the poem, you might try to relate the various tripartite groupings, for example:

- Should we see the debate between "salvation by works" and "salvation by grace" which underlay the Third and Fourth Visions as an attempt to balance the conflicting claims of the Father (who imposes law) with those of the Son and the Holy Spirit (who offer grace)? How does this relate to the conflict between justice and mercy in the First and Sixth Visions (Passus 4 and 18)?

- It appears that Langland moves from a psychology derived from Aristotle (embodied in the powers of the mind like Kynde Wit (see Langland's Psychology, p. 123) to one derived from St Augustine via Isidore (embodied in the three Powers of the Soul – Memory, Reason, and Free Will – which reflect the Father, Son and Holy Spirit: see The Powers of Soul, p. 192)? How should these different powers of the mind and soul be related to one another and to the triads of the poem?
- If the three Persons of the Trinity suggested marriage, virginity and widowhood to Abraham, should we see this as the reason why the Third Vision had so much to say about marriage, while the Fifth included Anima's attack on the virgin monks and friars, the Sixth concerns the virgin Christ, and that in the last Vision, Will, if not exactly a widower, is impotent?

Will looks in Faith's lap 253–275

If Faith epitomises obedience to God's law (Dowel), it is not surprising to find that he is in a sense incomplete, trapped by God's justice. For this part of the poem seems to be set before Jesus' incarnation, when both he and his descendants have been impounded by the Devil as forfeit for Adam's sin. They are waiting in a kind of infernal antechamber called Limbo, without pain but also without the sight of God, awaiting rescue by Jesus. Following *Luke* 16:22, Limbo is represented here as Abraham's bosom, where he holds the patriarchs and prophets in the folds of his garment:

> And I loked on his lappe: a laȝar lay þerinne
> Amonges patriarkes and prophetes pleyinge togideres. (255–256)

laȝar: leper / Lazarus, the poor man of *Luke* 16:19–31

These are the same Old Testament people who were the fallen fruit from the Tree of Charity (197).

In the final image of the Passus, Langland shows that they will be released from the 'poundfold' (prison) or 'daunger' (jurisdiction) of Lucifer only when Jesus is ready to stand surety for them as their 'borȝ' (pledge), body for body (263). This ancient form of 'mayn-prise' (264) is different from the more modern bail (also called 'maynprise', 4.112) which Meed was prepared to pay for Wrong, and which would have unjustly replaced punishment by an easy financial payment. The 'borȝ' simply transfers the punishment from the imprisoned descendants of Adam to Jesus himself. He then offers a 'wed' (security) of his own life, worth so much more than the lives of the imprisoned sinners. The line of thought is from Anselm's doctrine of the "satisfaction" paid by Jesus for man's sin, which far exceeded the worth of the sinners (*Cur Deus Homo* I.21; see Atonement, p. 227), but is the effect of so much legal terminology Langland's carefully constructed version?

> 'It is a precious present,' quod he, 'ac þe pouke it haþ attached, no line break should be used
> 'And me þerwiþ,' quod þat wye, 'may no wed vs quyte,
> Ne no buyrn be oure borȝ, ne brynge vs fram his daunger;
> Out of þe poukes poundfold no maynprise may vs fecche
> Til he come þat I carpe of: Crist is his name
> That shal deliuere vs som day out of þe deueles power,
> And bettre wed for vs legge þan we ben alle worþi –
> That is, lif for lif – or ligge þus euere
> Lollynge in my lappe, til swich a lord vs fecche.' (261–269)

poddke: devil; attached: claimed; wed: pledge; qyte: pay off; buyrn: man; borȝ: pledge; daunger: power; poundfold: lock-up; maynprise: bail, pledge; carpe: speak; legge: lay

Will responds by weeping for pity at their plight, which is then a cue for the appearance of another figure, Hope, who will look forward even more insistently to Jesus' triumph over Lucifer. The Passus ends, as it were, on a comma. The problem of man's inadequacy, which has been raised again and again on Will's journey, has been moved into a historical dimension, and shown to stem from man's Fall. But this historical dimension has also suggested a solution, as this new historical allegory moves towards the Redemption.

Further reading

On Augustine, see *On the Trinity*; Portalie; Pelikan, I, pp. 172ff. On Joachim of Fiore, see Reeves. On Abraham and Moses, see Smith, pp. 81–93.

Passus 17

The next Passus is a vital one for the structure of the poem. If we accept the early reader's rubric we can see Passus 17 as the second of three Passus on Dobet, concerned with God's charity towards mankind, and written not as a series of debates but as a vision which mirrors human history. However in it Langland seems to be doing two things at once. In the first place he continues the historical movement I have just mentioned, from Old Testament time (Passus 16–17) to Gospel time (Passus 18) and so to the present day (Passus 19–20). To establish this pattern, the Old Testament characters Abraham and Moses must be seen as one half of a balance, on the other half of which are the New Testament characters of Jesus and St Peter, both of them appearing as figures of Piers Plowman. Abraham and Moses represent the Old Law, Jesus and St Peter the New Law of the Gospels and the Church. But in contrast to this duple pattern, Langland needs to establish a tripartite structure, to show that Abraham, Moses and the Good Samaritan form a triad of Faith, Hope and Charity which mirrors the triad of the Father, Son and Holy Spirit. It is this vacillation between an opposed pair (of Old Testament with New Testament) and a developing triad (of the three Theological Virtues and the Trinity), using the same characters in different ways, which makes the Passus hard to disentangle. I have laid out the structure as a chart on p. 246.

The narrative is dramatic for a while, with Moses / Hope and Faith / Abraham taking part in the story of the Good Samaritan, but then the Samaritan delivers a sermon on the Holy Trinity with which most readers will dispense. If you do read it however you will find it contains some of the most inspired religious thought of the poem, expressing Langland's passionate but contradictory desires for God to forgive mankind, and for him to punish the 'unkynde'. The Passus is an *allegorical vision* and can be divided in the following way:

Will meets Hope and compares him unfavourably with Faith 1–47

The next Theological Virtue who appears is Hope, represented by the historical Moses, who received the Old Law on Mount Sinai (*Exodus* 20). The connection between Moses and Hope is not as natural as that between Abraham and Faith, though Smith cites St Augustine's teaching that good works based on the law of charity are a reasonable basis for Hope (pp. 82–3). Here he and Abraham represent Old Testament law, whose justice has condemned them to Lucifer's power. But whereas Abraham awaits a 'borȝ', Moses awaits a seal to authenticate his 'letters patent':

> 'Is it asseled?' I seide. 'May men see þi lettres?'
> 'Nay,' he seide, 'I seke hym þat haþ þe seel to kepe –
> And þat is cros and Cristendom, and Crist þeron to honge.
> And whan it is asseled so, I woot wel þe soþe –
> That Luciferis lordshipe laste shal no lenger!' (4–8)

asseled: sealed; kepe: guard

A 'letter patent' (open letter) was a government command on which the royal seal was hung so that the document remained open. On Moses' document it is not the Great Seal representing England, but the Cross to represent Christendom. As Keen has shown in detail, the image of Christ's crucified body as a Charter granting release can be found in other fourteenth-century poems, though Langland has changed it by making Christ 'hang' his body from the letters containing the Old Law under which mankind was condemned (see Atonement, p. 227). What does this image suggest about the relation between justice and mercy? And what has it got in common with Hawkyn's pardon in 14.190–195, or with the 'maynprise' image at the end of the previous Passus?

To Will at any rate Faith and Hope seem to represent different demands. He had learned from Scripture (10.353–372) that Moses' Ten Commandments are summed up as 'love God and your neighbour' (*Matthew* 22:37–40; see p. 000) but sees this injunction to love as something distinct from the injunction to believe in the Trinity which Abraham advocated (34). And he suspects that Moses, like Christ, will order him to 'Love your enemies' (*Matthew* 5:44, though this is *not* Mosaic law) so he rather charmingly opts for Faith's easier duty of believing in the Trinity:

> It is lighter to leeue in þre louely persones
> Than for to louye and lene as wel lorels as lele.
> 'Go þi gate,' quod I to *Spes;* 'so me God helpe,
> Tho þat lernen þi lawe wol litel while vsen it!' (44–47)

> lighter: easier; leeue: believe; lene: lend; lorels: scoundrels; lele: loyal people; Go thy gate: Be off!

This reminds us of the debate in Passus 10 between "salvation by works" and "salvation by faith", and St Paul's dictum that 'by the deeds of the law here shall no flesh be justified in [God's] sight' (*Romans* 3:20) and Augustine's comment that 'we are saved not by the law of works, but by the law of faith' (see above, p. 141). At this point Will is opting for Faith, but it will shortly appear that neither is sufficient without Christ's grace.

The Good Samaritan 48–124

Langland now "dramatises" the Parable of the Good Samaritan (*Luke* 10:30–6), the parable that answered the question begged by the young man who summarised the law in *Matthew* 22: 'Who is my neighbour?' (v.29). The Samaritan uses the usual Catholic interpretation of the parable, which was read as a symbolic representation of salvation history. The wounded man represents mankind wounded by Original Sin, unable to help himself:

> He myȝte neiþer steppe ne stande, ne stere foot ne handes,
> Ne helpe hymself sooþly, for *semyvif* he semed. (55–56)
>
> *semyvif*: half-alive

In the usual interpretation the Priest and the Levite represent the failure of Old Testament law to save mankind, but Langland has them played by Abraham and Moses, so it seems more natural to interpret them as the inadequacy of either faith or works to save mankind without grace. The Samaritan who takes him to '*lex Christi*, a graunge' (the law of Christ, a farm, 72) and binds his wounds, represents Christ who brings man to the New Law of love and faith and heals him with the sacraments. He tells Will that it is only he who can restore fallen mankind through a surreal but medicinal application of the sacraments of baptism, mass and penance, which remind us of the 'lechecraft' of Jesus in the previous Passus:

> 'Haue hem excused,' quod he, 'hir help may litel auaille:
> May no medicyne vnder molde þe man to heele brynge –
> Neiþer Feiþ ne fyn Hope, so festred be hise woundes,
> Wiþouten þe blood of a barn born of a mayde.
> And be he baþed in þat blood, baptised as it were,
> And þanne plastred wil penaunce and passion of þat baby,
> He sholde stonde and steppe – ac stalworþe worþ he neuere
> Til he have eten al þe barn and his blood ydronke.' (91–98)
>
> molde: world; heele: health; plastred: poulticed; stalworPe: strong

Although this is the first time that we have heard of these crucial sacraments of baptism and the Mass from the divine point of view, it

is not the first time that Will has been reminded of their importance
as the channel for God's grace (see Atonement, p. 227). In Passus 12
for example Ymaginatif defended Clergy from Will's attacks with the
argument that only Clergy could enact the sacraments and that these
save mankind, and in Passus 14 Patience showed Hawkyn how to
clean his coat through the same sacraments. But will a reliance on
the sacraments (which is what Will himself was showing in his most
reckless moments of Passus 10 and 11) not discourage men from
trying to obey beneficent law of love? How can faith (represented by
Abraham) and works (represented by Moses the law-giver) be
included in man's salvation if only grace (represented by the Good
Samaritan) is crucial? These are the questions which Will had
resolved all too glibly at 44–46, and now puts to the Samaritan:

> 'A, swete sire!' I seide þo, 'wher I shal bileue –
> And Hope afterward, he bad me to louye (125, 129).

The Samaritan's discourse on the Trinity 125–250

This question, and the whole issue of works and grace is finally
resolved in the Samaritan's sermon on the Trinity, which is based,
but not wholly dependent, on St Augustine's *De Trinitate*. The soul
suggests the Father when it remembers, the Son when it understands, and the Holy Spirit when it uses its free will to love (see
Powers of the Soul, p. 192). Love is the fulfilment of the human
being, as it is of the Divine Mind, and in the last part of *De Trinitate*
(as often in his work) Augustine insists that this love must be manifest in love of our neighbours:

> So it is God the Holy Spirit proceeding from God who fires man to
> the love of God and neighbour when he has been given to him, and
> he himself is love. Man has no capacity to love God except from God
> ... So the love which is from God and is God is distinctively the
> Holy Spirit; through him the charity of God is poured out in our
> hearts (*Romans* 5:5), and through it the whole triad dwells in us ...
> This is the reason why it is most apposite that the Holy Spirit, while

being God, should also be called the gift of God. And this gift, surely, is distinctively to be understood as being the charity which brings us through to God. (*De Trinitate* 14:31, 32)

This wonderful passage claims not only that all human charity is sent from God as a gift (which is what "grace" means), but that such charity expresses all three Persons of the Trinity in their reflection in the powers of the human soul. God's charity therefore precedes and activates man's charity by entering and transforming the human will. Is this what the Samaritan is saying?

The Samaritan's two analogies, that of the hand, and that of the torch, both convey the unity of the Trinity and the pre-eminence of the Spirit. The analogy with the hand probably derives both from a sixth-century hymn in which God 'holds the world in his fist', and from another Augustine text, *On the Spirit and the Letter* (see another probable reference on p. 000 above), in which the Holy Spirit is described as the 'finger of God' writing the law of love on men's hearts (Ch. 30, referring to *Exodus* 8:19). The Samaritan unpacks the image: the Father is the fist, the Son is the fingers extended to touch mankind, and the palm is the Holy Spirit. He suggests that although all three parts can be seen as the hand, to be hurt in the palm is more serious than to be hurt in fist or fingers (perhaps with the Crucifixion nails in mind). This, he says, is why the sin against the Holy Ghost is the least forgivable of sins.

The Samaritan's second metaphor, that of the torch, is even more original, and its meaning departs from Augustine's ideas, for here Langland demonstrate the reciprocity of God's charity with man's. The flame, representing the Holy Spirit, emanates from the wax (the Father) and the wick (the Son); together these create the 'warm fir' of the Holy Spirit which is poured as charity into the hearts of men' (*Romans* 5.5):

> And as wex and weke and warm fir togideres
> Fostren forþ a flawmbe and a fair leye
> So dooþ þe Sire and þe Sone and also *Spiritus Sanctus*
> Fostren forþ amonges folk loue and bileue,
> That alle kynne Cristene clenseþ of synnes. (207–212)

Fostren forþ: generate; leye: flame

This seems to convey Augustine's idea that 'the love which is from God and is God is distinctively the Holy Spirit'. But Augustine had insisted that the charity which burns in men's hearts ('God the Holy Spirit ... who fires man to the love of his neighbour') is a gift of God, and Langland seems unable to give up man's moral responsibility in this way. For him there will always be those who resist the law of love (the 'vkynde creatures') and these will quench the 'glowynge' (218, 224) of the Holy Spirit towards them.

In contrast man's charity to his fellow men blows the Holy Spirit into a flame, melting the power (and presumably the justice) of the Father and Son into forgiveness:

> So þat þe Holy Goost gloweþ but as a glede
> Til þat lele loue ligge on hym and blowe.
> And þanne flawmeþ he as fir on Fader and on *Filius*
> And melteþ hire my3t into mercy (224–227).

glede: coal; hire my3t: their power

This is virtually a reversal of Augustine's idea, for now it is man, and not God, who initiates the process by which 'the whole triad dwells in us'. For St Augustine 'we are not even able to will without an invitation from God' (though that invitation comes to all and we can freely reject it). But for Langland the invitation seems to be initiated by the human mind blowing God's charity into a flame of grace. We are therefore saved by works and grace together; grace makes up the shortfall in human morality. This develops Ymaginatif's semi-Pelagianism (see discussion on pp. 161–2; and Adams 1983, p. 394); it does not, as Augustine does, make human charity wholly the gift of God. And it answers Will's initial question at 125, for it shows that Faith and Love, Abraham and Moses, are essential prerequisites of Grace, the Samaritan.

Sinning against the Holy Ghost 251–352

However Will is already asking another question, one prompted by the Samaritan's insistence that if charity blows the Holy Spirit into forgiveness, then 'vnkyndenesse … quencheþ, as it were, / The grace of þe Holy Goost, Goddes owene kynde' (271–272). This makes unkindness the sin against the Holy Spirit, the unforgivable sin, of *Mark* 3:28–9:

> Verily I say unto you, all sins shall be forgiven unto the sons of men … But he that shall blaspheme against the Holy Spirit, hath never forgiveness, but is in danger of eternal damnation.

So Will very naturally asks:

> I pose I hadde synned so, and sholde now deye,
> And now am sory þat I so þe Seint Spirit agulte,
> Confesse me and crye his grace, God þat al made,
> And myldeliche his mercy aske – myghte I noȝt be saued? (295–298)

> I pose: I put it that; agulte: offended; myldeliche: humbly

Unkindness is a pretty general fault (see for example 9.156–157, 13.219, 14.70–74, 20.297 and White, pp. 95–110). and it is not surprising that Will, anxious as ever about his own salvation, asks whether he would ever be forgiven if he committed it. The Samaritan gives some guarded reassurance, but brings in yet another analogy, that of a royal pardon:

> Ac it is but selden yseiȝe, ler sooþnesse bereþ witnesse,
> Any creature be coupable bifore a kynges justice,
> Be raunsoned for his repentaunce þer alle reson hym dampneþ.
> For þer þat partie pursueþ þe peel is so huge
> That þe kyng may do no mercy til boþe men acorde
> And eyþer have equite, as holy writ telleþ:
> *Numquam dimittitur peccatum* … (301–306)

> selden: seldom; coupable: guilty; raunsoned: redeemed; dampneþ: condemn; þat partie: the other party (in the dispute); huge: outstanding; acorde: agree; equite: individualised justice; *Nunquam dimittitur* … : The sin is never forgiven until what is stolen is restored

The medieval king had a 'prerogative of pardon' to reprieve criminals ('do mercy') in certain circumstances. However this pardon only protected the criminal from punishment imposed by the Crown; a murdered man's kin retained their ancient legal right to bring a private suit or appeal (*peel*, 304) and so could force the pardoned murderer to make a financial settlement or 'acorde' with them so that they had 'equite' or justice. In the same way, suggests the Samaritan, the man who has been found 'coupable' (guilty) of unkyndeness must satisfy his victims by giving them compensation if he wants to receive the pardon of Christ. The principle that the penitent man must still perform some 'restitution' reminds us of the restitution demanded of Covetousness in Passus 5 (where the same quotation from Augustine is used, 5.271, see p. 84), of Hawkyn in Passus 14, and it foreshadows the terms of Jesus' pardon in Passus 18. As so often in the poem, the offer of mercy is countered by condition of justice:

> *Misericordia eius super omnia opera eius*
> Ac er his riȝtwisnesse to ruþe torne, som restitucion bihoueþ (314–315).

> *Misericordia ... eius*: his tender mercies are over all his works (*Psalms* 144:9); riȝtwisnesse to ruþe: justice to mercy; bihoueþ: needed

Even under the merciful law of Christ, men cannot be passive recipients of sacraments which carry that mercy, but must prove the sincerity of their repentance.

To drive home his warning against 'unkyndeness', the Samaritan gives an original interpretation to the proverbial and wryly comic story of the three evils which drive a husband from his house (317–350). For him the husband represents the Holy Spirit dwelling in man's heart, who can be driven out by 'oure wikked flessh' (the scolding wife), 'siknesses and oþere sorwes' (the rain dripping through the roof), and worst of all a failure in charity; this is the smoke that quenches the torch of the Holy Spirit (271):

> Ac þe smoke and þe smolder þat smyt in oure eiȝen,
> That is coueitise and vnkyndenesse, þat quencheþ Goddes mercy (343–344)

> eiȝhen: eyes

Then, as if reminded by his own words of his own responsibility to his fellow men, to 'louye hem lik hymself, and his lif amende' (350), the Samaritan rides off towards Jerusalem, closely followed by Faith and Hope. These characters had shown that man failed to keep the Law of Love in the past, and the Samaritan will now, as Jesus, perform the great act of God's charity in dying on the Cross, and so bring in a new age in which the Holy Spirit helps men to perform that law.

Further reading

On the Trinitarian analogies, see Frank; Galloway (1998). On the Good Samaritan, see Carruthers; Goldsmith; Smith. On Augustine, see *On the Trinity*; Portalie; Pelikan, I, pp. 172ff. On pardon, see Baldwin (1981a); Hurnard; Keen.

Further reading

The Sixth Vision: Passus 18

Passus 18 is the climax of the poem; if you read no other Passus in the original language, read this one. In it most of the oppositions of the poem find a resolution – the opposition between justice and mercy, between book-learning and 'kynde knowyng', between force and patience, between the Old Testament and the New, and of course between works and grace. It is the culmination of the Faith, Hope and Charity sequence, in which the Good Samaritan is transformed into Jesus and suffers the Crucifixion as a supreme act of charity towards men. This is at once a *historical narrative* and an *allegory* of the duel already introduced by Faith in Passus 16. The history comes from the gospel story of the Crucifixion and the apocryphal *Gospel of Nicodemus* or *Acts of Pilate*, in which a dead body narrates Christ's descent into Hell after the Crucifixion (see Atonement, p. 227). The allegory, is that of the "Four Daughters of God", which he probably derived from a Middle English version of Grosseteste's *Château d'Amour*. There is a wealth of other references and imagery, all transformed into a narrative at once ornate, realistic and more intellectually searching than the originals. The intellectual changes are focused on the task of reconciling God's justice and mercy, or in other words of showing the legality of the Atonement. The Passus therefore acts as a keystone of the poem's discussion of human salvation. But it can stand alone as a wonderful piece of poetry, working on symbolic, intellectual and vividly realistic levels at once.

The Passus can be divided into three narratives, as follows:

Passus 18	
Will falls asleep	1–7
Trial by battle	
Faith explains the joust	8–35
Trial and death of Jesus	36–74
Longeus	75–110
Four Daughters of God and Book	
Truth and Mercy	111–162
Righteousness and Peace	163–228
Book	229–258
Christ's debate with the Devils	
The Devils' argument	259–314
Christ enters Hell	315–327
Christ's argument	328–371
Pardon and Finale	372–433

Will falls asleep 1–7

Faith, Hope and Charity had brought the poem decisively into historical time, and Langland marks the end of this narrative by waking Will. Before he falls asleep again, Will indicates that he is also experiencing present time in the Church year. It will be remembered that he met Abraham on a mid-Lenten Sunday (16.172), and he now sleeps from Palm Sunday until Easter Day (18.6, 429). Many of the Latin quotations in this Passus are taken from the services of this highly significant period (see Adams 1976). Indeed the next few lines are full of the responses from Palm Sunday when Christians would process with branches around the Church, but which seem only to have put Will to sleep.

Atonement

Though St Paul insists that Christ redeemed mankind from sin by his death, he does not really explain how. The Church Fathers had taught that man needed redeeming because he had been condemned to Hell for the Original Sin of eating the forbidden fruit in Paradise. According to the apocryphal *Gospel of Nicodemus*, Jesus descended into Hell after his crucifixion and 'harrowed it' by binding Lucifer and rescuing the faithful Old Testament figures (see picture, p. 235). Thenceforward mankind is not automatically condemned to Hell upon death, but is judged by Christ. This rescue mission was seen in different ways through the long history of the Church:

(1) In the early Middle Ages Christ was often seen as simply defeating Satan at the gates of Hell; mankind could then be seen as rescued captives. This meaning was embodied in three early liturgical hymns sung at Eastertide (see St Jacques).

(2) Another very early explanation for Jesus' rescue of man suggested that because the Devil had tricked man into eating the forbidden fruit, he himself was tricked by Jesus' disguise as a man into letting him enter Hell, where he could break down its gates; this disguise was said to be the bait on the fishhook which caught Leviathan in *Job* 41 (see Pelikan, III, pp. 134–5).

(3) In the eleventh century the Archbishop Anselm developed a theory of the Atonement in his *Cur Deus Homo?* (Why Did God Become Man?), which satisfied his own obsession with '*rectitudo*' or "rightness" (Pelikan, III, p. 135) and which Langland seems to have known well. Because Original Sin itself violated justice, it rightly condemned man to death. This punishment could only be cancelled if an appropriate *quid pro quo* could be found, a "satisfaction" which would pay off the debt. Because Christ is perfect and divine, his sacrifice of himself to God on the Cross is a more than adequate satisfaction, and so it ransoms or "redeems" mankind. Hence Anselm's notion of satisfaction depends on his explanation of the dual nature of Christ, who is both man (and so liable for the debt of Original Sin) and God (able to pay it for all mankind). In *Piers Plowman*, how far does Jesus' speech to Satan about his own righteousness in freeing mankind depend on Langland's depiction of his double nature as Jesus (man and knight) and Christ (God and champion)?

The 'fruits' or saving effects of the Passion were communicated through baptism (which saves man from Original Sin), and through penance and the Mass (which save him from his own Actual Sin). Indeed those fruits were seen from the thirteenth century as making up a *Treasury of Merit*, a spiritual bank-balance on which any sinner could draw to pay for his sins, and for which a pardon was a kind of cheque. Langland does not appear to doubt that the sacraments are necessary for salvation, though he does seem to mistrust pardons, and to raise the question of whether it is ful-filling religious formalities, or acting upon Christian principles (and even Muslims or the righteous heathen can do this), which attracts God's saving grace, for (in the words of a Wycliffite preacher) 'ther cometh no pardon but of God for dowel and living in charity'.

Bibliography
Pelikan, III; Palmer (1952, 1955).

Trial by battle: Faith explains the joust 8–35

Will's dream of the Crucifixion, like many dreams, it is highly sym-bolic. Christ appears as Jesus riding the donkey on Palm Sunday, as the mounted Samaritan from the last Passus, and as a knight 'þat comeþ to be dubbed / To geten hym gilte spores on galoches ycouped' (slashed shoes, 13–14; Simpson suggests this refers to his nailed feet). The image of Christ as a knight fighting the Devil on the Cross was not original to Langland, but was part of a tradition of allegories which had developed from hymns and sequences sung during Holy Week and Easter (see St Jacques). In particular the Latin hymn called *Victimae paschali* describes a 'marvellous battle between Life and Death' (*Mors et vita duello / conflixere mirando*). Some texts inspired by this idea, such as the thirteenth-century *Ancrene Wisse*, depict the battle as a chivalric joust for the love of the Lady Anima (the soul); others, such as the early-fifteenth-century alliterative poem *Death and Life*, depict it more as a cosmic struggle. Langland's treat-ment is quite original. For him this is not so much a chivalric joust, where the best fighter won, as a trial by battle, 'where what triumphed was not brute force but Truth' (Pollock and Maitland, p. 600). Indeed though he continues to use the word 'joust', it is much closer to the trial ('juggement') referred to in Passus 16:

> And þanne sholde Iesus iuste þerfore, and bi iuggement of armes,
> Wheiþer sholde fonge þe fruyt – þe fend or hymselue. (95–96)

iuste: joust; iuggement of armes: trial by battle; fonge: take

Such trials by battle were still very occasionally fought in the four-teenth century, where they attracted enormous audiences. In the 1350s two were staged under Edward III's new Court of Chivalry to decide 'appeals' (private accusations) of treason, as at the beginning of Shakespeare's *Richard II*. But they could also be used in civil cases of a 'Writ of Right' when paid champions wearing their employers' arms would fight to determine the ownership of land, and this seems to be Langland's model for a fight which will decide the ownership of Piers' fruit (the patriarchs and prophets lying in Abraham's lap; on duels so, see Baldwin 1981b, 66). Faith is still our guide:

> Thanne I frayned at Feiþ what al þat fare bymente,
> And who sholde iuste in Ierusalem. 'Iesus,' he seide,
> 'And fecche þat þe fend claymeþ, Piers fruyt þe Plowman.' ...
> In Piers paltok þe Plowman þis prikiere shal ryde;
> For no dynt shal hym dere as *in deitate Patris*.'...
> Lif seiþ þat he [Deeþ] lieþ, and leieþ his lif to wedde
> That, for al þat Deeþ kan do, wiþinne þre daies to walke
> And fecche fro þe fend Piers fruyt þe Plowman,
> In Piers paltok þe Plowman þis prikiere shal ryde;
> For no dynt shal hym dere as *in deitate Patris*. (18–33)

frayned: asked; wedde: pledge; paltok: jacket; prikiere: horseman; dynt: blow; dere: harm; *deitate Patris*: divinity of the Father

The 'paltok' is at once the arms which this champion wears to fight the duel (compare 'secte' of 5.491), and the disguise which in another Latin Easter hymn, the *Pangue Lingua,* Jesus uses to trick the Devil into letting him enter Hell. And underlying both mean-ings it expresses the double nature of Christ as God and man at once (see Atonement, p. 227).

Trial by battle: trial and death of Jesus 36–74

There follows a vivid account of the unjust trial and death of Jesus' human self, still seen partly as a duel under the supervision of Pilate (37–50). As in the mystery plays the diabolic energy of the accusers is contrasted with patient non-violence, a patience which will conquer (*Patientes vincunt*) for he will defeat Death by dying. Faith promised Will in Passus 16 that this would happen:

> On cros vpon Caluarie Crist took þe bataille
> Ayeins deep and þe deuel, destruyed hir boþeres myȝtes –
> Deide, and deep fordide, and day of nyȝt made. (16.164–166)
>
> fordide: destroy

We are now given a much greater understanding of how this paradoxical triumph is achieved, When 'the lord of lif and of light þo leide hise eiȝen togideres' (59) he is still vitally alive, for we hear from a dead body (61, as in the *Gospel of Nicodemus*) that the battle is still going on in the Underworld:

> 'For a bitter bataille,' þe dede body seide;
> 'Lif and Deeþ in þis derknesse, hir oon fordooþ hir ooþer.' (64–65)
>
> fordooþ: destroy

There appear in fact to be two battles: Jesus' human nature has jousted and died on the Cross (thus paying for man's sin), but his divine nature is still fighting Death at the gates of Hell (59–64).

Trial by battle: Longeus 75–110

To make it clear that Jesus seems to have lost only the duel which he fought in his human nature, Langland finds a human opponent, Longeus. This was the name given in the Middle English *Gospel of Nicodemus* to the Roman centurion who thrust a spear into Jesus' dead body. Following a story in the Golden Legend (printed

Krochalis and Peters, Pt. 15), the writer explains he was a 'blynde knight' whose sight was miraculously restored when Jesus' blood touched his face (see Peebles). If Jesus is the human counterpart of Life, and champion of Piers, Longeus is the (unwilling) human counterpart of Death, and champion of the Jews:

> he was maad þat tyme
> To [iusten wiþ Iesus, þis blynde Iew Longeus].
> For alle þei were vnhardy, þat houed on horse or stode,
> To touchen hym or to tasten hym or taken hym doun of roode,
> But þis blynde bacheler ... (81–85)

> vnhardy: lacking in courage; houed: were there; tasten: handle; roode: cross

It is because they realise that Jesus is 'kny3t and kynges sone' (76) that the Jews choose a champion who cannot see him to fight him, for it was treason to be 'so hardy as to touch the body of our lord the king' (*Ordinances of War*, see Baldwin 1981a). But having put the spear into Jesus' side, and been cured of blindness, Longeus begs Jesus for 'grace'. In consequence Faith claims that Jesus has in fact "won":

> For youre champion chiualer, chief kny3t of yow alle,
> 3ilt hym recreaunt rennyng, ri3t at Iesus wille.
> For be þis derknesse ydo, Deeþ worþ yvenquisshed;
> And ye, lurdaynes, han ylost, for Lif shal have þe maistrye.
> And youre fraunchyse, þat fre was, fallen is in þraldom (99–103).

> recreaunt: cowardly surrender; ydo: over; lurdaynes: little lords; maistrye: victory;
> fraunchyse: freedom; Praldom: bondage

If a champion lost a trial by battle, he lost his civil rights, and Faith goes on to claim that this is what has happened to the Jews. The very few English Jews remaining after the Expulsion of 1290 were indeed legally unfree, serfs of the king. So there seems no doubt that in spite of his death Jesus has really won the battle which had been anticipated from Passus 16. Faith prophesies that Life will also win the supernatural battle against the Devil at the gates of Hell. It is there that Will goes next.

Four Daughters of God and Book 111–258

The dramatic episode that follows, the encounter between the Four Daughters of God, was no more invented by Langland than the allegory of Christ as a knight. Yet again, as Waldron shows in detail, he uses it in a very original way. The story was based on a verse from *Psalms* 85:10: 'Mercy and Truth are met together; righteousness and Peace have kissed each other', and developed into an allegorical story by several authors including the thirteenth-century French poet Robert Grosseteste in his *Chateau d'Amour*; this was a popular text and had been translated into Middle English by the time Langland was writing. He introduces an account of Christ's birth from the 'Castle' of the Virgin Mary, by telling the allegorical story of a king whose servant, Adam, has been imprisoned for disobedience. Two of his daughters, Mercy and Peace, plead for his release, but their request is scorned by Righteousness and Truth:

> I ne may forbere to tel hit þe
> Hou hit me þinkeþ a wonder þing
> Of Merci, my suster, wilnynge, ...
> Deliuere þe þral out of prison
> Þat swythe agulte. ... (Grosseteste, *Château*, 364–9).
>
> forbere: restrain myself; swythe agulte: exceedingly guilty

The quarrel causes Peace to leave the court, and is only resolved when the king's son offers to take the clothes of the prisoner and suffer the punishment on his behalf (521–554); eventually he will tell him 'þi rihte ichulle crauen / For icham of þi lynage' (I shall ask to defend your right for I am of your kin, 966–967). In a dialogue between Jesus and the Devil at the Temptation, Jesus both accuses the Devil of imprisoning man unjustly, for 'þou þorw treson to monkynde speke' (1068), and offers nevertheless to pay a ransom to release him (1114).

Langland has given the debate a new setting and time– the gates of Hell after Jesus' death. Jesus' speech will be made not to God but to the Devil, and the debate between the daughters very realistic, even funny. As in the sources, the initiative for releasing Adam and his descendants from the prison they have occupied since the Original Sin is taken by Mercy, assisted by Peace:

> And þat God haþ forgyuen and graunted me, Pees, and Mercy
> To be mannes meynpernour for eueremoore after. (183–184)

meynpernour: bail

This suggests that Mercy and Peace will provide the 'maynprise' for which Abraham was waiting (16.264) to release himself and the patriarchs and prophets lying in his lap (see above, p. 212). However Truth, representing God's justice as so often in the poem (see What is Truth?, p. 35), treats her words with even more contempt than her counterpart in the *Château d'Amour*:

> 'That þow tellest,' quod Trupe, 'is but a tale of waltrot!' (142).

Righteousness is equally against pardoning Mankind, for his abandonment of God's instructions for Satan's was a breach of faith – the other meaning of truth – and indeed 'ayeins reson' (see Alford 1988):

> Adam afterward, ayeins his defence,
> Freet of þat fruyt, and forsook, as it weere,
> The loue of Oure Lord and his loore boþe
> And folwede þat þe fend tauȝte and his felawes wille
> Ayeins reson – I, Rightwisnesse, recorde þus wiþ Truþe,
> That hir peyne be perpetuel and no preiere hem helpe.
> Forþi lat hem chewe as þeiþchosen, and chide we noȝt, sustres
> (194–200).

defence: prohibition; Freet: ate; loore: teaching; Forþi: therefore

Both Truth and Righteousness are therefore arguing for the principle explained by Reason in Passus 4 and validated in Truth's pardon in Passus 7, that '*nullum malum impunitum ... nullum bonum irremuneratum*' (no evil be unpunished, no good unrewarded, 18.391; see 4.143–144 and discussion, p. 000 above). So how is Langland to answer Truth and Righteousness without undermining the rest of his poem?

His answers take the form of a chain of metaphors and proofs, voiced by Mercy and Peace here and by Jesus in the next section (and it is worth distinguishing the kind of proof given to him from those spoken by the Daughters). Mercy suggests that the venom of Christ's death (like a dead scorpion) 'fordooþ' (destroys) the venom which Death brings to the world (the scorpion's bite). Later Jesus will make Lucifer drink the venom himself, and give mankind the drink of love instead (365–367). Even more daringly, Peace offers a proof of God's final mercy which echoes Patience's prayer in Passus 14 that the suffering poor 'That al hir lif han lyued in langour and in defaute' should eventually enjoy 'some manere ioye' like the birds and beasts to whom God sends 'somer, þat is hir souereyn ioye' (14.114–117). The natural progression from winter to summer appears in Passus 18 as the natural change of all things from 'wo into wele'(pain to joy):

'And I shal preie,' quod Pees, 'hir peyne moot have ende,
And wo into wele mowe wende at þe laste.
For hadde þei wist of no wo, wele hadde þei noȝt knowen;
For no wiȝt woot what wele is, þat neuere wo suffrede,
Ne what is hoot hunger, þat hadde neuere defaute' (202–206).

wele: happiness; wende: turn; wist: known; wiȝt: man; woot: knows; defaute: lack

The alliteration of 'woe' and 'well' here is educative: it gives 'kynde knowyng' to both Adam and to God himself:

'Forþi God, of his goodnesse, þe firste gome Adam,
Sette hym in solace and in souereyn murþe;
And siþþe he suffred hym synne, sorwe to feele –
To wite what wele was, kyndeliche to knowe it,
And after, God auntrede hymself and took Adames kynde
To wite what he haþ suffred in þre sondry places,
Boþe in heuene and in erþe – and now til helle he þenkep,
To wite what alle wo is, pat woot of alle ioye. (217–224)

gome: man; solace: happiness; suffred: allowed; kyndeliche: naturally, by experience; auntrede: ventured; kynde: nature; wite: know

This takes us back to Will's search throughout the Third and Fourth Visions to have 'kynde knowyng' of Dowel (8.57–58, 110; see

Kynde, Kynde Knowyng and Kynde Wit, p. 153), and here it seems that God himself pursues a corresponding search. The knowledge gained through suffering not only enables man to appreciate joy, but helps God to appreciate mankind's woe. Just as the Samaritan claimed that man's charity anticipated the Holy Spirit's in Passus 17, so now man's woe anticipates and precipitates Jesus' suffering. This gives dignity to man, and offers an explanation for the "problem of pain" – the question of why a good God allows suffering at all. Does it also illuminate Will's own journey?

Langland seems to decorate his narrative like a medieval Church with a richness of imagery, for he now introduces two more *exempla*, which both hint at Jesus' double nature as God and man, which Anselm had shown to be crucial to his rescue of mankind (see Atonement, p. 227). Both are from Biblical commentaries and so are spoken by the Book, who offers to self-immolate if they do not now come true (229–258). Drawing on Gregory, Book says that the four natural elements broke their own laws at Jesus' death, proving his divinity: fire witnessed his divinity through the star at his birth or

The Harrowing of Hell
(after an English alabaster bas-relief, Carcassonne Museum, 15th century)

the eclipse of the sun at his death; water through his disregard of its nature in walking on it (*Matthew* 14:29). And drawing on Hugh of St Cher he describes Jesus as '*Gigas* þe geaunt' (the double-natured giant, 253) whose divinity will be a 'gyn' (trick) to defeat the Devil (Kaske 1959). This speech acts as an introduction to Christ's first appearance in the poem.

Christ's debate with the Devils 259–371

Will, Book and the Four Daughters now witness the spirit of Jesus arrive there after the Crucifixion. The next Passus is taken from the 'Harrowing of Hell' episode in the *Gospel of Nicodemus*, though as usual Langland has changed things considerably (see picture on p. 235). He adds many realistic, even comic details influenced by the treatment of the episode in the mystery plays. More significantly, he continues to emphasise the *legality* of Jesus' deliverance of the souls from Hell. In the first place the metaphor of the trial by battle continues, though it has now become a battle between Life, meaning the divinity of Christ, clothed in light, and Death, or the Devil in the darkness. Whereas the duel between champions on earth had been like a Duel of Right to decide the ownership of Piers' fruit, this battle is like a Duel of Treason, fought by Christ in his own person on the issue of the Devil's deceit towards Adam (see Baldwin 1981a). He also gives Jesus a much longer and more legalistic speech than he had in the source, including several new proofs and metaphors of the justice in harrowing Hell. As Augustine put it, it was important that God 'deliver man from the devil's authority by beating him at the justice game, not the power game' (*De Trinitate* 18.17).

The devils are aware of Christ's superior power, and rush about in comic consternation (in C 20.291 they even have 'brazen guns'), but Lucifer reassures them that 'right and reson' – which we last heard being championed by Righteousness herself – has given him Mankind:

> If he reue me of my riȝt, he robbeþ me by maistrie;
> For by right and by reson þe renkes þat ben here

Body and soule beþ myne, boþe goode and ille. (276–278)

reue: deprive; maistrie: force; renkes: people

But Goblyn (like the Jesus in *Château d'Amour*) reminds him that
mankind is only theirs (the devils') by a 'treason':

> 'For God wol noȝt be bigiled,' quod Gobelyn, 'ne byiaped.
> We haue no trewe title to hem, for þoruȝ treson were þaei dampned.'
> (292–293)

bigiled: tricked; byiaped: fooled

As the Devils are accusing Lucifer of losing their joy not once but
twice, Christ, as in the *Gospel of Nicodemus*, shouts '*Rex Glorie*'
(King of Glory, *Psalms* 24) and bursts into Hell as light triumphs
over darkness:

> Lucifer loke ne myȝte, so light hym ablente.
> And þo þat Oure Lord louede, into his light he laughte (326–327).

ablente: blinded; laughte: caught

Although this may appear to be a triumph 'bi maistrie', its context
in a duel makes it also a triumph of justice, and Jesus is at pains to
explain this to the devils. He both accuses Lucifer of his treason in
deceiving Adam, and of offending against reason (which was what
Lucifer had claimed *he* was doing):

> For þe dede þat þei dide, þi deceite it made;
> Wiþ gile þow hem gete, ageyn alle reson. (334–335)

With poetic justice the beguiler has been beguiled (as in another
Easter hymn) because Jesus has tricked Satan into letting him enter
Hell. More justly, and in accordance with Anselm's "satisfaction
theory" of the Atonement, Jesus also pays a ransom:

> And al þat man haþ mysdo, I, man, wole amende it.
> Membre for membre was amendes by þe Olde Lawe,
> And lif for lif also – and by þat lawe I clayme

> Adam and al his issue at my wille herafter.
> And þat Deeþ in hem fordide, my deeþ shal releue ...
> So leue it noȝt, Lucifer, ayein þe lawe I fecche hem,
> But by right and by reson raunsone here my liges: (342–350)

mysdo: did wrong; amendes: cure; fordide: destroyed; liges: subjects

The Old Law of 'an eye for an eye' is the Judaic law which Christ
will fulfil by giving his life for Adam's, for *Non veni soluere legem set
adimplere* (I come not to replace the law but to fulfil, 359a; *Matthew*
5:17). By accepting the judgment of the law, Christ recovers his
power over both man and the Devil. Notice how the alliteration and
the use of the *caesura* in the middle of the line suggests the balance-
pans of Christ's justice and how the word-play conveys the replace-
ment of death and guile by life and 'good faith'. Indeed, in a
development of the Samaritan's image, Jesus says his life is sufficient
to bring back the fire of God's grace to where it has been quenched
by sin:

> And boþe quyke and quyte þat queynt was þoruȝ synne;
> And þat grace gile destruye, good feiþ it askeþ. (347–348)

quyke: bring to life; quyte: requite, pay for; queynt: quenched

And Jesus is also a fulfilment of the Samaritan in healing Mankind
with the medicine of love:

> For I þat am lord of lif, loue is my drynke,
> And for þat drynke today, I deide vpon erþe.
> I fauȝt so, me þursteþ yet, for mannes soule sake (366–368)

Here is an answer to Righteousness' challenge that people should
'chewe as Pei chosen' (200); it is Lucifer, the 'doctour of deeþ', and
not Adam, who must 'drynk þat þow madest' (365), while Christ
slakes his thirst on the drink of love (see 1.152 where Love 'eats his
fill'). As Jill Mann puts it, Christ 'is driven by a need ... which is as
concrete as hunger or thirst'– the need to love and to save (Mann
1979, 43).

Pardon and Finale 372–433

Jesus has now established the brotherhood with mankind through blood-shedding which has been alluded to throughout the poem (for example, 5.504, 11.301) and will be able to judge all men at the Lat Judgment:

> And þanne shal I come as a kyng, crouned, wiþ aungeles,
> And have out of helle alle mennes soules ... .
> Ac alle þat beþ myne hole breþeren, in blood and in baptisme,
> Shul noȝt be dampned to þe deeþ þat is wiþouten ende (372–378).

> hole: whole

Although Jesus seems here to confirm Will's claim that all 'þat is baptized beþ saaf' (10.345), he came only to save Christians from everlasting Hell, and retains the right to treat them with justice, indeed only to pardon them by the terms of English law (see Baldwin 1981a, pp. 73–5; Hurnard, pp. 171–213). The royal 'pre-rogative of mercy' could only be used to pardon murderers in certain restricted circumstances. One was when a hanging had been already performed but the rope broke. Another was when a king was actu-ally present at a hanging, and gave an instant reprieve. Jesus refers to both of these conditions (380–390), presumably to explain how he can justly pardon all those whom he finds now in Hell, and so who have already suffered one punishment, and who are also in his sight. But he makes an important proviso:

> Be it any þyng abouȝt, þe boldnesse of hir synnes,
> I may do mercy þoruȝ rightwisnesse, and alle my wordes trewe.
> (*Nullum mlura impunitum ...*) (389–390)

> Be it: so long as; abouȝt: paid for; nullum malum etc.: no evil shall go unpunished, no
> good unrewarded.

Jesus seems here to be referring to the same restriction on royal pardons as the Samaritan did when he spoke about the Holy Spirit's power to pardon unkindness (see above, p. 222):

That þe kyng may do no mercy til boþe men acorde
And eyþer have equite, as holy writ telleþ
Numquam dimittitur peccatum ... (17.305–306)

Nunquam dimittitur etc: the sin is not forgiven until restitution is made (Augustine
Epistle 153)

In neither case does the heavenly King's pardon release the sinner
from the obligation to make restitution to those whom he has
wronged, and possibly also to perform "satisfaction" in Purgatory; as
elsewhere in the poem, these Latin tags express the claims of justice
in the face of mercy (4.143–144, 5.271). In the next Passus we will
hear precisely how Piers' pardon must be 'abouȝt'. All through the
poem justice and mercy have jostled for pre-eminence, nowhere
more so than when pardons are on offer. Christ has paid the recompense 'body for body' on man's behalf and so given Faith his "mainprise" and hung the seal on Hope's pardon (see above, pp. 212–16).
It only remains for Jesus to sum up the judgement of his two duels;
by the Duel of Right on earth in Piers' arms he has won the right to
take possession of the souls in Hell; by the Duel of Treason before
the gates of Hell he has won the right to punish Lucifer:

'Thus by lawe,' quod Oure Lord, 'lede I wole fro hennes
Tho [leodes] þat I louede and leued in my comynge.
And for þi lesynge, Lucifer, þat þow leighe til Eue,
Thow shalt abyen it bittre!' – and bond hym wiþ cheynes. (401–404)

leodes: men; lesynge: lying; abyen: pay for it

So we return to liturgical time, with the quotes from the Ascension
Hymn and the general Hymn of Thanksgiving *Te deum laudamus*
(we praise thee, O God). Peace, restored by the resolution of the
debate, confirms that the natural, the social and the religious progression from 'wo to wele' has been achieved (compare 14.114–117,
18.202–206):

'After sharpest shoures,' quod Pees, 'moost shene is þe sonne; ...
 Ne no loue leuere, ne leuer frendes
Than after werre and wo, whan loue and pees ben maistres. (411–414)

shene: beautiful; leuer: dearer

Truth punningly calls for a "truce" (418) and the sisters fulfil *Psalms* 85:10 by kissing. Will hears the singing and ringing of the Easter Resurrection bells, and wakes to find it is Easter Day.

Further reading

For analogues, see *York Mystery Plays*; Grosseteste, *The Middle English Translations ... Château d'Amour*; Krochalis and Peters, Pts 24–5. On Christ allegory, see Baldwin 1981b; Birnes; Waldron (1986); Warner.

The Seventh Vision: Passus 19

Passus 19 is the first Passus of *Dobest* in the old rubric, and like Passus 18 is a single Vision. In the Trinitarian structure which underlies the *Vita*, it is under the protection of the Holy Spirit. It is dominated at first by Piers, who now fits into the succession of historical figures which was begun in Passus 16 with the appearance of Abraham. As was explained on p. 210, Faith and Hope together seem to represent the Father, the Samaritan / Jesus represents the Son, and this leaves Piers Plowman to represent the Holy Spirit. He appears in a new persona, that of St Peter, the first Pope, in this Passus, which therefore carries forward the history of the Faith into the early Church, though the last part concerns the corruption of the early ideals in Langland's own time. This corruption is allegorised as a *psychomachia*, a conflict between the Vices and the Remedies. The next Passus will take the story forward to the end of the world, which also looks very like the fourteenth century. These two Passus therefore introduce an *apocalyptic* element into the poem, in which characters and events taken from the *Apocalypse* (the Biblical book *Revelation*) are used to satirise present society.

Passus 19 is constructed in the following parts:

Passus 19	
The speech of Conscience	1–199
Vision of Christ as conqueror	1–68
Naming sequence	69–199
Unite	
The coming of the Holy Spirit and the foundation of the Church	200–336
The attack of Pride	337–412
Speech of the Lewed Vicar	413–485

Vision of Christ as conqueror 1–68

When Will has taken his Easter Eucharist he falls asleep and dreams of Piers as the conquering Christ:

> I fel eftsoones aslepe – and sodeynly me mette
> That Piers þe Plowman was peynted al blody,
> And corn in wiþ a cros bifore þe comune peple,
> And riȝt lik in alle lymes to Oure Lord Iesu. (5–8)
>
> eftsoones: again; mette: dreamed; lymes: limbs

This dream-like vision does several things. On one level it is Christ resurrected after his descent into Hell, as depicted in the picture on p. 245. On another it is Christ at the end of the world coming as judge (*Revelation* 14:19), as "prefigured" in Isaiah's vision of an angry deity:

> 'Who is this that cometh from Edom, with dyed garments … Why art thou red in thine apparel, and thy garments like him that treadeth in the winefat?' … 'I will tread them in mine anger … For the day of vengeance is in mine heart … ' (*Isaiah* 63:1–4).

On yet another level this is Piers Plowman, and Will asks Conscience, who has suddenly reappeared, to explain whether this is 'Iesus þe iustere' or 'Piers þe Plowman?' (10–11). Conscience answers rather obliquely by explaining that it is Christ the conqueror (12–62). But he is not one who follows Meed's advice to 'brenne and to bruttene, to bete adoun strengths' (C 3.237), but a paradoxical conqueror, one who conquers through shedding his 'herte blood' (58), following Patience's principle of *patientes vincunt* (see 15.155–158). He fights on behalf of his people, and gives them new laws and estates, but this is not earthly 'lordshipe or oþer large mede' but freedom from Hell and 'Places in paradis at hir partynge hennes', a spiritual lordship for those he ennobles by his blood (see Simpson 1985). But they must follow his path of suffering and patient poverty:

Christ with Cross

(after the Doubting Thomas window, All Saints' North St., York, 15th century)

Ac þe cause þat he comeþ þus wiþ cros of his passion
Is to wissen vs þerwiþ …
And se bi his sorwe þat whoso loueþ ioye,
To penaunce and to pouerte he moste puten hymseluen,
And muche wo in þis world wilnen and suffren. (63–67)

wissen: instruct; wilnen: desire

Naming sequence 69–199

Triad	In Passus 8–15	In Passus 16–19	In Passus 19
Dowel	Obedience to law	Faith and Hope (Abraham and Moses): Father	Jesus as knight Gives laws – judges
Dobet	Performance of charity	Charity (Samaritan) Son	Filius David as King Righteousness, reason and truth Healer
Dobest	Part of Church authority	Piers as Pope Holy Spirit	Christ as conqueror Giving gifts

As in Passus 16–17 Langland needs to turn two into three (see above, p. 210), and Conscience's strategy for doing this is to split the functions of the king into judging and healing, which suits the whole poem's distinction between Dowel (following the law) and Dobet (acting with charity). For example the gifts of the Magi can be seen as representing both justice ('Reson' and 'Rihtwisnesse', 87–89) and mercy ('Pitee', 93). Thus Jesus in his own life Does Well as a *judge* who gives the law, and Jesus as a *king* Does Better when he acts with charity in healing and feeding his people:

> In his Iuuentee þis Iesus at Iewene feeste
> Turnede water into wyn, as Holy Writ telleþ,
> And þere bigan God of his grace to do wel.
> For wyn is likned to lawe and lif of holynesse; …
> Thus he confortede carefulle and caughte a gretter name,
> The which was Dobet, where þat he wente.
> For deue þoruȝ hise doynges and dombe speke and herde (108–130)

> Iuuentee: youth; Iewene feste: Jewish feast; likned: compared; carefulle: the distressed; caughte: got; deue: deaf

Instead of repeating his earlier account of Christ as a conqueror (12–69), Conscience then gives a detailed account of the

Resurrection, which finishes the story told in Passus 18 (19.143–183), and then says that Jesus Does Best when he empowers St Peter to establish his Church:

> And whan þis dede was doon, Dobest he [þou]ȝte,
> And yaf Piers power, and pardon he grauntede:
> To alle maner men, mercy and forȝifnesse;
> [To] hym, myght men to assoille of alle manere synnes,
> In couenaunt þat þei come and kneweliche to paye
> To Piers pardon þe Plowman – Redde *quod debes*. (183–188)

yaf: gave; assoille: absolve; In couenaunt: on condition

In fact St Peter was given the 'power of the keys' rather earlier in Jesus' life than Conscience suggests, in a passage which was seen by the Church as establishing the Pope as head of the Church, and gave him and his clergy the 'keys of the Kingdom of Heaven' and the power to 'bind and loose' men from Actual Sin, through the Sacrament of Penance (*Matthew* 16:18–19; see p. 24 and picture on p. 25, where St Peter holds the keys to Heaven and Hell).

This is clearly a defining moment for a poem about Piers, who is here given a new *persona* as the Rock (*Petrus* / Peter) on which Jesus founded his Church (*Matthew* 16:18). Moreover like Christ at the moment of releasing the patriarchs and prophets from the bonds of Original Sin, St Peter's pardon for Actual Sin must be 'abouȝt' (paid for, 18.389) through performing penance:

> To Piers pardon þe Plowman – *Redde quod debes*.
> Thus haþ Piers power, be his pardon paied,
> To bynde and vnbynde boþe here and ellis (188–190).

be: as long as; ellis: elsewhere (that is, in Heaven)

This was indeed part of the theology of penance, for as Duns Scotus put it, 'the [absolving] sentence of the priest ... absolves from the debt of eternal punishment, but it binds to the debt of temporal punishment' (Palmer 1952, p.217). We are back to the principle quoted by the Samaritan that '*non dimmititur peccatum donec restitutatur ablatum*' (the sin is not cancelled until restitution has been made, 17.304–306, 5. 274). The alternative to paying this "debt" seems to be the fearful justice of Piers' old pardon in Passus 6, for Conscience warns:

> And what persone paieþ it nouȝt, punysshen he þenkeþ,
> And demen hem at domesday, boþe quyke and dede –
> The goode to þe Godhede and to greet ioye,
> And wikkede to wonye in wo wiþouten ende. (196–199)

demen: judge; quyke: living; wonye: dwell

However there is a crucial difference, for those who do pay their debts in penance and restitution seem to have access to Jesus' mercy rather than his judgment. Whereas Piers and then Will had sought throughout the poem for individual Dowel as the means of salvation, now the corporate sacrament of penance is instituted as a support for those who (inevitably) fail. Grace will come with the Holy Spirit to pardon sin, so long as those wronged by one's sin are compensated. The correct use of penance will therefore be the pivot on which the rest of the poem turns.

The coming of the Holy Spirit and the foundation of the Church 200–336

Langland now completes his Father (Abraham and Moses) and Son (Samaritan and Jesus) sequence by initiating a new Age of the Spirit, which begins when the Holy Spirit or 'Paraclete' descends to the Apostles at Pentecost.

> And there appeared unto [the Apostles] cloven tongues as of fire, and
> it sat upon each of them. And they were all filled with the Holy Spirit
> and began to speak with other tongues (*Acts* 2:3–4)

For Langland this is the moment when the Age of the Law (Dowel), following the Atonement (Dobet), is replaced by the Age of Grace. The representative of this Third Age is St Peter transformed into Piers Plowman, who receives the Holy Spirit with his fellows from grace:

> and þanne cam, me þou3te,
> Oon *Spiritus Paraclitus* to Piers and to hise felawes. ...
> And þanne bigan Grace to go wiþ Piers Plowman,
> And counseillede hym and Conscience þe comune to sompne.
>
> (201– 215)

Spiritus Paraclitus: the Spirit of the Comforter; sompne: summon

Langland combines this with St Paul's account of the distribution of personal 'gifts' within the Church:

> Now there are diversities of gifts, but the same Spirit ... For to one is given, by the Spirit, the word of wisdom; to another, the word of knowledge ... ; to another the gifts of healing, by the same Spirit ... For by one Spirit were we all baptised into one Body (*1 Cor.* 12:4–9)

It is therefore clear that this Third Age is the Age of the Church, when men should work together for salvation, receiving God's grace through the sacraments. And it soon transpires that this Third Age is also the last, for grace is equipping them not just for the new Church of *Acts* but also for the 'last time' when St John predicted that 'Antichrist shall come' (*1 John* 2:18):

> For I wole dele today and dyuyde grace
> To alle kynne creatures þat kan hise fyue wittes –
> Tresour to lyue by to hir lyues ende,
> And wepne to fighte wiþ þat wole neuere faille.
> For Antecrist and hise al þe world shul greue,
> And acombre þee, Conscience, but if Crist þee helpe. (216–221)

dyuyde: share; kynne: kinds; kan: use; hise: his followers; acombre: overcome

The gifts which then follow (230–252) can be seen as repeating the estates of the Prologue, 'the crafts of a whole society ... clerical, commercial, manual, martial and contemplative skills (Simpson 1990, p. 223; see also 1985). Or they can be seen as more inward gifts, to use against the psychological enemies of 'Pride', 'Coueitise' and 'Vnkyndenesse' ... 'Ydelnesse' and 'Enuye' (224–229). These are typically Langlandian vices, and are opposed by activities which have been used throughout the poem: the labour which gives 'a lele lif and a trewe', the 'wit' of 'prechours' and 'prentices of lawe', the fervour for justice which recovers 'þat vnriȝffully was wonne', and the 'pouerte and pacience' of the religious life (232–250). We may recognise in these crafts the characters of Piers, Wit and Study, Reason, and Patience – characters who have represented ideals at different points in the poem. The gifts are then individual and moral as well as social, and, as in the Samaritan's lecture on the Holy Spirit, grace is activated through personal effort and the moral behaviour which has underpinned the whole poem.

Grace then sets up a social structure modelled on the manorial estate, but with Conscience as king:

> And crouneþ Conscience kyng, and makeþ Craft youre stiward,
> And after Craftes conseil cloþeþ yow and fede ...
> My prowor and my plowman Piers shal ben on erþe (258–262).

Craft: skill; stiward: steward, deputy; prowor: purveyor

Compare these lines with Prologue 116–119; the ingredients are similar but do they combine the "horizontal" (social) and "vertical" (moral and religious) axes in the same way? One difference could be that in Passus 19 there is a greater dependence on moral and religious faculties: Conscience controls Craft, and Piers seems to be a cleric receiving penance, not a real ploughman feeding the people (see White, p. 38). It is in fact possible to interpret the passage not only as an analysis of the Church as a whole, but also of individual Christians whose conscience, skills, and obedience to Church discipline fit them for receiving God's grace. Such an interpretation can run alongside the more social analysis offered by Simpson (1985), and is particularly illuminating when Piers begins to plough. Having acquired from Grace a plough-team which represents 'Clergy' (the learning of the Church), Piers begins to cultivate the individual soul:

> And Grace gaf Piers greynes – cardynales vertues,
> And sew it in mannes soule, and siþen he tolde hir names. (276–277)

greynes: seeds; sew: sow

These 'greynes' are the four Cardinal Virtues of antiquity which were added to the three Theological Virtues to make up the Seven Virtues of the Christian soul (see Moral Lists, p. 93). In Langland's version each Cardinal Virtue is called '*Spiritus*', possibly, as Bloomfield suggests (1962, p. 220), to show they are 'infused' with the Holy Spirit. Although they appear at first to betray their pagan origin in being more pragmatic than ideal, they have some affinity with the moral teachers of the *Vita*. Prudence has similar powers to Wit and Inwit; Temperance is like the 'mesure' praised by Holy Church, and Fortitude has similar qualities to Patience:

> And whoso ete of þat seed hardy was euere
> To suffren al þat God sente, siknesse and angres. (292–293)
>
> hardy: daring; angres: sorrows

The 'cheef seede', *Spiritus Iusticie*, does 'equyte to alle eueneforþ his power' (311), like Reason in Passus 4, though Langland also points out its vulnerability to guile (rather as Milton does when describing the angels' inability to spy hypocrisy). All four Virtues are Christianised by 'harrowing' with the doctors of the Church, and so the soul is prepared by teaching, by developing moral virtue, and by grace, for the war against Vice.

The individual soul is then given a clear institutional protection: a barn of Unity which binds them together and acts as an Ark in a sea of troubles (see the picture of the Ark, p. 120, and note the Cross on the mast). All the virtues and gifts already given by Grace are now supplemented by the sacraments, particularly those which convey the saving effects of Christ's Passion: baptism, the mass, and penance (see Atonement, p. 227). Consequently the barn is built on a foundation mixed out of Christ's blood:

> And of his baptisme and blood þat he bledde on roode
> He made a manere morter, and mercy it highte. (326–327)
>
> manere mortar: a kind of mortar

The priests are made village policemen or 'haywards' to administer the crucial sacrament of penance, driving the 'cart of Contricion and Confession' (334–335) under the authority of the Pope, Piers Plowman:

> For I make Piers þe Plowman my procuratour and my reue,
> And registrer to receyue *Redde quod debe*. (260–261)

procuratour: agent; registrer: registrar; *Redde quod debe*: render what is owed

Piers' conditional pardon allows men's failure to obey the law of charity to be forgiven, so long as they share (in penance or restitution) in the suffering which earned them that pardon. Their hearts will thus be prepared for Grace, who, it will be remembered, has been setting up this society, working with the Pope to help men "grow truth". But then they both depart, leaving Unite under the leadership of the individual conscience:

> Þe while hymself wente
> As wide as þe world is, wiþ Piers to tilie truþe
> And þe lo[nd] of bileue, þe lawe of Holy Chirche. (335–337)

tilie: till, cultivate

Where do they go? this is the last we hear of either of them. Does their disappearance express Langland's semi-Pelagianism by leaving men and women to find grace by performing the sacraments and by imitating Piers, cultivating truth for themselves (rather than, as Augustine would say, receiving virtue as the gift of grace)? Or does it express Langland's despair for his own world?

The attack of Pride 337–412

Medieval literature abounds in allegories of a war between Vice and Virtue, mostly derived from the *Psychomachia* of Prudentius (348–410), which, according to Bloomfield, 'was to be the chief source of the medieval literature of moral conflict, and to have a wide general influence on medieval allegory'(1952, p. 62). This Latin poem begins with a series of individual battles between Vices and Remedies (Anger against Patience, Voluptuousness against Sobriety and so on), all allegorised as women. Although Pride leads the attack, it is the defeat of Avarice which wins the war, using hypocrisy to corrupt the clergy:

And with a veil of piety [Avarice] hides
Her snaky locks, ... and she may excuse
Under the name of Love her offspring –
Her theft and pillage and rapacity (558–563).

In Passus 19 too a principal weapon that Pride and his followers use
is deceit – calling Vice by the name of Virtue:

Wiþ swiche colours and queyntise comeþ Pride y-armed,
Wiþ þe lord þat lyueþ after þe lust of his body (355–356).

colours: banners; queyntise: deceptions; lust: pleasure

In Prudentius' allegory, the Virtues retreat into a fortified camp
under the leadership of Concordia (Unity), where they wait 'till
Christ our God is present with his grace' (910). So too in Passus 19,
Conscience calls his followers into the Barn of Unite because he feels
they will fail 'but Grace were wiþ vs' (363). Grace can now only be
reached through the sacraments, and Conscience and Kynde Wit
(who had appointed the Clergy in Prol. 114), teach the Christians
how to use baptism and penance. Not all the Christians repent, but
most do, and as Anima had said (15.270ff.), the purity of this early
Church provides the leadership:

Clennesse of þe comune and clerkes clene lyuynge
Made Vnitee Holy Chirche in holynesse stonde. (383–384)

A third channel of grace, the mass, is then offered to the Christians
(388) but with the original stipulation that the sacrament should be
taken after completing penance (as a Lenten confession usually preceded the Easter Mass for Langland's contemporaries):

Here is breed yblessed, and Goddes body þervnder.
Grace, þoruȝ Goddes word, gaf Piers power,
... as ofte as þei hadde nede, þo þat hadde ypaied
To Piers pardon þe Plowman, *Redde quod debes*. (389–394)

ypaied: paid; *Redde quod debes*: render what you owe

However Langland is less optimistic than Prudentius, who gives the

Virtues the victory. A brewer, resurrected from Meed's or Covetousness's fellowship in Passus 3 and 5, refuses to repay his ill-gotten gains. Conscience sees this as a breach of the very justice which underlies Piers' pardon, and threatens him with damnation:

> 'Caytif!' quod Conscience, 'cursede wrecche!
> Vnblessed artow, brewere, but if þee God helpe.
> [Saue] þow lyue by loore of *Spiritus Iusticie*,
> The chief seed þat Piers sew, ysaued worstow neuere.' (407–410)

Caytif: scoundrel; loore: teaching; worstow: will you be

Once again Langland is showing that the sacraments (grace) and the virtues (law) must work together if Unite is to survive.

Speech of the Lewed Vicar 413–485

There then steps forward a curious figure – a vicar, that is to say, a cleric without a living of his own who is paid to work in another priest's church. Like Recklessness in the C-text he is dissociated from the author by his title ('lewed' means ignorant; 'reckless' means care-less) and seems to voice criticisms of the Church which Will dare not speak in his own voice, though they do appear elsewhere in the poem. After a scathing attack on the Cardinals (reminiscent of Prol. 107–110) he makes the point made by Patience in Passus 13.207–211 and by Anima in Passus 15.538–542, that the Church has no business to be taking part in wars. The B-text attack on the Pope here may refer to the battles between the Popes after their Schism of 1379, and in the C-text to the Despenser Crusade of 1383 (see p. 199). The vicar contrasts the imperfect actual Pope with Piers Plowman in some of the most memorable lines in the poem, lines which recall the sunshine of 18.411:

> Inparfit is þat Pope þat al peple sholde helpe,
> And s[ou]deþ hem þaat sleeþ swiche as he sholde saue.
> A[c] wel worþe Piers þe Plowman, þat pursueþ God in doynge,
> *Qui pluit super iustos et iniustos* at ones,
> And sent þe sonne to saue a cursed mannes tilþe

As brighte as to þe beste man or to þe beste womman. (432–437)

Inparfit: faulty; soudep: pays; sleep: slays; wel worp: well be to; *Qui pluit* … : who raineth upon the just and the unjust; tilpe: crops

Is this Lewed Vicar an early follower of Wycliffe? They too supposedly said:

it is not leueful to sle any man, neiþer … Sarasines, neiþer paynemes, be battel … (Hudson 1978, p. 20)

leueful: lawful

for who is in most charite is beste herde of god, be he schepeherde or lewid man, or in þe chirche or in þe feld; & who kepiþ wel þe hestis of god schal haue pardon & þe blisse of heuene (Wyclif *Sermons*, 238, quoted Godden 1990, p. 53).

herde: guardian; lewid: ignorant; hestis: commands

Or is he a reader of Franciscan Apocalyptic prophecies, looking for the 'Angelic Pope' who was said to be coming with the Last World Emperor to 'repair the whole globe' (Reeves, pp. 67–8)? And if we too are moved by the poetry to accept this as a true characterisation of Piers Plowman, does his readiness to save 'a wastour and wenches of þe stewes' (439) undermine the principle established in the *Visio* (by an earlier Piers Plowman) that wasters must work, and only a few lines earlier in this very Passus, that prostitutes who did not pay their spiritual debts in penance and restitution should be refused pardon (19.371)? Does Langland long for a Christ who will offer salvation to all Christians (as Christ almost did at 18.378–379), or for a Christ who will embody the principles of Truth?

In the Lewed Vicar's experience the world practises neither mercy nor truth, for the laity follow the Pope's bad example and twist the Cardinal Virtues to 'sowne, as by siȝte, somwhat to wynnyng' (tend, as I see it, towards profit, 457). Two lay characters step forward and frankly confirm this claim. The first is a lord:

Thanne louȝ þer a lord, and 'By þis light!' seide,
'I holde it riȝt and reson of my reue to take
Al þat myn auditour or ellis my styward

Counseilleþ me bi hir acounte and my clerkes writynge.
Wiþ *Spiritus Intellectus* þei toke þe reues rolles,
And wiþ *Spiritus Fortitudinis* fecche it – wole [he, nel he].' (463–468)

lou3: laughed; *Spiritus Intellectus*: spirit of understanding; wole he, nel he: whether he
will or not

The reeve (village steward) of a manor would submit accounts of
expenses and sales to the lord's auditors, who would check them for
consistency not only with that year's records, but also with records
of other years and even with the 'extent' or general survey of the
manor (the 'clerkes' writing'), where he might 'chaunce to fynd
fewer acres then they telle you of, and more quarters sowed then
neede was' (*Walter of Henley*, p. 313). Under the Statute of
Accompte, the reeve could then be imprisoned until he made up the
difference, as in 14.105–109, where Patience suggested God making
'allowaunce' for the poor and ignorant (see p. 182, and also
10.470–471). Here the lord is selfishly exploiting his reeve under
the colour of 'prudence.'

The unjust lord is followed by a tyrannical king:

'I am kyng wiþ croune þe comune to rule, …
And if me lakkeþ to lyue by, þe lawe wole I take it
Ther I may hastilokest it haue – for I am heed of lawe: …
And what I take of yow two, I take it at þe techynge
Of *Spiritus Iusticie* – for I iugge yow alle.
So I may boldely be housled, for I borwe neuere (470–479).

hastilokest: quickest; *Spiritus Iusticie*: spirit of justice; be housled: take the Eucharist;
borwe: borrow

This king speaks like the Roman Emperor, whose will was 'animate
justice' and who could over-ride written law, including property law
(see Baldwin 1981a, p. 8). But in England such disregard of property rights was seen as tyranny. Indeed it would be one reason for
deposing Richard II in 1399 that he apparently claimed that 'the
life of every one of his lieges, together with their lands, … goods
and chattels, was subject to his own pleasure, apart from any
[lawful] forfeiture' (Tuck 1973, pp. 209–10). The king's delusion
that he never borrows simply indicates how much he is in debt to

God and man; he is certainly not ready to 'be housled' (take the Eucharist, 479).

It is not this king but Conscience who has been appointed king of Unite, but Conscience seems content to leave this king in control of the political sphere. He even allows him to take resources he needs to defend the realm, taken *ad defendendum* (to defend) his realm, not *ad deprehendendum* (to fleece it, A 483). But he has no way of enforcing this condition, of making the king rule 'in reson, right wel and in trupe' (542). Is Conscience demonstrating the egalitarian nature of the society of the Church, which guides but does not direct men towards truth? Or is he showing a weakness that betrays he is only a natural, not a grace-given faculty (see Langland's Psychology, p. 123 and Introduction, p. 16)? On this equivocal note ends this first Vision of the new Church, already changing the very virtues on which it is built to suit the old vices of pride and avarice. Though grace still seems to be present in the sacraments, we have been warned that Unite also stands by cleanness in its leaders. One of them, Conscience, may already be compromising his principles, and even Piers Plowman seems to be remembered only as a recklessly generous rebel. Where is the poem going? Is Langland going to destroy all that he has built up?

Further reading

On gifts of grace, see Simpson (1985); Davlin (1996). On Sins, see Bloomfield (1952). On sowing of Cardinal Virtues, see Aers (1980), Ch. 3; Baldwin (1981a); Bloomfield (1952), pp. 133ff.

The Eighth Vision: Passus 20

Passus 20 is the culmination of the poem as well as of *Dobest*. In it we see the failure of Langland's Church to protect those values which have become crucial to the poem: charity, patient poverty, justice. The Church is threatened not only by individual sin but also by weak leadership and an institutional disunity which prevents it from healing and helping the sinner. The clergy have been seen as frequently corrupt throughout the poem, but now Langland focuses on how the inclusion of the unstable friars in their ranks has weakened them even further. These so undermine the crucial sacrament of penance that charity becomes dangerously naïve, poverty becomes an excuse for flattery, and justice bypassed. Even the individual conscience seems lost in a world without Grace or Piers Plowman, and Christ seems to have been replaced by Antichrist. And yet the values of the poem are not diminished but reconfirmed by this tragic close, which in any case seems only to be a staging-post on the journey.

The Passus beings with a long waking episode, and then Will has a dream which mirrors his own old age as well as the dissolution of the Church. In form it continues the dramatic *Psychomachia* of the previous Passus and develops into an *apocalyptic vision* of the last days of the world. As Emmerson, historian of Antichrist, puts it:

> The exegetical interpretation of a few biblical texts, coupled with sibylline legends and encouraged by apocalyptic expectations of the imminent end, grew into a widespread and complex body of beliefs that were discussed in theological *compendia*, illustrated in a wide variety of art media, and developed in homilies, histories, plays, and allegorical poems. In the medieval view of history, Antichrist will play the crucial final role in the battle between good and evil on earth. (p. 203)

In Apocalyptic style the Unite is assailed by the Three Enemies: the World, the Flesh and the Devil represented by Antichrist, with the friars as his followers. Together they force Unite to lose the fight against Sin.

The Passus can be divided into the following sections:

Passus 20	
The speech of Need	1–51
The coming of Antichrist and the assault on the Flesh	52–68
The Battle	69–226
The siege of Unite	227–272
The fall of Unite	273–387

Who is Need?

At the beginning of this the last Passus of the *Vita*, as at the beginning of the first, Will has a long waking conversation. The first was with two friars, and since the second – with Need – concerns the legitimacy of begging, a topic of peculiar and current interest to the friars, Clopper has suggested that Need must also be a friar (1997, pp. 93–7). But as Will has no idea where his next meal is coming from (3), it seems pretty clearly to be his own Need, which 'afrounted me foule and faitour me called' (confronted me and called me a hypocrite, 5). But what is he suggesting? Szitya sums up the position of earlier critics:

> Some see Nede as a virtue, the "regulating principle of temperance" [Bloomfield, Clopper] and the culmination of the poem's praise of temperance and poverty. Others, however [Adams, Scase], see Nede as a smooth-talking vice, with specious arguments that distort the ideals of *mesure* and patient poverty in the service of acquisitiveness or worse, petty theft. (Szitya, pp. 268–90)

You can decide where you stand as you read his speech and see the use that the friars make of his name in the last part of the Passus.

The speech of Need 1–51

When Piers gave the new Christians a pardon, it was on the condition that the Christians paid their debts in penance and restitution. But the 'foule' character Need seems to offer to override this principle, in the same way as the Lord in 19.463–468 had used *Spiritus Prudencie*, and the king in 19.469–479 had used *Spiritus Iusticie*, to justify stealing. Will is hungry; if he 'nome na moore þan nede þee tauȝte' (if you take no more than Need requires, 9), then he can take what he needs without needing to pay it back in the future. Even Aquinas allowed that necessity excused theft (*S. T.* II.1.q.66 a.7 quoted Carruthers p. 161; see also Fitzralph quoted Szittya, p. 270). But can we trust Need himself? When he brags that he can act by 'sleiȝte', or 'wiþouten conseil of Conscience,' or that – like the tyrant king – he 'neuere shal falle in dette', should we not conclude that the passage completes the corruption of the Cardinal Virtues to which he himself alludes (27–35)?

Then Need suddenly changes his tone and says he is simply obeying the supreme virtue of *Spiritus Temperancie*, because he lives a life of patient poverty. He is 'as lowe as a lomb', and lives like Christ himself (who speaks in the middle of the following quotation):

> And God al his grete ioye goostliche he lefte,
> And cam and took mankynde and bicam nedy. ...
> That he seide in his sorwe on þe selue roode, ...
> 'Ther nede haþ ynome me, þat I moot nede abide
> And suffre sorwes ful soure, þat shal to ioye torne.' (40–47)

> goostliche: really, essentially; ynome: seized; abide: endure

His words seem to invoke the Kynde Knowyng through suffering of Patience, of Mercy and of Christ on the Cross. So the problem seems to be this: the needy man is living a truly Christian life – until his very need drives him to take what he needs from others. Need promises to 'nymeþ hym vnder maynprise' (stand surety for him, 17) but we might find this kind of 'maynprise' uncomfortably close to Meed's (4.88) and conclude that his theft will put him in debt to Piers' pardon.

The discussion looks forward to the involvement of the friars in the destruction of Unite. They had always claimed that they begged because they had need, and indeed throughout the poem Langland has attempted to judge beggars according to their need. Truth's pardon in Passus 7 was denied to false beggars, who are 'in dette' (79), but 'hir borʒ is God Almyʒty' (surety, 80) and he will pay the debts of those who 'haue need' (66). Need now goes further and says that real destitution allows more than begging; it allows you to break the law. We will see how the laws are broken by the needy at the end of the Passus.

The coming of Antichrist and the assault on the flesh 52–68

Will's only response to Need's ambiguous challenge is to fall asleep and dream of the coming of Antichrist 'in mannes forme' (53). This section of the poem is within the tradition of *apocalyptic* or *eschatological* writing – writing which reveals the Last Days in a series of prophecies, such of those of Joachim of Fiore (see p. 210). Such accounts took their authority from the Bible. Jesus himself had predicted that 'many will come in my name saying 'I am Christ'' (*Matthew* 24:5), which seems to lie behind St John's warning of 'Antichrists' in his second *Letter*:

> For many deceivers are entered into the world, who confess not that Jesus Christ cometh in the flesh. This is a deceiver and an antichrist. (*2 John* 1:7).

In other *Letters* and in the book of *Revelation* (the '*Apocalypse*'), the implication is that these Last Days are already here:

there would be mockers In the last time who should walk after their own ungodly lusts (*Jude* 18).

There shall come 'lying prophets' and 'false teachers' (*2 Peter* 2:1–2).

[n the] last days [men will be] lovers of their own selves, covetous, boasters, proud, boasters … without natural affection, … incontinent … despisers of those who are good … For of this sort are they who creep into houses. [*penetrans domus*] (*2 Timothy* 3:1–6).

Jesus had also predicted natural disasters for the Last Days:

the end is not at once … [for first] nation shall rise against nation, and great earthquakes shall be in different places, and famines and pestilences (*Luke* 21:9–10)

As you read the rest of the Passus, see how many parallels you can find with these Biblical passages in the kind of vices which the followers of Antichrist display, and the way the action proceeds.

The literary texts developed from such prophecies often vilify the friars. In the thirteenth century monks like Willliam of St Armour sees them as those who come in the Last Days to 'creep into houses'(see the extract above), or as the false prophets of *Revelation* 16:13 (whose lies leap from their mouths like frogs; see Emmerson, p. 23 and picture on p. 263). and in Langland's England similar attacks were made both by figures within the Church, like Richard Fitzralph (discussed above, p. 187), and by the followers of Wycliffe who were moving towards leaving it (see Szittya, pp. 62–3, 139–51). Langland is therefore by no means unique then in putting friars into Antichrist's army – though they are not the only clerics there:

Antecrist cam þanne, and al þe crop of truþe
Torned it [tid] vp-so-doun, and ouertilte þe roote, …
Freres folwede þat fend, for he gaf hem copes,
And religiouse reuerenced hym and rongen hir belles (53–59).

ouertilte: upturned; copes: capes; religiouse: monks

The 'fools' who resist joining the enemy came from this tradition, for several groups claimed the honour of being the 'witnesses' who remained faithful in *Revelation* 11, or the fools whom St Paul says are 'the wise in this age' (*I Cor* 3.18).

A friar as follower of Antichrist

(after Lincoln College, Oxford, MS16, 14th century)

The Battle 69–227

The battle between the Vices and the inhabitants of Unite which takes up most of the rest of the Passus is a traditional part of apocalyptic prophecy, where the Dragon with Seven Heads (see picture on p. 43) was interpreted as the Seven Deadly Sins warring against the Woman clothed with the Sun, interpreted as the Church (*Revelation* 12, 17). On one side are the fools, the Cardinal Virtues, fighting not as personified abstractions, but as human individuals, and Nature (Kynde) who sends illnesses and natural disasters to (rather surprisingly) increase faith. On the other side are the Vices, Antichrist, and those who have joined them – most notably, the friars. How are we to see these enemies of Unite? Szittya suggests that they corresponds loosely to the Three Temptations of Lust of the Flesh, Lust of the Eyes and the Pride of Life, which plagued Will in Passus 11, so that we find we are following a personal as well as an institutional battle (Szittya, p. 274). But I will group them as the Three Enemies of the World, the Flesh and the Devil (as Antichrist with the friars), as these categories are more distinct from each other than the Three Temptations (see Moral Lists, p. 93, which also lists the Remedies).

Conscience's first defences are against Sins of the Flesh, epitomised by 'a lord þat lyeþ after likyng of body' (71; see also 19.386) and attacked by Kynde (Nature) and Death. Kynde sends the pestilences which Christ warned of (*Luke* 21:10), and which frighten the Christians into good behaviour as Hunger had long ago frightened Piers' lazy labourers (6.172ff.). The writing is dramatic and even comic in its lists of diseases, and appropriate allegorical details:

> The lord þat lyued after lust þo aloud cryde
> After Confort, a knyght, to come and bere his baner. (90–91)

In order for the allegory to work Langland has had to metamorphose the Sins into this sinful lord, who presumably slays his own sin in his fear of Death – though this does not stop Death from coming:

> Deeþ cam dryuynge after and al to duste passhed
> Kynges and knyghtes, kaysers and popes. (100–101)

> passhed: dashed; kaysers: emperors

Conscience therefore, again like Piers in Passus 6, has pity on his own people and asks Kynde to leave them alone. This will not be the only time when Conscience's "kindness" is misplaced.

The allegory now moves to Vices associated throughout the poem with the World: Covetousness, Pride, Lechery, and Sloth. Although the Sins have a frightening edge that was absent from their more human incarnations in Passus 5, the battle continues to be lively and full of perceptive and witty detail; note for example that Lechery uses laughter as a weapon against Conscience, and Covetousness is both predatory ('hungriliche', 123) and deceitful. Fortune and Life join the assault as Fortune, Covetousness of Eyes, and Pride of Parfyt Lyving had done in Passus 11 (3–15), Life mocking 'hendeness' and 'Holynesse' (143; as predicted in *Jude* 18), and Fortune encouraging the Christians to believe in their own self-sufficiency and immortality. Luckily Elde is still waiting in the wings to unveil their lies, as he had done long ago in 11.25ff.

The allegory also replays some of the satirical encounters of the *Visio*:

> Symonye hym s[ue]de to assaille Conscience, ...
> And cam to þe Kynges counseille as a kene baroun,
> And kneled to Conscience in Court afore hem alle,
> And garte Good Feiþ flee and Fals to abide,
> And boldeliche bar adoun wiþ many a bright noble
> Muche of þe wit and wisdom of Westmynstre Halle. (126–133)

> assaille: assault; kene: bold; abide: stay; noble: coin

Here Simony, the venal civil lawyer who was the follower of Meed and the protector of False in Passus 2, is allowed to tilt against Good Faith and Wisdom in the Court of Common Pleas where private cases were brought, and generally won by the richest suitor (see Secular Law Courts, p. 65). His offer of easy compensation ('Tak þis vp amendement') was the cry of Meed to Peace in Passus 4, and Simony is resurrected from Passus 2 to corrupt the Consistory Court, while Sloth reintroduces the venal juror from Passus 2 and 4 (see p. 48).

The personal level of the allegory then takes centre stage as Elde, on his way to beat Life, takes a short cut over Will's head:

> And Elde anoon after hym, and ouer myn heed yede,
> And made me balled bifore and bare on þe croune;
> 'Sire yuele ytauȝt Elde,' quod I, 'vnhende go wiþ þe!'
> Siþ whanne was þe wey ouer mennes heddes?
> Haddestow be hende,' quod I, 'þow woldest haue asked leeue!'
> 'Ye leue, lurdeyn?' quod he, and leyde on me wiþ age (183–189).

> balled bifore: bald in front; yuele ytauȝt: badly brought up; vnhende: discourtesy; hende: polite; lurdeyn: sluggard

Elde's rough manners are comic, certainly, but the passage is also a deft return to the issue of Need which had opened the Passus. Will's age and decrepitude makes him so needy that he might even become destitute, and he cries for help to Kynde, commander of Elde, who answers:

> 'If þow wolt be wroken, wend into Vnitee, ...
> And loke þow konne some craft er þow come þennes.' (204–206)
> wroken: avenged; konne: learn; er: before

Entering the protection of the Church, which deals with matters eternal, will be a kind of revenge on Elde. But Unite had been founded on the basis that its members each had a craft (19.230–252; see above, p. 249), and Will seems, as always, destitute of craft or wealth. He asks how he should avoid begging for support in Unite, apparently taking Piers' requirement to 'pay what you owe' in a social rather than a religious, penitential sense, and reluctant to follow Ned's advice and simply take the food and clothes he now needs:

> 'Counseilleþ me, Kynde,' quod I, 'what craft be best to lerne?'
> 'Lerne to loue,' quod Kynde, 'and leef alle oþere.'
> 'How shal I come to catel so, to cloþe me and to feede?'
> 'And þow loue lelly, lakke shal þee neuere
> Weede ne worldly mete, while þi lif lasteþ.' (207–211)
> leef: leave; catel: possessions; lelly: faithfully; weede: clothes

No doubt he then expects Conscience to ask him to work, as Reason did in C6, but he *is* destitute, and is in any case too old to learn any craft but love. Kynde's words are kind, indeed beautiful, but what kind of love do they refer to? Is it the love for God which can transform 'solicitude' (anxiety about one's physical needs) into patient reliance on God's will? Or is it charity, Holy Church's 'best tresure' which St Paul said was owed by all Christians to each other (Owe no man anything but to love one another ... [for] love is the fulfilling of the law', *Romans* 13:8–10; see Frank, p. 168)? If Will can learn both patience and love he will indeed *redde quod debet*, and find the 'kynde knowyng' for which he has been searching since the beginning of the poem. Does he do so? He certainly begins in the right way, by entering Unite and paying his religious debts in penance, but we hear no more about him and it soon transpires that Unite is not a place of real safety.

Who are the friars in Antichrist's army?

The enemy in this, the last phase of the battle, is an outsider, as in Prudentius' *Psychomachia* where Concordia is threatened by the heretics Plotinus and Arius (794, see above p. 253). In Langland's poem, Unite is threatened by the friars. But, as explained in Monks and Friars on p. 197, St Francis' vision of a brotherhood who wandered the world begging their food and teaching the poor seems very close to Langland's ideal of patient poverty. Why should they threaten the Church more than the rich and cruel lords of the earth?

One answer may be that it was because they *were* outsiders. Unlike the secular clergy of the parish, who were under the control of the bishops, the friars were licensed by the Pope himself in the early thirteenth century. And yet they shared with the secular clergy a priestly 'cure of souls' in three areas of competence: preaching, burying the dead, and most importantly, hearing confession and giving penance. This weakened the very centre of the Church's fight against sin, by allowing the sinner to avoid the (healing) shame of confessing to his own parish priest, and to pay for his sins in alms to friars rather than in genuine penance and restitution. This corruption is a result of the friars' need, for they were supposed to own no property and had no way of earning money apart from exercising this flawed "cure of souls". So Langland's contemporary, Bishop Fitzralph, saw their very independence of the Church hierarchy, and so of control by the bishops, as a threat to the unity that Church and to the Holy Spirit which had founded it – in language strongly reminiscent of Passus 20:

> Such an exemption [from ecclesiastical control] ... divides or splits
> the ecclesiastical hierarchy, which the Holy Spirit, through Christ's

apostles, instituted in conformity to the celestial hierarchy ... Procuration of privileges is contrary to that other law 'Thou shalt not covet'. (*On the Salvation of the Poor*, quoted Szittya, pp. 139, 141; see also Clopper, pp. 72–6)

The siege of Unite 227–272

Unite is now seen as closed, under siege, and suffering from the corrupt Church leadership who Anima in Passus 15 had warned would ruin it. The institutional vices of the clergy which have already preoccupied the poem – Sloth, Covetousness, Pride – reappear associated with the stock figure of the Irish priest; only the friars offer to help:

> Conscience cryede, 'Help, Clergie, or ellis I falle
> Thoruȝ inparfite preestes and prelates of Holy Chirche!'
> Freres herden hym crye, and comen hym to helpe;
> Ac for þei kouþe noȝt wel hir craft, Conscience forsook hem. (228–231)

The only craft which Grace (as founder of Unite) would recognise in the friars would be obedience to their Rule of poverty and holiness. As Scase shows in her study of the new 'anticlericism', fourteenth-century critics of the friars generally found a remedy in a return to their ideal of poverty, in which they would be stripped of their profitable but corrupting 'cure of souls' and returned to living by begging alone, 'coveting' neither property nor responsibility (pp. 23–5; see also Clopper, p. 98). It is to make this very point that Need suddenly returns, warning Conscience against the friars' 'cure of souls':

> Nede neghede þo neer, and Conscience he tolde
> That [freres] come for coueitise to haue cure of soules:
> 'And for þei are pouere, parauenture, for patrymonye hem failleþ,
> Thei wol flatere, to fare wel, folk þat ben riche.
> And siþen þei chosen chele and cheitiftee pouerte –
> Lat hem chewe as þei chose, and charge hem with no cure. (232–237)

neghede þo: then came close; cure of soules: care of parishioners; parauenture: perhaps; patrymonye: endowments; fare: get on; siþen: since; cheitiftee pouerte: destitution; charge: burden

Is Need satirising the miracle-working faith in *fiat voluntas tua* (Thy will be done, *Matthew* 6:10) advocated by Patience in Passus 14.48–69, with his sarcastic challenge that they should 'lyue by aungeles foode' (241), as St Francis was supposed to have done? Conscience however has another alternative, one which accords with some contemporary thinkers: that the friars should cease to be a kind of fifth column of outsiders within the Church, and become insiders. With supreme charity he invites them all into Unite:

> And seide, 'Sires, sooþly welcome be ye alle
> To Vnitee and Holy Chirche – ac o þyng I yow preye:
> Holdeþ yow in vnitee, and haueþ noon enuye
> To lered ne to lewed, but lyueþ after youre reule. (244–247)

lered: learned; lewed: ignorant

Indeed such a return to their Rule would have satisfied many critics – including one group of friars themselves, the 'Franciscan Spirituals', who had been driven underground in 1328 because they opposed all the activities which contravened St Francis' ideal of absolute poverty, including the cure of souls. It will be remembered that in Passus 5 it was Wrath who taught the friars to use their 'spiritualte' merely as an excuse for despising each other (5.147–148). Conscience promises that if they end both their quarrels and their envy of 'lordshup', he will give what they need, so that they do not have to take or borrow anything:

> And I wol be youre boruȝ, ye shal haue breed and cloþes
> And oþere necessaries ynowe – yow shal no þyng lakke,
> Wiþ þat ye leue logik; and lerneþ for to louye! …
> And if ye coueite cure, Kynde wol yow telle
> That in mesure God made alle manere þynges (248–250).

boruȝ: pledge; ynowe: enough; cure: care of parishioners; mesure: proportion

Their need will justify his charity, rather than (as in Need's own statement earlier) justifying their corrupting demands. They will then discover, like Patience or Hawkyn, or presumably, Will, the value of 'mesure' or self-limitation (Temperance), and that 'the

highest form of Temperance is to throw oneself utterly on God'
(Bloomfield 1962, p. 142).

However, as Conscience now goes on to show, the friars' whole
organisation seems to betray Temperance, which presupposes 'that in
mesure God made alle manere þynges', while the friars are so successful that they 'wexen out of noumbre!' (254, 269). Can
Conscience, the king of Unite, afford to support so many extra pas-
sengers? His anxiety about this takes up nearly 20 lines (253–272)
and echoes a frequent clerical criticism of the friars, voiced by
Fitzralph, that their numbers are as uncontrollable as the followers of
Antichrist (Bloomfield 1962, pp. 144–6; Szittya, p. 280).

The fall of Unite 273–387

It is from this point in the allegory that the friars' privilege of
hearing penance becomes the crucial factor in the fall of Unite.
Doubting that Conscience will support them, they hurry to the
Universities to learn arguments in favour of their ownership of property (which they could only do 'in common', 276), and they get the
bishop's leave to resume their cure of penitent souls (325–328).
These income streams will remove their need to beg, but also replace
their dependence on God by a dependence on flattery and manipu-
lation of others. In an angry aside Langland warns that they will care
for souls as the Westminster sanctuary cares for creditors, that is to
say, by offering them sanctuary from the law of *redde quod debes*
(285–289; see Baldwin 1982). And If Envy is driving the friars to
offer easy penances to the inhabitants of Unite, Hypocrisy is driving
those inhabitants to change their message (as in 2 *Peter* 2:2):

> Ypocrisie at þe yate harde gan fighte,
> And woundede wel wikkedly many a wys techere
> That wiþ Conscience acordede and Cardynale Vertues. (302–304)
>
> acordede: agreed

It is much easier to pretend to be following Conscience and
the Cardinal Virtues than to actually do it, but the consciousnesses

of failure and sin (Contrition) is already a step on the road to recovery.

Meanwhile inside Unite, Shrift is acting like the traditional parish priest, curing the sickness of sin by first investigating ('groping', 364) the sinner and then imposing a painful ointment of penance and restitution (see The Sacrament of Penance, p. 89, and picture of a priest with a whip on p. 90). But they find his 'sharp salue' (painful cure, 306) of *redde quod debes* (giving what you owe – penance and restitution, 309) indeed very painful. Although he knows that this is the best medicine (319), Conscience is suddenly moved by their suffering to 'suffre' the friar to offer easier penances (323). If he is the natural form of conscience, he seems moved by his very nature to be kind and not just or wise (see Langland's Psychology, p. 123). The new 'leech' (physician) is recognised by Peace as the lecher who earned his name *'penetrans domus'* by penetrating women as houses (348; see 2 Timothy 3:1–6). Both Will and the friars had been told to learn the craft of love, but this physician seems merely crafty. In Passus 3 Conscience had rejected the king's demand that he kiss Meed with hauteur, but now he and Hende-Speche (gracious speech, 349) seem blinded by optimistic kindness, hoping that the friar will help the sinners to love God for his mercy and to become more charitable:

> He may se and here, so may bifalle,
> That Lif þoruȝ his loore shal leue Coueitise,
> And be adrad of Deeþ and wiþdrawe hym fram Pryde,
> And acorde wiþ Conscience and kisse hir eiþer ooþer.' (351–354)

> bifalle: happen; loore: teaching; leue: abandon; adrad: fear

Can we distinguish Conscience's naïve kindness here from the charity which had attracted grace throughout the poem? The ideals of love and reconciliation which had seemed so satisfying seem now to be self-deceiving and dangerous.

In practice the sinners become friends not with Conscience but with the friars, who offer to enrol them in their fraternity 'for a litel siluer' (368). They are so encouraged by this easy forgiveness that they put their own contrition to sleep, and are again susceptible to

Sloth and Pride. The friars' corruption of the sacrament of penance undermines the principle of justice on which Unite depends – the principle of redde quod debes, of penance, of relying on Dowel as well as on grace (semi-Pelagianism). Thus to safeguard this fragile balance, the cure of souls must be taken from the friars, who have softened and corrupted penance in order to supply their own needs, for they cannot rely on the charity of the Christians. Langland can see no hope for the Church which does not include an endowment ('fyndyng', 384) for the friars; their Orders must become more like those of the monks, who had long seen that 'Poverty which has the necessities of life, not desiring any other things, … is more perfect' (Monk of Bury quoted Bloomfield 1962, p. 148). But in order that the friars should be given their home, Conscience once again (as in 13.215) prepares to leave his. Like Piers in Passus 7, Will in Passus 8, Conscience in Passus 13, and Hawkyn in Passus 14, he too will become a pilgrim:

> And walken as wide as þe world lasteþ,
> To seke Piers þe Plowman, þat Pryde myȝte destruye,
> And þat freres hadde a fyndyng, þat for nede flateren
> And siþþe he gradde after Grace, til I gan awake. (382–387)

> fyndyng: endowment; gradde: cried aloud

Is the cry for Grace an appeal for the Holy Spirit, who founded Unite, to restore it by his gift, since Dowel has failed? The poet wakes up but the poem goes on.

Conclusion to this *Guidebook*

So we come to the end of this *Guidebook*. I hope that you enjoyed the journey and that you will see it as only the first stage along the road to understanding Piers Plowman. Now you have a sense of the shape of the whole poem, you can start to read it properly for yourself, using the rich library of studies and contextualisations, to some of which I have referred. Perhaps you will study its subtle language, or recover the complexity of ideas which I have had to simplify, or pursue one theme (such as the role of Truth) throughout the poem, or work out your own interpretation of Piers himself. But whatever you do, I hope you will continue to read this most fascinating and wise of poems.

Further reading

On apocalyptic literature, see Reeve; Kerby-Fulton (1990); Kurdlich; Little. On Need, see Adams (1978); Hewett-Smith; Clopper, pp. 93–7; Kim; Mann (2005). On Friars and Langland, see Clopper; Szittya; Scase.

Bibliography

Abbreviations

EC	Essays in Criticism
JEGP	Journal of English and German Philology
Med. Aev.	Medium Aevum
MP	Modern Philology
N&Q	Notes and Queries
NM	Neuphilologische Mitteilungen
PMLA	Publications of the Modern Language Association of America
RES	Review of English Studies
Rot. Parl.	Rotuli Parliamentorum
Stat. Realm	Statutes of the Realm
SP	Studies in Philology
YLS	Yearbook of Langland Studies

Dictionary

Middle English Dictionary (1956–), ed. H. Kurath and and S. M. Kuhn (Ann Arbor: University of Michigan Press).

Accessible editions

The text used in this Guide is taken from:
Schmidt, A.V.C. (ed.) (1995a) *Piers Plowman: A Parallel Text Edition* (London: Longmans).

The translations are mainly derived from the same-page glosses in:
Schmidt, A.V.C. (ed.) (1995b) *Piers Plowman: the B-text*, 3rd edition (London: Everyman).

The reader will also find useful the text with facing-page translation in:
The Norton Critical Edition of Piers Plowman (2006), ed. E. Robertson and S. A. Shepherd (New York: Norton).

See also:

Duggan, H. N. (1994) The Piers Plowman electronic archive (Mosaic), http://Jefferson.village.virginia.edu/piers/report94.html

Pearsall, D. A. (ed.) (1978) *Piers Plowman: An Edition of the C-text* (London: Edward Arnold).

Pearsall, D. A. and Scott, K. (eds) (1992) *Piers Plowman: a Facsimile of Bodlean Library, Oxford, MS Douce, 104* (Cambridge: Brewer).

Rigg, A. G. and Brewer, C. (eds) (1983) *Piers Plowman: the Z version* (Toronto: Pontifical Institute of Mediaeval Studies).

Translations

Donaldson, E. T. (1990) *Will's Vision of Piers Plowman: an alliterative verse translation*, ed. E. D. Kirk and J. A. Anderson (New York and London: Norton). Used in Norton edition.

Goodridge, J. F. (1959) *Langland: Piers the Plowman* (Harmondsworth: Penguin).

Schmidt, A. V. C. (1992) *William Langland: Piers Plowman* (Oxford: Oxford University Press).

Bible

The Bible used is the Authorised Version.

Bibliographies

'Annual Bibliography' in *YLS* (East Lansing, 1987–).

Pearsall, D. A. (1990) *An annotated critical Bibliography of Langland* (New York and London, Harvester Wheatsheaf).

Primary texts

Aquinas, St T. (1964) *Summa Theologica, Vol. II (1a 75–83) Man* (Cambridge: Blackfriars).

Augustine, St (1991) *Confessions*, trans. H. Chadwick (Oxford, Oxford University Press).

Augustine, St (1925) *On the Spirit and the Letter*, trans. W. J. Sparrow Simpson (London, New York and Toronto: Macmillan (now Palgrave Macmillan)).

Augustine, St (1991) *The Trinity*, in *The Works of St Augustine: a Translation for the 21st Century*, trans. E. Hill (New York: New City Press).

Barr, H. (ed.) (1993) *The Piers Plowman Tradition* (London: Everyman).

The Book of Vices and Virtues: a fourteenth century English translation of the Somme le Roi of Lorens d'Orléans (1942) ed. W. Nelson Francis (London: Oxford University Press).

Bracton, H. (1968) *Bracton on the Laws and Customs of England*, 4 vols, ed. G. E. Woodbine, trans. S. E.Thorne (Cambridge, MA: Harvard University Press).

Burgo, J. de. *Pupilla Oculi* (Argentini, 1518).

Dean, J. M. (ed.) (1996) *Medieval English Political Writing* (Kalamazoo: Medieval Institute Publications).

Fasciculus Morum: a Fourteenth-Century Preachers' Handbook (1989) ed. and trans. S.Wenzel (University Park: Penn State University Press).

The Gospel of Nicodemus in *The Apocryphal New Testament: a Collection of Apocryphal Christian Literature in an English Translation*, Text A (1993) ed. J. K. Elliott (Oxford: Clarendon Press), pp. 190–204. *See also* Hulme.

Gower, J. (1968) 'In Praise of Peace' and 'Vox Clamantis' in *Complete Works of John Gower*, ed. G. C. Macaulay (Oxford: Clarendon Press).

Grosseteste, R. (1967) *The Middle English Translations of Robert Grosseteste's Château d'Amour*, ed. K. Sajavaara (Helsinki: Modern Language Society).

Henley, Walter of, *see* Walter.

Historical Poems, *see* Robbins.

Hoccleve, T. (1999) *The Regiment of Princes*, ed. C. R. Blyth, (Kalamazoo: Medieval Institute Publications).

Hudson, A. (ed.) (1978) *Selections from English Wycliffite Writings* (Cambridge: Cambridge University Press).

Hulme, W. H. (ed.) (1907) The Middle English Harrowing of Hell and Gospel of Nicodemus (London: Early English Text Society, Extra Series No. 100).

Krochalis, J. and Peters, E. (eds and trans.) (1975) *The World of Piers Plowman* (Philadelphia: University of Pennsylvania Press).

Macrobius (1952) *Commentary on the Dream of Scipio*, trans. W. H. Stahl (New York: Columbia University Press).

The Parliament of the Three Ages, see *Wynnere and Wastoure*.

Political prophecy, *see* Dean.

Pupilla Oculi, *see* Burgo.

Political Poems and Songs, see Wright.

Prudentius (1965) *The Poems of Prudentius*, trans. M. C. Eagan, Fathers of the Church Vol. 52 (Washington, DC: Catholic University of America Press), 2, 558–63.

Robbins, R. H. (ed.) (1959) *Historical Poems of the XIVth and XVth Centuries* (New York: Columbia University Press).

Ross, W. O. (ed.) (1940) *[Medieval] Middle English Sermons* (London: Early English Text Society, Ordinary Series No. 209).

Rotuli Parliamentorum (1935) (London: Offices of the Royal Historical Society).

Select Cases before the King's Council 1243–1482 (1918) ed. L. F. Leedham and J. F. Baldwin (London: Seldon Society, No. 35).

Select Cases in Chancery 1364–1471 (1896) ed. W. P. Bailon (London: Seldon Society, No. 10).

The Simonie, The Prophecies of Merlin, see Dean.

Statutes of the Realm, Vols I and II (London, 1810, 1816).

Summa Virtutum de Remediis Animae (1984) ed. S.Wenzel (Athens, GA: University of Georgia Press).

Walter of Henley and Other Treatises on Estate Management and Accounting (1971) ed. D. Oschinsky (Oxford: Clarendon Press).

Wright, T. (ed.) (1859, 1861) *Political Poems and Songs*, 2 vols, Rolls Series No. 252 (London: Longman Green).

Wycliff, J. (1880) *The English Works of Wyclif*, ed. F. D. Mathew (London: Early English Text Society, Ordinary Series No. 74).

Wycliffite Writings, see Hudson.

Wynnere and Wastoure and *The Parliament of the Three Ages* (1992) ed. W. Ginsburg (Kalamazoo: Medieval Institute Publications).

Secondary texts

Adams, R. (1976) 'Langland and the liturgy revisited', *SP* 73, 266–84.

Adams, R. (1983) 'Piers's pardon and Langland's semi-Pelagianism', *Traditio* 39, 367–418.

Adams, R. (1985) 'The reliability of the rubrics in the B-text of *Piers Plowman*', *Med. Aev.* 54, 208–31.

Adams, R. (1988) 'Langland's theology' in Alford (1988c), pp. 87–116.

Aers, D. (1980) *Chaucer, Langland and the Creative Imagination* (London: Routledge and Kegan Paul, 1980).

Aers, D. (1988) *Community, Gender and Individual Identity* (London and New York: Routledge, 1988).

Aers, D. (1994) 'Class, gender, medieval criticism and *Piers Plowman*' in Harwood and Overing, pp. 59–75.

Aers, D. (2002) 'The sacrament of the altar and Piers Plowman and the late medieval Church in England' in Dimmick et al., pp. 63–80.

Alford, J. (1974) 'Haukyn's Coat', *Med. Aev.* 43, 133–8.

Alford, J. (1988a) *Piers Plowman: Glossary of Legal Diction* (Cambridge: Brewer).

Alford, J. (1988b) 'The idea of Reason in *Piers Plowman*' in *Medieval English Studies Presented to George Kane*, ed. D. Kennedy et al. (Woodbridge: Boydell & Brewer), pp. 199–215.

Alford, J. (ed.) (1988c) *A Companion to Piers Plowman* (Berkeley: University of California Press).

Alford, J. (1992) *Piers Plowman: a Guide to the Quotations* (Binghamton: Center for Medieval and Early Renaissance Studies).

Astell, A.W. (1999) *Political Allegory in Late Medieval England* (Ithaca: Cornell University Press).

Baldwin, A. (1981a) *The Theme of Government in Piers Plowman* (Cambridge: Brewer).

Baldwin, A. (1981b) 'The double duel in *Piers Plowman* B.XVIII and C XXI', *Med. Aev.* 50, 64–78.

Baldwin, A. (1982) 'A reference in Piers Plowman to the Westminster Sanctuary', *N&Q*, New Series, 29: 106–8.

Baldwin, A. (1988a) 'The Historical context' in Alford (1988c).

Baldwin, A. (1988b) 'Sacramental perfection in Pearl, Patience and Cleanness' in *Genres, Themes and Images in English Literature from the Fourteenth to the Fifteenth Century*, ed. P. Boitani and A. Torti (Tubingen: Narr), pp. 125–40.

Baldwin, A. (1994) 'The Debt narrative in *Piers Plowman*' in *Art and Context in Late Medieval English Narrative*, ed. R. R. Edwards (Cambridge: Brewer), pp. 37–50.

Baldwin, A. (2002) 'Patient politics in *Piers Plowman*', *YLS* 15, 99–108.

Barnie, J. (1974) *War in Medieval English Society:Social Values and the Hundred Years' War* (Ithaca: Cornell University Press).

Barney, S.A. 'Langland's mighty line' in Hewett-Smith, pp. 103–17.

Bennett, H. S. (1968) *The Pastons and their England*, 2nd edition (Cambridge: Cambridge University Press).

Benson, C. D. (2004) 'The history of the Langland Myth' in *Public Piers Plowman* (Philadelphia: Penn State University Press).

Besserman, L. (1979) *The Legend of Job in the Middle Ages* (Cambridge, MA and London: Harvard University Press).

Birnes, W. (1975) 'Christ as advocate: the legal metaphor in Piers Plowman', *Annuale Medievale* 16, 71–93.

Bishop, L. M. (1998) 'Dame Study and Women's Literacy', *YLS* 12, 97–115.

Blanch, R. (ed.) (1969) *Style and Symbolism in Piers Plowman* (Knoxville: University of Tennessee Press).

Bloomfield, M. W. (1952) *The Seven Deadly Sins* (East Lansing: Michigan State University Press).

Bloomfield, M. W. (1962) *Piers Plowman as a Fourteenth-century Apocalypse* (New Brunswick: Rutgers University Press).

Bowers, J. M. (1995) 'Writing the author's life', *YLS* 9, 65–90.

Braswell, M. F. (1983) *The Medieval Sinner* (London: Associated University Presses).

Bullock-Davies, C. (1978) *Menestrellorum Multitudo* (Cardiff: University of Wales Press).

Burrow, J. (1965) 'The action of Langland's Second Vision', *EC* 15, 247–68; repr. in Blanch, pp. 209–27.

Burrow, J. A. (1982) *Medieval Writers and their Work* (Oxford: Oxford University Press).

Burrow, J. A. (1993) *Langland's Fictions* (Oxford: Clarendon Press).

Carruthers, M. J. (1973) *The Search for St Truth: a Study of Meaning in Piers Plowman* (Evanston: Northwestern University Press).

Chambers, R. W. (1924) 'Long Will, Dante, and the Righteous Heathen', *Essays and Studies* 9, 50–69.

Clark-Maxwell, W. G. (1929) 'Some letters of confraternity', *Archaeologica* 25 and 29.

Clopper, L. M. (1997) *Songes of Rechelesnesæ* (Ann Arbor: University of Michigan Press).

Cole, A. (2003) 'William Langland's Lollardy', *YLS* 17, 25–54.

Cooper, H. (1991) 'Gender and personification in Piers Plowman', *YLS* 5, 31–48.

Davenport, W. A. (1988) 'Patterns in Middle English dialogues' in Kennedy et al., pp. 127–46.

Davlin, M. C. (1971) 'Kynde Knowyng as a Major Theme in Piers Plowman B', *RES*, New Series, 22, 1–19.

Davlin, M. C. (1981) 'Kynde Knowyng as a Middle English equivalent for "Wisdom" in Piers Plourman B', *Med. Aev.* 50, 5–17.

Davlin, M. C. (1989) *A Game of Heuene* (Cambridge: Brewer).

Davlin, M. C. (1996) '*Piers Plowman* and the Gospel and First Epistle of John', *YLS* 10, 89–127.

d'Entrèves, P. (1951, 1970) *Natural Law* (London: Hutchinson).

Dimmick, J., Simpson, J. and Zeeman, N. (eds.) (2002) *Images, Idolatry and Iconoclasm in Late Medieval England* (Oxford: Oxford University Press).

Dobson, R. B. (1970) *The Peasants' Revolt of 1381* (London: Macmillan (now Palgrave Macmillan)).

Donaldson E. T. (1949) *The C-text and its Poet* (New Haven: Yale University Press).

Dronke, P. (1981) '*Arbor caritatis*' in *Medieval Studies for J. A. W .Bennett*, ed. P. L. Heyworth (Oxford: Clarendon Press), pp. 207–53.

Emmerson, R. K. (1981) *Antichrist in the Middle Ages: A Study of Medieval Apocalypticism, Art and Literature* (Seattle: University of Washington Press).

Finke, L. A. (1993) 'Truth's treasure: allegory and meaning in *Piers Plowman*' in Trigg, pp. 84–98.

Fleming, J. V. (1977) *An Introduction to the Franciscan Literature of the Middle Ages* (Chicago: Franciscan Herald Press).

Fowler, D. (1999) 'Will's *Apologia pro vita suä*', *YLS* 13, 35–48.

Frank, R. W. (1957) *Piers Plowman and the Scheme of Salvation* (New Haven: Yale University Press).

Gaffney, W. (1931) 'The allegory of the Christ-knight in *Piers Plowman*', *PMLA* 46, 155–68.

Galloway, A. (1995) 'The rhetoric of riddling in late medieval England', *Speculum* 70, 68–105.

Galloway, A. (1998) 'Intellectual pregnancy: metaphysical femininity and the social doctrine of the Trinity in *Piers Plowman*', *YLS* 12, 117–52.

Galloway, A. (2001) 'Making history legal: Piers Plowman and the rebels of fourteenth-century England' in Hewett-Smith, pp. 7–39.

Godden, M. (1984) '[Piers] Plowmen and hermits in Langland's *Piers Plowman*', *RES*, New Series, 35, 129–63.

Godden, M. (1990) *The Making of Piers Plowman* (London: Longmans).

Goldsmith, M. (1981) *The Figure of Piers Plowman* (Cambridge: Brewer).

Hanna, R. III (1978) 'Patience in the Middle Ages' in *The Triumph of Patience*, ed. G. K. Schiffhorst (Orlando: University Presses of Florida).

Hanna, R. III (1993) *William Langland* Authors of the Middle Ages No. 3 (Aldershot: Variorum).

Hanna, R. III (1997) 'Will's work' in *Written Work: Langland Labour and Authorship*, ed. S. Justice and K. Kirby-Fulton (Philadelphia: University of Pennsylvania Press), pp. 23–66.

Hanna, R. III (2001) 'Emendations to a 1993 *Vita*', *YLS* 14, 185–98.

Hanna, R. III (2002) 'Langland's Ymaginatif: images and the limits of poetry' 81–94 in *Images, Idolatory and Iconoclasm in Late Medieval England*, ed. J. Dimmick, J. Simpson and N. Zeeman (Oxford: Oxford University Press), pp. 81–94.

Harding, A. (1973) *The Law Courts of Medieval England* (London: Allen and Unwin).

Harwood, B. J. (1983) 'Langland's Kynde Knowyng and the Quest for Christ', *MP* 80, 242–55.

Harwood, B. and Overing, G.,R. (1994) *Class and Gender in Early English Literature* (Bloomington: Indiana University Press).

Harwood, B. J. and Smith, R. F. (1970) 'Inwit and the Castle *of Caro* in *Piers Plowman*', *NM*, 648–54.

Helmholz, R. H. (1974) *Marriage Litigation in Medieval England* (London: Cambridge University Press).

Hewett-Smith, K. M. (ed.) (2001a) *Langland's Piers Plowman: a Book of Essays* (New York & London: Routledge).

Hewett-Smith, K. M. (2001b) 'Nede hath no lawe: poverty and the destabilisation of allegory in the final visions of *Piers Plowman*' in Hewett-Smith, pp. 233–53.

Hudson, A. (1988) 'The legacy of *Piers Plowman*' in Alford (1988), pp. 251–66.

Hilton, R. H. (1969) *The Decline of Serfdom in Medieval England* (London: Macmillan (now Palgrave Macmillan)).

Holmes, G. (1975) *The Good Parliament* (Oxford: Clarendon Press).

Howard, D. R. (1966) *The Three Temptations: Medieval Man in Search of the World* (Princeton: Princeton University Presss).

Hurnard, N. D. (1969) *The King's Pardon for Homicide before AD 1377* (Oxford: Clarendon Press).

Hussey, S. S. (ed.) (1969) *Piers Plowman: Critical Approaches* (London: Methuen).

Jenkins, P. (1969) 'Conscience, the frustration of allegory' in Hussey, pp. 125–42.

Jeffrey, D. (1975) *The Early English Lyric and Franciscan Spirituality* (Lincoln, NE: University of Nebraska Press).

Johnson, D. E. (1997) 'Persen with a pater-noster paradys other heuene', *YLS* 5, 77–89.

Jones, E. (1997) 'Langland and hermits', *YLS* 11, 67–86.

Jones, H. (1914) 'Ymaginatif in *Piers Plowman*', *JEGP* 13, 583–8.

Justice, S. (1993) 'The genres of *Piers Plowman*' in Trigg, pp. 99–118.

Justice, S. (1994) *Writing and Rebellion: England in 1381* (Berkeley and London: University of California Press).

Kaske, R.E. (1959) 'The speech of Book in *Piers Plowman*', *Anglia* 77, 117–44.

Kaske, R. E. (1963) 'Ex vi transitionis', *JEGP* 62, 32–60; repr. in Blanch, pp. 228–63.

Kaulbach, E. (1985) 'The "vis imaginative" and the reasoning powers of Imaginatif in the B-text of *Piers Plowman*', *JEGP* 84, 16–29.

Keen J. A. (2002) *The Charters of Christ and Piers Plowman: Documenting Salvation* (Oxford: Peter Lang).

Kemp, S. (1990) *Medieval Psychology*, Contributions in Psychology No. 14 (New York: Greenwood).

Kennedy, E. D. et al. (eds) (1988) *Piers Plowman: Medieval English Studies Presented to George Kane* (Cambridge: Brewer).

Kerby-Fulton, K. *Reformist Apocalypticism and Piers Plowman* (Cambridge: Cambridge Unversity Press).

Kolve, V. A. (1972) 'Everyman and the parable of the talents' in *Medieval English Drama*, ed. J. Taylor and A. Nelson (Chicago: University of Chicago Press), pp. 316–40.

Lambert, M. (1977) *Medieval Heresy* (London: Edward Arnold).

Lawton, D. A. (ed.) (1982) *Middle English Alliterative Poetry and its Literary Background* (Woodbridge: Brewer).

Lawton, D. A. (1988) 'Alliterative style' in *A Companion to Piers Plowman*, ed. J. A. Alford (Berkeley: University of California Press), pp. 223–50.

Lees, C. (1994) 'Gender and exchange in *Piers Plowman*' in Harwood and Overing, pp. 112–90.

Lewis, L. (1995) 'Langland's Tree of Charity and Usk's Wexing Tree', *N&Q*, New Series 42 [240], 429–33.

Lucas, A. M. (1983) *Women in the Middle Ages* (New York: St Martin's Press).

McFarlane, K. B. (1973) *The Nobility of Later Medieval England* (Oxford: Clarendon Press).

McKisack, M. (1959) *The Fourteenth Century*, Oxford History of England (Oxford: Clarendon Press).

Maguire, S. (1949) 'The significance of Hawkyn, *Activa Vita* in *Piers Plowman*', *RES*, Original Series 25, 97–109.

Mann, J. (1973) *Chaucer and Medieval Estates Satire* (Cambridge: Cambridge University Press).

Mann, J. (1979) 'Eating and drinking in *Piers Plowman*', *Essays and Studies*, New Series 32, 26–43.

Mann, J. (1991) *Geoffrey Chaucer* (Atlantic Highlands: Humanities Press)

Mann, J. (1994) 'The power of the alphabet: a reassessment of the relation between the A and B versions of Piers Plowman', *YLS* 8, 21–50.

Middleton, A. (1982a) 'The audience and public of *Piers Plowman*' in *Middle English Alliterative Poetry and its Literary Background*, ed. D. Laton (Cambridge: Brewer), pp. 101–23, 147–54.

Middleton, A. (1982b) 'Narration and the invention of experience: episodic form in *Piers Plowman*' in *The Wisdom of Poetry: Essays in Early English Literature in Honour of Morton W. Bloomfield*, ed. L. D. Benson and S. Wenzel (Kalamazoo: Medieval Institute Publications), pp. 91–122.

Middleton, A. (1997) 'Acts of vagrancy; the C-version autobiography and the Statute of 1388' in *Written Work: Langland, Labor and Authorship*, ed. S. Justice and K. Kirby-Fulton (Philadelphia: University of Pennsylvania Press) , pp. 208–317.

Mitchell, A. C. (1969) 'Lady Meed and the Art of Piers Plowman' in Blanch, pp. 174–93.

Morgan, G. (1987) 'The meaning of Kynde Wit, Conscience and Reason in the Vision of *Piers Plowman*', *MP* 84, 351–8.

Owst, G. R. (1966 [1933]) *Literature and Pulpit in Medieval England* (Cambridge: Cambridge University Press).

Palmer, I. J. N. (1972) *England, France and Christendom, 1377–99* (London: Routledge and Kegan Paul).

Palmer, P. F. (1955) *Sacraments and Worship* (Westminster, MD: Newman Press).

Palmer, P. F. (1959 [1952]) *Sacraments and Forgiveness* (Westminster, MD: Newman Press).

Pantin, W. A. (1955) *The English Church in the Fourteenth Century* (Cambridge: Cambridge University Press).

Pearsall, D. A. (1988) 'Poverty and poor people in *Piers Plowman*' in Kennedy et al., pp. 167–85.

Pearsall. D. A. (1997) 'Langland's London' in Justice and Kerby-Fulton, pp. 185–207.

Paxson, J. J. (2001) 'Inventing the subject and the personification of Will in *Piers Plowman*' in Hewett-Smith, pp. 195–231.

Peebles, J. (1911) *The Legend of Longinus* (Baltimore: Bryn Mawr College).

Pelikan, J. (1971 [1923–]) *The Christian Tradition: a History of the Development of Doctrine*, 5 vols (Chicago and London: University of Chicago Press).

Pollock, F. and Maitland, F. W. (1895) *The History of English Law before the Time of Edward I* (Cambridge: Cambridge University Press).

Portalie, E. (1960) *Guide to the Thought of Saint Augustine*, trans R. J. Bastian (London: Burns & Oates).

Potts, T. C. (1980) *Conscience in Medieval Philosophy* (Cambridge: Cambridge University Press).

Putnam, B. (1908) *The Enforcement of the Statutes of Labourers during the First Decade after the Black Deth 1349–1359* (New York: Columbia College).

Quirk, R. (1953) 'Langland's use of Kynde Wit and Inwit', *JEGP* 52, 182–95.

Reeves, M. (1976) *Joachim of Fiore and the Prophetic Future: Studies in Historial Thinking* (London: SPCK).

Robertson, D. W. and Huppé, B. F. (1951) *Piers Plowman and Scriptural Tradition* (Princeton: Princeton University Press).

Roest, B. (2000) *A History of Franciscan Education* (Leiden and Boston, MA: Brill).

Rosenthal, J. T. (1972) *The Purchase of Paradise* (London: Routledge and Kegan Paul).

Russell, J. B. (1977) *The Devil: Perceptions of Evil from Antiquity to Primitive Christianity* (Ithaca and London: Cornell University Press).

St Jacques, R. (1967) 'Langland's Christ-knight and the liturgy', *Review of University of Ottowa* 37, 146–58.

Samuels, M. L. (1988) 'Language and grammar' in Alford (1988c) , pp. 201–22.

Saul, N. (1997) *Richard II* (New Haven: Yale University Press).

Scase, W. (1989) *Piers Plowman and New Anticlericalism* (Cambridge: Cambridge Unversity Press).

Scattergood, J. (2000) *The Lost Tradition* (Dublin: Four Courts Press).

Schmidt, A. V. C. (1969) 'Langland and scholastic philosophy', *Med. Aev.* 38, 134–56.

Schmidt, A. V. C. (1987) *The Clerkly Maker* (Cambridge: Brewer).

Sheehan, M. M. (1971) 'Formation and stability of marriage in 14C England: evidence of an Ely register', *Medieval Studies* 33, 28–63.

Shepherd, S. H. (2001) 'Langland's Romances' in Hewett-Smith, pp. 69–82.

Simpson, J. (1985) 'Spiritual and earthly nobility in *Piers Plowman*', *NM* 83, 467–81.

Simpson, J. (1986a) 'From reason to affective knowledge', *Med. Aev.* 55, 1–23.

Simpson, J. (1986b) 'The role of *Scientia* in Piers Plowman' in *Medieval English Religious and Ethical Literature: Essays in Honour of G. H. Russell*, ed. G. Kratzmann and J. Simpson (Cambridge: Brewer), pp. 49–65.

Simpson, J. (1987) 'Spirituality and economics in Passus I–VII of the B-text', *YLS* 1, 83–103.

Simpson, J. (1990) *Piers Plowman: an Introduction to the B-text* (London and New York: Longman).

Simpson, J. (2001) 'The power of impropriety: authorial naming in *Piers Plowman*' in Hewett-Smith, pp. 145–65.

Simpson, J. (2002) 'The rule of medieval imagination' in Dimmick et al., pp. 4–24.

Smith, B. (1966) *Traditional Imagery of Charity in Piers Plowman* (The Hague and Paris: Mouton).

Somerset, F. et al. (eds) (2003) *Lollards and Their Influence in Late Medieval England* (Woodbridge: Boydell).

Spearing, A. C. (1976) *Medieval Dream Poetry* (Cambridge: Cambridge University Press).

Stokes, M. (1984) *Justice and Mercy in Piers Plowman* (London: Croom Helm).

Szittya, P. (1986) *The Antifraternal Tradition in Medieval England* (Princeton: Princeton University Press).

Tambling, J. (1990) *Confession: Sexuality, Sin, the Subject* (Manchester: Manchester University Press).

Tavormina, M. T. (1995) *Kindly Similitude: Marriage and Family Life in Piers Plowman* (Cambridge: Brewer).

Taylor, R. (1911) *The Political Prophecy of England* (New York: Columbia College).

Tentler, J. N. (1977) *Sin and Confession on the Eve of the Reformation* (Princeton: Princeton University Press).

Trigg, S. (1993) *Medieval English Poetry* (London: Longmans).

Trigg, S. (1998) 'The traffic in medieval women: Alice Perrers, feminist criticism and *Piers Plowman*', *YLS* 12, 5–29.

Troyer, H. W. 'Who is Piers Plowman?' in Blanch, pp. 156–73.

Tuck, R. (1973) *Richard II and the English Nobility* (London: Edward Arnold).

Turville-Petre, T. (1977) *The Alliterative Revival* (Cambridge: Brewer).

Waldron, R. A. (1986) 'Langland's originality: the Christ-knight and the Harrowing of Hell' in *Medieval English Religious and Ethical Literature: Essays in Honour of G. H. Russell*, ed. G. Katzmann and J. Simpson (Cambridge: Brewer), pp. 66–81.

Walker, S. S. (1987) 'Punishing convicted ravishers', *Journal Medieval History* 13, 237–50.

Warner, L. (2005) 'John But and the other works that Will wrought', *N&Q*, New Series 52, 13–18.

Wenzel, S. (1988) 'Medieval sermons' in Alford (1988c), pp. 155–74.

White, H. (1988) *Nature and Salvation in Piers Plowman* (Cambridge: Brewer).

Wilkinson, B. (1952) *Constitutional History of England II* (London: Longmans), Chs 6, 9.

Wunderli, R. M. (1981) *London Church Courts and Society on the Eve of the Reformation* (Cambridge, MA: Medieval Academy of America).

Index

The most important references are given in bold; references to pictures are given in italics. Allegorical characters are all included and are given a capital letter (for example, Clergy), while concepts are in lower case (truth). References to modern critics are not indexed, nor medieval works, nor people mentioned only once.